ESTHER RUTH JONAH

DECIPHERED

by Stephen Gabriel Rosenberg Ph.D

DEVORA
PUBLISHING
JERUSALEM ◆ NEW YORK

ESTHER, RUTH, JONAH DECIPHERED:
The Complete Hebrew and English Text with a New Historical Commentary
Published by DEVORA PUBLISHING COMPANY

Text Copyright © 2004 by Stephen Gabriel Rosenberg
Cover and Book Design: Benjie Herskowitz
Editor: Chaya Leader

Library of Congress Cataloging-in-Publication Data

Bible. O.T. Esther. Hebrew. 2004.
   Esther, Ruth, Jonah Deciphered: the complete Hebrew and English text with a new Historical Commentary / by Stephen Gabriel Rosenberg.
      p. cm.
   Includes bibliographical references.
   ISBN 1-930143-90-7 (hc : alk. paper) 1. Bible. O.T. Esther – Commentaries. 2. Bible. O.T. Ruth – Commentaries. 3. Bible. O.T. Jonah – Commentaries. I. Rosenberg, Stephen (Stephen G.) II. Bible. O.T. Esther. English. 2004. III. Bible. O.T. Ruth. Hebrew. 2004. IV. Bible. O.T. Ruth. English. 2004. V. Bible. O.T. Jonah. Hebrew. 2004. VI. Bible. O.T. Jonah. English. 2004. VII. Title.
   BS1375.R67 2004
   221 – dc22

                              2004004616
   ISBN: 1-930143-90-7 (HC)

Email: sales@devorapublishing.com
Web Site: www.devorapublishing.com

Printed in Israel

to Nurith
Yardenna
Jeremy
Saul
David
and their
mother Marion

∽ CONTENTS ∽

᚛ AUTHOR'S PREFACE ᚛

I have concentrated on three books of the Hebrew Bible that cry out for some basic explanation, if they are not to fall into the category of fable or fairy story. For some people belief is enough, but for most of us understanding is a necessary ingredient.

These three books of Esther, Ruth and Jonah are well known to Jews and Christians alike. In the synagogue they are read each year on the festivals of Purim (Esther), Shavuoth or Pentecost (Ruth) and Yom Kippur, the Day of Atonement (Jonah); nevertheless, it is my view that they have still not been fully explained. To the Christians they are also well known as divine literature and as good stories and I hope they will appreciate a fuller understanding of the history and logic that I think underlies these three books.

It is of course the beauty of these great works that they can bear constant explanation and elucidation, and each age will leave its imprint on them. I hope that my views can be accepted as an interpretation that is, like everything else, a child of its time.

My teacher in these matters has been the late Rabbi Shmuel Sperber who revealed to me the profound unity of our ancient Hebrew texts. In carrying out his principles of learning, I have interacted with many fellow students in several synagogues who have helped me to develop some of the ideas expressed in this book.

My profound thanks to them all and to my wife Marion, who has stood by my side and helped me throughout.

Stephen Gabriel Rosenberg
London and Jerusalem, 5764/2004

7

≈ *FOREWORD* ≈

Esther, Ruth and Jonah are three books of the Hebrew Bible that each tell one dramatic tale. They are written in relatively simple Hebrew, they relate in whole or in part to events outside the land of Israel. Each book is dominated by one hero or heroine. Yet each book contains a number of unexplained mysteries, which we will try to resolve with the use of historical, archaeological and textual tools.

The Book of Esther is wholly set in a foreign land, unlike any of the other Biblical books except Daniel. But whereas Daniel is mainly written in official Aramaic and contains a variety of tales and visions, Esther tells, in classical Hebrew interspersed with words from the Persian, a story that is self-contained, romantic and racy. The wicked Haman, first minister to the Persian Empire, plans to destroy all its Jewish population, but the beautiful Queen Esther, a Jewish girl recently taken into the king's harem, overturns his evil plans. Could Esther really change the mind of Ahasuerus, king of the most powerful empire in the East?

The Book of Ruth tells the life of Naomi: she goes abroad and acquires a heathen daughter-in-law who becomes the great-grandmother of David, the king. The story moves between two countries and two cultures and between town and countryside, but again it is completely self-contained and couched in plain Hebrew. Although set in the period of the Judges, it is not part of that Book as are the other stories of that period, such as Jephthah's daughter or Samson

9

and Delilah. Does Ruth have a message not related to the Book of Judges?

Jonah is quite unlike the other writing prophets, major or minor. The Book is in prose virtually throughout and describes Jonah's actions rather than any prophecy. Part of his story takes place on the high seas and part of it abroad in Nineveh, or so it appears on the surface. Did Jonah really go to Nineveh, and why was Nineveh so important to Israel?

These three books have further factors in common. They tell of events that appear to be less than credible, yet they are not fairy stories. The Jews of the Persian Empire are threatened with death, but given eleven months' notice of their day of destruction. Is that credible? Naomi and Ruth, from very different backgrounds and cultures, become so close to each other that the founder of the Davidic dynasty comes to have a non-Jewish great-grandmother. This seems to be an arrangement made in heaven; so who is the mysterious stranger, named *Peloni-Almoni*, who nearly upsets the apple cart? Most incredible of all is the wretched Jonah, tossed on the high seas, swallowed by a great fish and spewed back on to land and forced to go to Nineveh. Can this really be believed?

Another important factor common to all three books is their ending. In each case the conclusion reveals part of their true significance, somewhat different from the general belief. Esther ends on a mundane note of taxation at variance with its otherwise exotic settings. The ending to Ruth indicates the unorthodox genealogy not only of David but also of Solomon and his son Rehoboam. In the case of Jonah, God insists that the welfare of the hordes of Nineveh is more important to Him than that of Jonah himself. And all three tales, as an element of their self-containment, are built on a symmetrical structure that reveals a most satisfying literary format. In this chiastic form it is worth noting that in each of the three Books, the turning point comes in a scene shrouded in darkness. In Esther, it is the sleepless night of the king when he orders the royal diary to be read to him. In Ruth it is the love scene between Ruth and Boaz in the granary at night. And in Jonah it is the time when he is trapped in darkness, in the belly of the great fish.

It must also be said that these books, particularly Esther and Jonah, have spawned a tremendous popular and critical literature from writers and scholars of many different disciplines, religions and shades of opinion. It is certainly not my purpose to compete with these many experts, and I have not attempted, or been able to, reproduce all their points of view and arguments. I would only say that in spite of years of critical study by scholars, most of the points of explanation that I offer have, as far as I have been able to ascertain, not been advanced before. Does that make them invalid? I leave that to the reader to judge. To my mind they are essential to a proper understanding of these three books.

There are a few technical points to clarify. Concerning the texts, I have used my own translation in certain cases. I have done so in order to provide as literal a translation as I can, even though I am sure my version is not as elegant as many others. It may also vary in many cases from the fine JPS (1985) translation that we are printing alongside the Hebrew text. But to completely understand the original text, and to be able to build on it, literalness is the essential key. To give one example, in the last sentence of Jonah, the JPS translation says, "…in which there are more than one hundred and twenty thousand persons who do not yet know their right hand from their left…." (4:11). The word "yet" does not appear in the original Hebrew; the translation follows the idea of the great medieval commentator Rashi (ad loc.) who says it refers to the children, who do not *yet* know their right from their left. But this is his interpretation and should not be part of the translation. I hope it will become clear in this and other cases that the Hebrew text *as it stands* is all-important.

The transliteration of the Hebrew follows the semi-popular notation, without the use of diacritical signs, rather than the much more complicated scholarly versions. The spelling of proper names of people and places follows that used in the standard translations of the Hebrew Bible. In all cases, I hope that readers with the ability will, wherever possible, consult the original Hebrew. I must thank my wife Marion for checking the transliterations.

The Hebrew text is all-important, but as I cannot pretend to be an expert on the chronology of Biblical Hebrew, I have not indulged in long analyses of language in relation to dating. I must leave that approach to other expert studies of which there are many, but I would point out that it is not an exact science and I have indicated in places what I think, based on content and context, could be the general dating of the texts in question.

To settle exact historical dates is always difficult. The problem is particularly acute in the case of the events reflected in Jonah, where I refer to several of the Israelite kings, the Arameans and the Assyrians. In general matters I have used the dates in Miller and Hayes 1986 (see references), but for the kings of Judah and Israel I have relied on Galil 1996, who has given the best analysis to date of their complex chronology.

References to traditional and modern sources are all given in the text in brackets, and full details of each work will be found in the Bibliography at the end of this volume.

❧ LIST OF ILLUSTRATIONS ❧

LIST OF ILLUSTRATIONS, *continued*

All drawings and
maps by the author

ESTHER
RUTH
JONAH
DECIPHERED

by Stephen Gabriel Rosenberg Ph.D

Book of Esther

1 ¹It happened in the days of Ahasuerus – that Ahasuerus who reigned over a hundred and twenty-seven provinces from India to Ethiopia. ²In those days, when King Ahasuerus occupied the royal throne in the fortress Shushan, ³in the third year of his reign, he gave a banquet for all the officials and courtiers – the administration of Persia and Media, the nobles and the governors of the provinces in his service. ⁴For no fewer than a hundred and eighty days he displayed the vast riches of his kingdom and the splendid glory of his majesty. ⁵At the end of this period, the king gave a banquet for seven days in the court of the king's palace garden for all the people who lived in the fortress Shushan, high and low alike. ⁶[There were hangings of] white cotton and blue wool, caught up by cords of fine linen and purple wool to silver rods and alabaster columns; and there were couches of gold and silver on a pavement of marble, alabaster, mother-of-pearl, and mosaics. ⁷Royal wine was served in abundance, as befits a king, in golden beakers, beakers of varied design. ⁸And the rule for the drinking was, "No restrictions!" For the king had given orders to every palace steward to comply with each man's wishes. ⁹In addition, Queen Vashti gave a banquet for women, in the royal palace of King Ahasuerus.

¹⁰On the seventh day, when the king was merry with wine, he ordered Mehuman, Bizzetha, Harbona, Bigtha, Abagtha, Zethar, and Carcas, the seven eunuchs in attendance on King Ahasuerus, ¹¹to bring Queen Vashti before the king wearing a royal diadem, to display her beauty to the peoples and the officials; for she was a beautiful woman. ¹²But Queen Vashti refused to come at the king's command conveyed by the eunuchs. The king was greatly incensed, and his fury burned within him.

¹³Then the king consulted the sages learned in procedure. (For it was the royal practice [to turn] to all who were versed in law and precedent. ¹⁴His closest advisers were Carshena, Shethar, Admatha, Tarshish, Meres, Marsena, and Memucan, the seven ministers of Persia and Media who had access to the royal presence and occupied the first place in the

מגילת אסתר

א **וַיְהִ֗י** בִּימֵי֙ אֲחַשְׁוֵר֔וֹשׁ ה֣וּא אֲחַשְׁוֵר֔וֹשׁ הַמֹּלֵ֖ךְ מֵהֹ֑דּוּ א

ב וְעַד־כּ֔וּשׁ שֶׁ֥בַע וְעֶשְׂרִ֖ים וּמֵאָ֣ה מְדִינָֽה: בַּיָּמִ֖ים הָהֵ֑ם

כְּשֶׁ֣בֶת ׀ הַמֶּ֣לֶךְ אֲחַשְׁוֵר֗וֹשׁ עַ֚ל כִּסֵּ֣א מַלְכוּת֔וֹ אֲשֶׁ֖ר בְּשׁוּשַׁ֥ן

ג הַבִּירָֽה: בִּשְׁנַ֣ת שָׁל֔וֹשׁ לְמָלְכ֔וֹ עָשָׂ֣ה מִשְׁתֶּ֔ה לְכָל־שָׂרָ֖יו

וַעֲבָדָ֑יו חֵ֣יל ׀ פָּרַ֣ס וּמָדַ֗י הַֽפַּרְתְּמִ֛ים וְשָׂרֵ֥י הַמְּדִינ֖וֹת לְפָנָֽיו:

ד בְּהַרְאֹת֗וֹ אֶת־עֹ֙שֶׁר֙ כְּב֣וֹד מַלְכוּת֔וֹ וְאֶ֨ת־יְקָ֔ר תִּפְאֶ֖רֶת

ה גְּדוּלָּת֑וֹ יָמִ֣ים רַבִּ֔ים שְׁמוֹנִ֥ים וּמְאַ֖ת יֽוֹם: וּבִמְל֣וֹאת ׀ הַיָּמִ֣ים

הָאֵ֗לֶּה עָשָׂ֣ה הַמֶּ֡לֶךְ לְכָל־הָעָ֣ם הַנִּמְצְאִים֩ בְּשׁוּשַׁ֨ן הַבִּירָ֜ה

לְמִגָּד֣וֹל וְעַד־קָטָ֗ן מִשְׁתֶּ֖ה שִׁבְעַ֣ת יָמִ֑ים בַּחֲצַ֕ר גִּנַּ֖ת בִּיתַ֥ן

ו הַמֶּֽלֶךְ: ח֣וּר ׀ כַּרְפַּ֣ס וּתְכֵ֗לֶת אָחוּז֙ בְּחַבְלֵי־ב֣וּץ וְאַרְגָּמָ֔ן

עַל־גְּלִ֥ילֵי כֶ֖סֶף וְעַמּ֣וּדֵי שֵׁ֑שׁ מִטּ֣וֹת ׀ זָהָ֣ב וָכֶ֗סֶף עַ֚ל רִֽצְפַ֣ת

ז בַּֽהַט־וָשֵׁ֖שׁ וְדַ֥ר וְסֹחָֽרֶת: וְהַשְׁק֗וֹת בִּכְלֵ֣י זָהָ֔ב וְכֵלִ֖ים מִכֵּלִ֣ים

ח שׁוֹנִ֑ים וְיֵ֥ין מַלְכ֛וּת רָ֖ב כְּיַ֥ד הַמֶּֽלֶךְ: וְהַשְּׁתִיָּ֥ה כַדָּ֖ת אֵ֣ין אֹנֵ֑ס

כִּי־כֵ֣ן ׀ יִסַּ֣ד הַמֶּ֗לֶךְ עַ֚ל כָּל־רַ֣ב בֵּית֔וֹ לַעֲשׂ֖וֹת כִּרְצ֥וֹן

ט אִישׁ־וָאִֽישׁ: גַּ֚ם וַשְׁתִּ֣י הַמַּלְכָּ֔ה עָשְׂתָ֖ה מִשְׁתֵּ֣ה נָשִׁ֑ים

י בֵּ֚ית הַמַּלְכ֔וּת אֲשֶׁ֖ר לַמֶּ֥לֶךְ אֲחַשְׁוֵרֽוֹשׁ: בַּיּוֹם֙ הַשְּׁבִיעִ֔י כְּט֥וֹב

לֵב־הַמֶּ֖לֶךְ בַּיָּ֑יִן אָמַ֡ר לִ֠מְהוּמָ֠ן בִּזְּתָ֨א חַרְבוֹנָ֜א בִּגְתָ֣א

וַאֲבַגְתָ֗א זֵתַ֤ר וְכַרְכַּס֙ שִׁבְעַת֙ הַסָּ֣רִיסִ֔ים הַמְשָׁ֣רְתִ֔ים אֶת־פְּנֵ֖י

יא הַמֶּ֖לֶךְ אֲחַשְׁוֵרֽוֹשׁ: לְ֠הָבִיא אֶת־וַשְׁתִּ֧י הַמַּלְכָּ֛ה לִפְנֵ֥י הַמֶּ֖לֶךְ

בְּכֶ֣תֶר מַלְכ֑וּת לְהַרְא֨וֹת הָֽעַמִּ֤ים וְהַשָּׂרִים֙ אֶת־יָפְיָ֔הּ כִּֽי־

יב טוֹבַ֥ת מַרְאֶ֖ה הִֽיא: וַתְּמָאֵ֞ן הַמַּלְכָּ֣ה וַשְׁתִּ֗י לָבוֹא֙ בִּדְבַ֣ר

הַמֶּ֔לֶךְ אֲשֶׁ֖ר בְּיַ֣ד הַסָּרִיסִ֑ים וַיִּקְצֹ֤ף הַמֶּ֙לֶךְ֙ מְאֹ֔ד וַחֲמָת֖וֹ

יג בָּעֲרָ֥ה בֽוֹ: וַיֹּ֣אמֶר הַמֶּ֔לֶךְ לַחֲכָמִ֖ים יֹדְעֵ֣י הָֽעִתִּ֑ים

יד כִּי־כֵן֙ דְּבַ֣ר הַמֶּ֔לֶךְ לִפְנֵ֕י כָּל־יֹדְעֵ֖י דָּ֣ת וָדִ֑ין וְהַקָּרֹ֣ב אֵלָ֗יו

כַּרְשְׁנָ֤א שֵׁתָר֙ אַדְמָ֣תָא תַרְשִׁ֔ישׁ מֶ֥רֶס מַרְסְנָ֖א מְמוּכָ֑ן

kingdom.) [15]"What," [he asked,] "shall be done, according to law, to Queen Vashti for failing to obey the command of King Ahasuerus conveyed by the eunuchs?"

[16]Thereupon Memucan declared in the presence of the king and the ministers: "Queen Vashti has committed an offense not only against Your Majesty but also against all the officials and against all the peoples in all the provinces of King Ahasuerus. [17]For the queen's behavior will make all wives despise their husbands, as they reflect that King Ahasuerus himself ordered Queen Vashti to be brought before him, but she would not come. [18]This very day the ladies of Persia and Media, who have heard of the queen's behavior, will cite it to all Your Majesty's officials, and there will be no end of scorn and provocation!

[19]"If it please Your Majesty, let a royal edict be issued by you, and let it be written into the laws of Persia and Media, so that it cannot be abrogated, that Vashti shall never enter the presence of King Ahasuerus. And let Your Majesty bestow her royal state upon another who is more worthy than she. [20]Then will the judgment executed by Your Majesty resound throughout your realm, vast though it is; and all wives will treat their husbands with respect, high and low alike."

[21]The proposal was approved by the king and the ministers, and the king did as Memucan proposed. [22]Dispatches were sent to all the provinces of the king, to every province in its own script and to every nation in its own language, that every man should wield authority in his home and speak the language of his own people.

2 [1]Some time afterward, when the anger of King Ahasuerus subsided, he thought of Vashti and what she had done and what had been decreed against her. [2]The king's servants who attended him said, "Let beautiful young virgins be sought out for Your Majesty. [3]Let Your Majesty appoint officers in every province of your realm to assemble all the beautiful young virgins at the fortress Shushan, in the harem under the supervision of Hege, the king's eunuch, guardian of the women. Let them be provided with

שִׁבְעַת שָׂרֵי ׀ פָּרַס וּמָדַי רֹאֵי פְּנֵי הַמֶּלֶךְ הַיֹּשְׁבִים רִאשֹׁנָה

בַּמַּלְכוּת: כְּדָת מַה־לַעֲשׂוֹת בַּמַּלְכָּה וַשְׁתִּי עַל ׀ אֲשֶׁר טז
לֹא־עָשְׂתָה אֶת־מַאֲמַר הַמֶּלֶךְ אֲחַשְׁוֵרוֹשׁ בְּיַד הַסָּרִיסִים:

וַיֹּאמֶר מומכן* לִפְנֵי הַמֶּלֶךְ וְהַשָּׂרִים לֹא עַל־הַמֶּלֶךְ לְבַדּוֹ מְמוּכָן יז
עָוְתָה וַשְׁתִּי הַמַּלְכָּה כִּי עַל־כָּל־הַשָּׂרִים וְעַל־כָּל־הָעַמִּים

אֲשֶׁר בְּכָל־מְדִינוֹת הַמֶּלֶךְ אֲחַשְׁוֵרוֹשׁ: כִּי־יֵצֵא דְבַר־ יז
הַמַּלְכָּה עַל־כָּל־הַנָּשִׁים לְהַבְזוֹת בַּעְלֵיהֶן בְּעֵינֵיהֶן
בְּאָמְרָם הַמֶּלֶךְ אֲחַשְׁוֵרוֹשׁ אָמַר לְהָבִיא אֶת־וַשְׁתִּי

הַמַּלְכָּה לְפָנָיו וְלֹא־בָאָה: וְהַיּוֹם הַזֶּה תֹּאמַרְנָה ׀ שָׂרוֹת יח
פָּרַס־וּמָדַי אֲשֶׁר שָׁמְעוּ אֶת־דְּבַר הַמַּלְכָּה לְכֹל שָׂרֵי

הַמֶּלֶךְ וּכְדַי בִּזָּיוֹן וָקָצֶף: אִם־עַל־הַמֶּלֶךְ טוֹב יֵצֵא דְבַר־ יט
מַלְכוּת מִלְּפָנָיו וְיִכָּתֵב בְּדָתֵי פָרַס־וּמָדַי וְלֹא יַעֲבוֹר אֲשֶׁר
לֹא־תָבוֹא וַשְׁתִּי לִפְנֵי הַמֶּלֶךְ אֲחַשְׁוֵרוֹשׁ וּמַלְכוּתָהּ יִתֵּן

הַמֶּלֶךְ לִרְעוּתָהּ הַטּוֹבָה מִמֶּנָּה: וְנִשְׁמַע פִּתְגָם הַמֶּלֶךְ אֲשֶׁר־ כ
יַעֲשֶׂה בְּכָל־מַלְכוּתוֹ כִּי רַבָּה הִיא וְכָל־הַנָּשִׁים יִתְּנוּ יְקָר

לְבַעְלֵיהֶן לְמִגָּדוֹל וְעַד־קָטָן: וַיִּיטַב הַדָּבָר בְּעֵינֵי הַמֶּלֶךְ כא

וְהַשָּׂרִים וַיַּעַשׂ הַמֶּלֶךְ כִּדְבַר מְמוּכָן: וַיִּשְׁלַח סְפָרִים כב
אֶל־כָּל־מְדִינוֹת הַמֶּלֶךְ אֶל־מְדִינָה וּמְדִינָה כִּכְתָבָהּ וְאֶל־
עַם וָעַם כִּלְשׁוֹנוֹ לִהְיוֹת כָּל־אִישׁ שֹׂרֵר בְּבֵיתוֹ וּמְדַבֵּר כִּלְשׁוֹן

עַמּוֹ: אַחַר הַדְּבָרִים הָאֵלֶּה כְּשֹׁךְ חֲמַת הַמֶּלֶךְ ב א
אֲחַשְׁוֵרוֹשׁ זָכַר אֶת־וַשְׁתִּי וְאֵת אֲשֶׁר־עָשָׂתָה וְאֵת

אֲשֶׁר־נִגְזַר עָלֶיהָ: וַיֹּאמְרוּ נַעֲרֵי־הַמֶּלֶךְ מְשָׁרְתָיו יְבַקְשׁוּ ב

לַמֶּלֶךְ נְעָרוֹת בְּתוּלוֹת טוֹבוֹת מַרְאֶה: וְיַפְקֵד הַמֶּלֶךְ ג
פְּקִידִים בְּכָל־מְדִינוֹת מַלְכוּתוֹ וְיִקְבְּצוּ אֶת־כָּל־נַעֲרָה־
בְתוּלָה טוֹבַת מַרְאֶה אֶל־שׁוּשַׁן הַבִּירָה אֶל־בֵּית הַנָּשִׁים
אֶל־יַד הֵגֶא סְרִיס הַמֶּלֶךְ שֹׁמֵר הַנָּשִׁים וְנָתוֹן תַּמְרֻקֵיהֶן:

וְהַנַּעֲרָה אֲשֶׁר תִּיטַב בְּעֵינֵי הַמֶּלֶךְ תִּמְלֹךְ תַּחַת וַשְׁתִּי ד

their cosmetics. ⁴And let the maiden who pleases Your Majesty be queen instead of Vashti." The proposal pleased the king, and he acted upon it.

⁵In the fortress Shushan lived a Jew by the name of Mordecai, son of Jair son of Shimei son of Kish, a Benjaminite. ⁶[Kish] had been exiled from Jerusalem in the group that was carried into exile along with King Jeconiah of Judah, which had been driven into exile by King Nebuchadnezzar of Babylon. – ⁷He was foster father to Hadassah – that is, Esther – his uncle's daughter, for she had neither father nor mother. The maiden was shapely and beautiful; and when her father and mother died, Mordecai adopted her as his own daughter.

⁸When the king's order and edict was proclaimed, and when many girls were assembled in the fortress Shushan under the supervision of Hegai, Esther too was taken into the king's palace under the supervision of Hegai, guardian of the women. ⁹The girl pleased him and won his favor, and he hastened to furnish her with her cosmetics and her rations, as well as with the seven maids who were her due from the king's palace; and he treated her and her maids with special kindness in the harem. ¹⁰Esther did not reveal her people or her kindred, for Mordecai had told her not to reveal it. ¹¹Every single day Mordecai would walk about in front of the court of the harem, to learn how Esther was faring and what was happening to her.

¹²When each girl's turn came to go to King Ahasuerus at the end of the twelve months' treatment prescribed for women (for that was the period spent on beautifying them: six months with oil of myrrh and six months with perfumes and women's cosmetics, ¹³and it was after that that the girl would go to the king), whatever she asked for would be given her to take with her from the harem to the king's palace. ¹⁴She would go in the evening and leave in the morning for a second harem in charge of Shaashgaz, the king's eunuch, guardian of the concubines. She would not go again to the king unless the king wanted her, when she would be summoned by name.

¹⁵When the turn came for Esther daughter of Abihail – the uncle of Mordecai, who had adopted her as his own daughter – to go to the king, she did not ask for anything but what Hegai, the king's eunuch, guardian

ה וַיִּיטַב הַדָּבָר בְּעֵינֵי הַמֶּלֶךְ וַיַּעַשׂ כֵּן: אִישׁ יְהוּדִי הָיָה בְּשׁוּשַׁן הַבִּירָה וּשְׁמוֹ מָרְדֳּכַי בֶּן יָאִיר בֶּן־שִׁמְעִי

ו בֶּן־קִישׁ אִישׁ יְמִינִי: אֲשֶׁר הָגְלָה מִירוּשָׁלַיִם עִם־הַגֹּלָה אֲשֶׁר הָגְלְתָה עִם יְכָנְיָה מֶלֶךְ־יְהוּדָה אֲשֶׁר הֶגְלָה

ז נְבוּכַדְנֶצַּר מֶלֶךְ בָּבֶל: וַיְהִי אֹמֵן אֶת־הֲדַסָּה הִיא אֶסְתֵּר בַּת־דֹּדוֹ כִּי אֵין לָהּ אָב וָאֵם וְהַנַּעֲרָה יְפַת־תֹּאַר וְטוֹבַת

ח מַרְאֶה וּבְמוֹת אָבִיהָ וְאִמָּהּ לְקָחָהּ מָרְדֳּכַי לוֹ לְבַת: וַיְהִי בְּהִשָּׁמַע דְּבַר־הַמֶּלֶךְ וְדָתוֹ וּבְהִקָּבֵץ נְעָרוֹת רַבּוֹת אֶל־שׁוּשַׁן הַבִּירָה אֶל־יַד הֵגָי וַתִּלָּקַח אֶסְתֵּר אֶל־בֵּית

ט הַמֶּלֶךְ אֶל־יַד הֵגַי שֹׁמֵר הַנָּשִׁים: וַתִּיטַב הַנַּעֲרָה בְעֵינָיו וַתִּשָּׂא חֶסֶד לְפָנָיו וַיְבַהֵל אֶת־תַּמְרוּקֶיהָ וְאֶת־מָנוֹתֶהָ לָתֵת לָהּ וְאֵת שֶׁבַע הַנְּעָרוֹת הָרְאֻיוֹת לָתֶת־לָהּ מִבֵּית

י הַמֶּלֶךְ וַיְשַׁנֶּהָ וְאֶת־נַעֲרוֹתֶיהָ לְטוֹב בֵּית הַנָּשִׁים: לֹא־ הִגִּידָה אֶסְתֵּר אֶת־עַמָּהּ וְאֶת־מוֹלַדְתָּהּ כִּי מָרְדֳּכַי צִוָּה

יא עָלֶיהָ אֲשֶׁר לֹא־תַגִּיד: וּבְכָל־יוֹם וָיוֹם מָרְדֳּכַי מִתְהַלֵּךְ לִפְנֵי חֲצַר בֵּית־הַנָּשִׁים לָדַעַת אֶת־שְׁלוֹם אֶסְתֵּר וּמַה־

יב יֵעָשֶׂה בָּהּ: וּבְהַגִּיעַ תֹּר נַעֲרָה וְנַעֲרָה לָבוֹא ׀ אֶל־הַמֶּלֶךְ אֲחַשְׁוֵרוֹשׁ מִקֵּץ הֱיוֹת לָהּ כְּדָת הַנָּשִׁים שְׁנֵים עָשָׂר חֹדֶשׁ כִּי כֵּן יִמְלְאוּ יְמֵי מְרוּקֵיהֶן שִׁשָּׁה חֳדָשִׁים בְּשֶׁמֶן הַמֹּר

יג וְשִׁשָּׁה חֳדָשִׁים בַּבְּשָׂמִים וּבְתַמְרוּקֵי הַנָּשִׁים: וּבָזֶה הַנַּעֲרָה בָּאָה אֶל־הַמֶּלֶךְ אֵת כָּל־אֲשֶׁר תֹּאמַר יִנָּתֵן לָהּ לָבוֹא

יד עִמָּהּ מִבֵּית הַנָּשִׁים עַד־בֵּית הַמֶּלֶךְ: בָּעֶרֶב ׀ הִיא בָאָה וּבַבֹּקֶר הִיא שָׁבָה אֶל־בֵּית הַנָּשִׁים שֵׁנִי אֶל־יַד שַׁעֲשְׁגַז סְרִיס הַמֶּלֶךְ שֹׁמֵר הַפִּילַגְשִׁים לֹא־תָבוֹא עוֹד אֶל־הַמֶּלֶךְ

טו כִּי אִם־חָפֵץ בָּהּ הַמֶּלֶךְ וְנִקְרְאָה בְשֵׁם: וּבְהַגִּיעַ תֹּר־אֶסְתֵּר בַּת־אֲבִיחַיִל ׀ דֹּד מָרְדֳּכַי אֲשֶׁר לָקַח־לוֹ לְבַת לָבוֹא אֶל־הַמֶּלֶךְ לֹא בִקְשָׁה דָּבָר כִּי אִם אֶת־אֲשֶׁר יֹאמַר הֵגַי

of the women, advised. Yet Esther won the admiration of all who saw her.

[16]Esther was taken to King Ahasuerus, in his royal palace, in the tenth month, which is the month of Tebeth, in the seventh year of his reign. [17]The king loved Esther more than all the other women, and she won his grace and favor more than all the virgins. So he set a royal diadem on her head and made her queen instead of Vashti. [18]The king gave a great banquet for all his officials and courtiers, "the banquet of Esther." He proclaimed a remission of taxes for the provinces and distributed gifts as befits a king.

[19]When the virgins were assembled a second time, Mordecai sat in the palace gate. [20]But Esther still did not reveal her kindred or her people, as Mordecai had instructed her; for Esther obeyed Mordecai's bidding, as she had done when she was under his tutelage.

[21]At that time, when Mordecai was sitting in the palace gate, Bigthan and Teresh, two of the king's eunuchs who guarded the threshold, became angry, and plotted to do away with King Ahasuerus. [22]Mordecai learned of it and told it to Queen Esther, and Esther reported it to the king in Mordecai's name. [23]The matter was investigated and found to be so, and the two were impaled on stakes. This was recorded in the book of annals at the instance of the king.

3 [1]Some time afterward, King Ahasuerus promoted Haman son of Hammedatha the Agagite; he advanced him and seated him higher than any of his fellow officials. [2]All the king's courtiers in the palace gate knelt and bowed low to Haman, for such was the king's order concerning him; but Mordecai would not kneel or bow low. [3]Then the king's courtiers who were in the palace gate said to Mordecai, "Why do you disobey the king's order?" [4]When they spoke to him day after day and he would not listen to them, they told Haman, in order to see whether Mordecai's resolve would prevail; for he had explained to them that he was a Jew. [5]When Haman saw that Mordecai would not kneel or bow low to him, Haman was filled with rage. [6]But he disdained to lay hands on Mordecai alone; having been told who Mordecai's people were, Haman plotted to do away with all the

סְרִיס־הַמֶּלֶךְ שֹׁמֵר הַנָּשִׁים וַתְּהִי אֶסְתֵּר נֹשֵׂאת חֵן בְּעֵינֵי

טז כָל־רֹאֶיהָ: וַתִּלָּקַח אֶסְתֵּר אֶל־הַמֶּלֶךְ אֲחַשְׁוֵרוֹשׁ אֶל־בֵּית
מַלְכוּתוֹ בַּחֹדֶשׁ הָעֲשִׂירִי הוּא־חֹדֶשׁ טֵבֵת בִּשְׁנַת־שֶׁבַע

יז לְמַלְכוּתוֹ: וַיֶּאֱהַב הַמֶּלֶךְ אֶת־אֶסְתֵּר מִכָּל־הַנָּשִׁים
וַתִּשָּׂא־חֵן וָחֶסֶד לְפָנָיו מִכָּל־הַבְּתוּלוֹת וַיָּשֶׂם כֶּתֶר־

יח מַלְכוּת בְּרֹאשָׁהּ וַיַּמְלִיכֶהָ תַּחַת וַשְׁתִּי: וַיַּעַשׂ הַמֶּלֶךְ
מִשְׁתֶּה גָדוֹל לְכָל־שָׂרָיו וַעֲבָדָיו אֵת מִשְׁתֵּה אֶסְתֵּר וַהֲנָחָה

יט לַמְּדִינוֹת עָשָׂה וַיִּתֵּן מַשְׂאֵת כְּיַד הַמֶּלֶךְ: וּבְהִקָּבֵץ בְּתוּלוֹת

כ שֵׁנִית וּמָרְדֳּכַי יֹשֵׁב בְּשַׁעַר־הַמֶּלֶךְ: אֵין אֶסְתֵּר מַגֶּדֶת
מוֹלַדְתָּהּ וְאֶת־עַמָּהּ כַּאֲשֶׁר צִוָּה עָלֶיהָ מָרְדֳּכַי וְאֶת־
מַאֲמַר מָרְדֳּכַי אֶסְתֵּר עֹשָׂה כַּאֲשֶׁר הָיְתָה בְאָמְנָה

כא אִתּוֹ: בַּיָּמִים הָהֵם וּמָרְדֳּכַי יוֹשֵׁב בְּשַׁעַר־הַמֶּלֶךְ קָצַף בִּגְתָן
וָתֶרֶשׁ שְׁנֵי־סָרִיסֵי הַמֶּלֶךְ מִשֹּׁמְרֵי הַסַּף וַיְבַקְשׁוּ לִשְׁלֹחַ

כב יָד בַּמֶּלֶךְ אֲחַשְׁוֵרוֹשׁ: וַיִּוָּדַע הַדָּבָר לְמָרְדֳּכַי וַיַּגֵּד לְאֶסְתֵּר

כג הַמַּלְכָּה וַתֹּאמֶר אֶסְתֵּר לַמֶּלֶךְ בְּשֵׁם מָרְדֳּכָי: וַיְבֻקַּשׁ
הַדָּבָר וַיִּמָּצֵא וַיִּתָּלוּ שְׁנֵיהֶם עַל־עֵץ וַיִּכָּתֵב בְּסֵפֶר דִּבְרֵי

ג הַיָּמִים לִפְנֵי הַמֶּלֶךְ:   אַחַר | הַדְּבָרִים הָאֵלֶּה גִּדַּל

א הַמֶּלֶךְ אֲחַשְׁוֵרוֹשׁ אֶת־הָמָן בֶּן־הַמְּדָתָא הָאֲגָגִי וַיְנַשְּׂאֵהוּ

ב וַיָּשֶׂם אֶת־כִּסְאוֹ מֵעַל כָּל־הַשָּׂרִים אֲשֶׁר אִתּוֹ: וְכָל־עַבְדֵי
הַמֶּלֶךְ אֲשֶׁר־בְּשַׁעַר הַמֶּלֶךְ כֹּרְעִים וּמִשְׁתַּחֲוִים לְהָמָן
כִּי־כֵן צִוָּה־לוֹ הַמֶּלֶךְ וּמָרְדֳּכַי לֹא יִכְרַע וְלֹא יִשְׁתַּחֲוֶה:

ג וַיֹּאמְרוּ עַבְדֵי הַמֶּלֶךְ אֲשֶׁר־בְּשַׁעַר הַמֶּלֶךְ לְמָרְדֳּכָי מַדּוּעַ

ד אַתָּה עוֹבֵר אֵת מִצְוַת הַמֶּלֶךְ: וַיְהִי בְּאָמְרָם* אֵלָיו יוֹם כְּאָמְרָם
וָיוֹם וְלֹא שָׁמַע אֲלֵיהֶם וַיַּגִּידוּ לְהָמָן לִרְאוֹת הֲיַעַמְדוּ

ה דִּבְרֵי מָרְדֳּכַי כִּי־הִגִּיד לָהֶם אֲשֶׁר־הוּא יְהוּדִי: וַיַּרְא הָמָן

ו כִּי־אֵין מָרְדֳּכַי כֹּרֵעַ וּמִשְׁתַּחֲוֶה לוֹ וַיִּמָּלֵא הָמָן חֵמָה: וַיִּבֶז
בְּעֵינָיו לִשְׁלֹחַ יָד בְּמָרְדֳּכַי לְבַדּוֹ כִּי־הִגִּידוּ לוֹ אֶת־עַם

Jews, Mordecai's people, throughout the kingdom of Ahasuerus.

⁷In the first month, that is, the month of Nisan, in the twelfth year of King Ahasuerus, pur – which means "the lot" – was cast before Haman concerning every day and every month, [until it fell on] the twelfth month, that is, the month of Adar. ⁸Haman then said to King Ahasuerus, "There is a certain people, scattered and dispersed among the other peoples in all the provinces of your realm, whose laws are different from those of any other people and who do not obey the king's laws; and it is not in Your Majesty's interest to tolerate them. ⁹If it please Your Majesty, let an edict be drawn for their destruction, and I will pay ten thousand talents of silver to the stewards for deposit in the royal treasury." ¹⁰Thereupon the king removed his signet ring from his hand and gave it to Haman son of Hammedatha the Agagite, the foe of the Jews. ¹¹And the king said, "The money and the people are yours to do with as you see fit."

¹²On the thirteenth day of the first month, the king's scribes were summoned and a decree was issued, as Haman directed, to the king's satraps, to the governors of every province, and to the officials of every people, to every province in its own script and to every people in its own language. The orders were issued in the name of King Ahasuerus and sealed with the king's signet. ¹³Accordingly, written instructions were dispatched by couriers to all the king's provinces to destroy, massacre, and exterminate all the Jews, young and old, children and women, on a single day, on the thirteenth day of the twelfth month – that is, the month of Adar – and to plunder their possessions. ¹⁴The text of the document was to the effect that a law should be proclaimed in every single province; it was to be publicly displayed to all the peoples, so that they might be ready for that day.

¹⁵The couriers went out posthaste on the royal mission, and the decree was proclaimed in the fortress Shushan. The king and Haman sat down to feast, but the city of Shushan was dumbfounded.

4 ¹When Mordecai learned all that had happened, Mordecai tore his clothes and put on sackcloth and ashes. He went through the city,

מָרְדֳּכָי וַיְבַקֵּשׁ הָמָן לְהַשְׁמִיד אֶת־כָּל־הַיְּהוּדִים אֲשֶׁר
ז בְּכָל־מַלְכוּת אֲחַשְׁוֵרוֹשׁ עַם מָרְדֳּכָי׃ בַּחֹדֶשׁ הָרִאשׁוֹן
הוּא־חֹדֶשׁ נִיסָן בִּשְׁנַת שְׁתֵּים עֶשְׂרֵה לַמֶּלֶךְ אֲחַשְׁוֵרוֹשׁ
הִפִּיל פּוּר הוּא הַגּוֹרָל לִפְנֵי הָמָן מִיּוֹם ׀ לְיוֹם וּמֵחֹדֶשׁ
ח לְחֹדֶשׁ שְׁנֵים־עָשָׂר הוּא־חֹדֶשׁ אֲדָר׃ וַיֹּאמֶר הָמָן
לַמֶּלֶךְ אֲחַשְׁוֵרוֹשׁ יֶשְׁנוֹ עַם־אֶחָד מְפֻזָּר וּמְפֹרָד בֵּין הָעַמִּים
בְּכֹל מְדִינוֹת מַלְכוּתֶךָ וְדָתֵיהֶם שֹׁנוֹת מִכָּל־עָם וְאֶת־דָּתֵי
ט הַמֶּלֶךְ אֵינָם עֹשִׂים וְלַמֶּלֶךְ אֵין־שֹׁוֶה לְהַנִּיחָם׃ אִם־עַל־
הַמֶּלֶךְ טוֹב יִכָּתֵב לְאַבְּדָם וַעֲשֶׂרֶת אֲלָפִים כִּכַּר־כֶּסֶף
י אֶשְׁקוֹל עַל־יְדֵי עֹשֵׂי הַמְּלָאכָה לְהָבִיא אֶל־גִּנְזֵי הַמֶּלֶךְ׃
וַיָּסַר הַמֶּלֶךְ אֶת־טַבַּעְתּוֹ מֵעַל יָדוֹ וַיִּתְּנָהּ לְהָמָן בֶּן־
יא הַמְּדָתָא הָאֲגָגִי צֹרֵר הַיְּהוּדִים׃ וַיֹּאמֶר הַמֶּלֶךְ לְהָמָן הַכֶּסֶף
יב נָתוּן לָךְ וְהָעָם לַעֲשׂוֹת בּוֹ כַּטּוֹב בְּעֵינֶיךָ׃ וַיִּקָּרְאוּ סֹפְרֵי
הַמֶּלֶךְ בַּחֹדֶשׁ הָרִאשׁוֹן בִּשְׁלוֹשָׁה עָשָׂר יוֹם בּוֹ וַיִּכָּתֵב
כְּכָל־אֲשֶׁר־צִוָּה הָמָן אֶל אֲחַשְׁדַּרְפְּנֵי־הַמֶּלֶךְ וְאֶל־הַפַּחוֹת
אֲשֶׁר ׀ עַל־מְדִינָה וּמְדִינָה וְאֶל־שָׂרֵי עַם וָעָם מְדִינָה וּמְדִינָה
כִּכְתָבָהּ וְעַם וָעָם כִּלְשׁוֹנוֹ בְּשֵׁם הַמֶּלֶךְ אֲחַשְׁוֵרֹשׁ נִכְתָּב
יג וְנֶחְתָּם בְּטַבַּעַת הַמֶּלֶךְ׃ וְנִשְׁלוֹחַ סְפָרִים בְּיַד הָרָצִים
אֶל־כָּל־מְדִינוֹת הַמֶּלֶךְ לְהַשְׁמִיד לַהֲרֹג וּלְאַבֵּד אֶת־כָּל־
הַיְּהוּדִים מִנַּעַר וְעַד־זָקֵן טַף וְנָשִׁים בְּיוֹם אֶחָד בִּשְׁלוֹשָׁה
עָשָׂר לְחֹדֶשׁ שְׁנֵים־עָשָׂר הוּא־חֹדֶשׁ אֲדָר וּשְׁלָלָם לָבוֹז׃
יד פַּתְשֶׁגֶן הַכְּתָב לְהִנָּתֵן דָּת בְּכָל־מְדִינָה וּמְדִינָה גָּלוּי
טו לְכָל־הָעַמִּים לִהְיוֹת עֲתִדִים לַיּוֹם הַזֶּה׃ הָרָצִים יָצְאוּ
דְחוּפִים בִּדְבַר הַמֶּלֶךְ וְהַדָּת נִתְּנָה בְּשׁוּשַׁן הַבִּירָה וְהַמֶּלֶךְ
ד א וְהָמָן יָשְׁבוּ לִשְׁתּוֹת וְהָעִיר שׁוּשָׁן נָבוֹכָה׃ וּמָרְדֳּכַי
יָדַע אֶת־כָּל־אֲשֶׁר נַעֲשָׂה וַיִּקְרַע מָרְדֳּכַי אֶת־בְּגָדָיו וַיִּלְבַּשׁ
שַׂק וָאֵפֶר וַיֵּצֵא בְּתוֹךְ הָעִיר וַיִּזְעַק זְעָקָה גְדוֹלָה וּמָרָה׃

crying out loudly and bitterly, [2]until he came in front of the palace gate; for one could not enter the palace gate wearing sackcloth. – [3]Also, in every province that the king's command and decree reached, there was great mourning among the Jews, with fasting, weeping, and wailing, and everybody lay in sackcloth and ashes. – [4]When Esther's maidens and eunuchs came and informed her, the queen was greatly agitated. She sent clothing for Mordecai to wear, so that he might take off his sackcloth; but he refused. [5]Thereupon Esther summoned Hathach, one of the eunuchs whom the king had appointed to serve her, and sent him to Mordecai to learn the why and wherefore of it all. [6]Hathach went out to Mordecai in the city square in front of the palace gate; [7]and Mordecai told him all that had happened to him, and all about the money that Haman had offered to pay into the royal treasury for the destruction of the Jews. [8]He also gave him the written text of the law that had been proclaimed in Shushan for their destruction. [He bade him] show it to Esther and inform her, and charge her to go to the king and to appeal to him and to plead with him for her people. [9]When Hathach came and delivered Mordecai's message to Esther, [10]Esther told Hathach to take back to Mordecai the following reply: [11]"All the king's courtiers and the people of the king's provinces know that if any person, man or woman, enters the king's presence in the inner court without having been summoned, there is but one law for him – that he be put to death. Only if the king extends the golden scepter to him may he live. Now I have not been summoned to visit the king for the last thirty days."

[12]When Mordecai was told what Esther had said, [13]Mordecai had this message delivered to Esther: "Do not imagine that you, of all the Jews, will escape with your life by being in the king's palace. [14]On the contrary, if you keep silent in this crisis, relief and deliverance will come to the Jews from another quarter, while you and your father's house will perish. And who knows, perhaps you have attained to royal position for just such a crisis." [15]Then Esther sent back this answer to Mordecai: [16]"Go, assemble all the Jews who live in Shushan, and fast in my behalf; do not eat or drink for three days, night or day. I and my maidens will observe the same

ב וַיָּב֗וֹא עַ֣ד לִפְנֵ֣י שַֽׁעַר־הַמֶּ֑לֶךְ כִּ֣י אֵ֥ין לָב֛וֹא אֶל־שַׁ֥עַר

ג הַמֶּ֖לֶךְ בִּלְב֥וּשׁ שָֽׂק׃ וּבְכָל־מְדִינָ֣ה וּמְדִינָ֗ה מְקוֹם֙ אֲשֶׁ֨ר

דְּבַר־הַמֶּ֤לֶךְ וְדָתוֹ֙ מַגִּ֔יעַ אֵ֤בֶל גָּדוֹל֙ לַיְּהוּדִ֔ים וְצ֥וֹם וּבְכִ֖י

ד וּמִסְפֵּ֑ד שַׂ֣ק וָאֵ֔פֶר יֻצַּ֖ע לָֽרַבִּֽים׃ וַתָּבֹ֩אנָה֩ נַעֲר֨וֹת אֶסְתֵּ֜ר וַתָּב֡וֹאנָה*

וְסָרִיסֶ֗יהָ וַיַּגִּ֣ידוּ לָ֔הּ וַתִּתְחַלְחַ֥ל הַמַּלְכָּ֖ה מְאֹ֑ד וַתִּשְׁלַ֨ח

בְּגָדִ֜ים לְהַלְבִּ֣ישׁ אֶֽת־מָרְדֳּכַ֗י וּלְהָסִ֥יר שַׂקּ֛וֹ מֵעָלָ֖יו וְלֹ֥א

ה קִבֵּֽל׃ וַתִּקְרָא֩ אֶסְתֵּ֨ר לַהֲתָ֜ךְ מִסָּרִיסֵ֤י הַמֶּ֙לֶךְ֙ אֲשֶׁ֣ר הֶעֱמִ֣יד

לְפָנֶ֔יהָ וַתְּצַוֵּ֖הוּ עַֽל־מָרְדֳּכָ֑י לָדַ֥עַת מַה־זֶּ֖ה וְעַל־מַה־זֶּֽה׃

ו וַיֵּצֵ֥א הֲתָ֖ךְ אֶֽל־מָרְדֳּכָ֑י אֶל־רְח֣וֹב הָעִ֔יר אֲשֶׁ֖ר לִפְנֵ֥י

ז שַֽׁעַר־הַמֶּֽלֶךְ׃ וַיַּגֶּד־ל֣וֹ מָרְדֳּכַ֔י אֵ֖ת כָּל־אֲשֶׁ֣ר קָרָ֑הוּ וְאֵ֣ת ׀

פָּרָשַׁ֣ת הַכֶּ֗סֶף אֲשֶׁ֨ר אָמַ֤ר הָמָן֙ לִשְׁקוֹל֙ עַל־גִּנְזֵ֣י הַמֶּ֔לֶךְ

ח בַּיְּהוּדִיִּ֖ים* לְאַבְּדָֽם׃ וְאֶת־פַּתְשֶׁ֣גֶן כְּתָֽב־הַ֠דָּת אֲשֶׁר־נִתַּ֨ן בַּיְּהוּדִ֖ים

בְּשׁוּשָׁ֤ן לְהַשְׁמִידָם֙ נָ֣תַן ל֔וֹ לְהַרְא֥וֹת אֶת־אֶסְתֵּ֖ר וּלְהַגִּ֣יד

לָ֑הּ וּלְצַוּ֣וֹת עָלֶ֗יהָ לָב֨וֹא אֶל־הַמֶּ֧לֶךְ לְהִֽתְחַנֶּן־ל֛וֹ וּלְבַקֵּ֥שׁ

ט מִלְּפָנָ֖יו עַל־עַמָּֽהּ׃ וַיָּב֖וֹא הֲתָ֑ךְ וַיַּגֵּ֣ד לְאֶסְתֵּ֔ר אֵ֖ת דִּבְרֵ֥י

יא מָרְדֳּכָֽי׃ וַתֹּ֤אמֶר אֶסְתֵּר֙ לַהֲתָ֔ךְ וַתְּצַוֵּ֖הוּ אֶֽל־מָרְדֳּכָֽי׃ כָּל־

עַבְדֵ֣י הַמֶּ֡לֶךְ וְעַם־מְדִינ֨וֹת הַמֶּ֜לֶךְ יֹֽדְעִ֗ים אֲשֶׁ֣ר כָּל־אִ֣ישׁ

וְאִשָּׁ֡ה אֲשֶׁ֣ר יָבֽוֹא־אֶל־הַמֶּלֶךְ֩ אֶל־הֶחָצֵ֨ר הַפְּנִימִ֜ית אֲשֶׁ֣ר

לֹֽא־יִקָּרֵ֗א אַחַ֤ת דָּתוֹ֙ לְהָמִ֔ית לְבַ֞ד מֵאֲשֶׁ֨ר יֽוֹשִׁיט־ל֧וֹ

הַמֶּ֛לֶךְ אֶת־שַׁרְבִ֥יט הַזָּהָ֖ב וְחָיָ֑ה וַאֲנִ֗י לֹ֤א נִקְרֵ֙אתִי֙ לָב֣וֹא

יב אֶל־הַמֶּ֔לֶךְ זֶ֖ה שְׁלוֹשִׁ֥ים יֽוֹם׃ וַיַּגִּ֣ידוּ לְמָרְדֳּכָ֔י אֵ֖ת דִּבְרֵ֥י

יג אֶסְתֵּֽר׃ וַיֹּ֥אמֶר מָרְדֳּכַ֖י לְהָשִׁ֣יב אֶל־אֶסְתֵּ֑ר אַל־תְּדַמִּ֣י

יד בְנַפְשֵׁ֔ךְ לְהִמָּלֵ֥ט בֵּית־הַמֶּ֖לֶךְ מִכָּל־הַיְּהוּדִֽים׃ כִּ֣י אִם־

הַחֲרֵ֣שׁ תַּחֲרִישִׁי֮ בָּעֵ֣ת הַזֹּאת֒ רֶ֣וַח וְהַצָּלָ֞ה יַעֲמ֤וֹד לַיְּהוּדִים֙

מִמָּק֣וֹם אַחֵ֔ר וְאַ֥תְּ וּבֵית־אָבִ֖יךְ תֹּאבֵ֑דוּ וּמִ֣י יוֹדֵ֔עַ אִם־לְעֵ֣ת

טו כָּזֹ֔את הִגַּ֖עַתְּ לַמַּלְכֽוּת׃ וַתֹּ֥אמֶר אֶסְתֵּ֖ר לְהָשִׁ֥יב אֶֽל־מָרְדֳּכָֽי׃

טז לֵךְ֩ כְּנ֨וֹס אֶת־כָּל־הַיְּהוּדִ֜ים הַֽנִּמְצְאִ֣ים בְּשׁוּשָׁ֗ן וְצ֣וּמוּ עָלַ֡י

fast. Then I shall go to the king, though it is contrary to the law; and if I am to perish, I shall perish!" [17]So Mordecai went about [the city] and did just as Esther had commanded him.

5 [1]On the third day, Esther put on royal apparel and stood in the inner court of the king's palace, facing the king's palace, while the king was sitting on his royal throne in the throne room facing the entrance of the palace. [2]As soon as the king saw Queen Esther standing in the court, she won his favor. The king extended to Esther the golden scepter which he had in his hand, and Esther approached and touched the tip of the scepter. [3]"What troubles you, Queen Esther?" the king asked her. "And what is your request? Even to half the kingdom, it shall be granted you."

[4]"If it please Your Majesty," Esther replied, "let Your Majesty and Haman come today to the feast that I have prepared for him." [5]The king commanded, "Tell Haman to hurry and do Esther's bidding." So the king and Haman came to the feast that Esther had prepared.

[6]At the wine feast, the king asked Esther, "What is your wish? It shall be granted you. And what is your request? Even to half the kingdom, it shall be fulfilled." [7]"My wish," replied Esther, "my request – [8]if Your Majesty will do me the favor, if it please Your Majesty to grant my wish and accede to my request – let Your Majesty and Haman come to the feast which I will prepare for them; and tomorrow I will do Your Majesty's bidding."

[9]That day Haman went out happy and lighthearted. But when Haman saw Mordecai in the palace gate, and Mordecai did not rise or even stir on his account, Haman was filled with rage at him. [10]Nevertheless, Haman controlled himself and went home. He sent for his friends and his wife Zeresh, [11]and Haman told them about his great wealth and his many sons, and all about how the king had promoted him and advanced him above the officials and the king's courtiers.

[12]"What is more," said Haman, "Queen Esther gave a feast, and besides the king she did not have anyone but me. And tomorrow too I am invited by her along with the king. [13]Yet all this means nothing to me

וְאַל־תֹּאכְלוּ וְאַל־תִּשְׁתּוּ שְׁלֹשֶׁת יָמִים לַיְלָה וָיוֹם גַּם־אֲנִי
וְנַעֲרֹתַי אָצוּם כֵּן וּבְכֵן אָבוֹא אֶל־הַמֶּלֶךְ אֲשֶׁר לֹא־כַדָּת

יז וְכַאֲשֶׁר אָבַדְתִּי אָבָדְתִּי: וַיַּעֲבֹר מָרְדֳּכָי וַיַּעַשׂ כְּכֹל אֲשֶׁר־

ה א צִוְּתָה עָלָיו אֶסְתֵּר: וַיְהִי | בַּיּוֹם הַשְּׁלִישִׁי וַתִּלְבַּשׁ
אֶסְתֵּר מַלְכוּת וַתַּעֲמֹד בַּחֲצַר בֵּית־הַמֶּלֶךְ הַפְּנִימִית נֹכַח
בֵּית הַמֶּלֶךְ וְהַמֶּלֶךְ יוֹשֵׁב עַל־כִּסֵּא מַלְכוּתוֹ בְּבֵית

ב הַמַּלְכוּת נֹכַח פֶּתַח הַבָּיִת: וַיְהִי כִרְאוֹת הַמֶּלֶךְ אֶת־
אֶסְתֵּר הַמַּלְכָּה עֹמֶדֶת בֶּחָצֵר נָשְׂאָה חֵן בְּעֵינָיו וַיּוֹשֶׁט
הַמֶּלֶךְ לְאֶסְתֵּר אֶת־שַׁרְבִיט הַזָּהָב אֲשֶׁר בְּיָדוֹ וַתִּקְרַב

ג אֶסְתֵּר וַתִּגַּע בְּרֹאשׁ הַשַּׁרְבִיט: וַיֹּאמֶר לָהּ הַמֶּלֶךְ מַה־לָּךְ
אֶסְתֵּר הַמַּלְכָּה וּמַה־בַּקָּשָׁתֵךְ עַד־חֲצִי הַמַּלְכוּת וְיִנָּתֵן

ד לָךְ: וַתֹּאמֶר אֶסְתֵּר אִם־עַל־הַמֶּלֶךְ טוֹב יָבוֹא הַמֶּלֶךְ

ה וְהָמָן הַיּוֹם אֶל־הַמִּשְׁתֶּה אֲשֶׁר־עָשִׂיתִי לוֹ: וַיֹּאמֶר הַמֶּלֶךְ
מַהֲרוּ אֶת־הָמָן לַעֲשׂוֹת אֶת־דְּבַר אֶסְתֵּר וַיָּבֹא הַמֶּלֶךְ

ו וְהָמָן אֶל־הַמִּשְׁתֶּה אֲשֶׁר־עָשְׂתָה אֶסְתֵּר: וַיֹּאמֶר הַמֶּלֶךְ
לְאֶסְתֵּר בְּמִשְׁתֵּה הַיַּיִן מַה־שְּׁאֵלָתֵךְ וְיִנָּתֵן לָךְ וּמַה־

ז בַּקָּשָׁתֵךְ עַד־חֲצִי הַמַּלְכוּת וְתֵעָשׂ: וַתַּעַן אֶסְתֵּר וַתֹּאמַר

ח שְׁאֵלָתִי וּבַקָּשָׁתִי: אִם־מָצָאתִי חֵן בְּעֵינֵי הַמֶּלֶךְ וְאִם־
עַל־הַמֶּלֶךְ טוֹב לָתֵת אֶת־שְׁאֵלָתִי וְלַעֲשׂוֹת אֶת־בַּקָּשָׁתִי
יָבוֹא הַמֶּלֶךְ וְהָמָן אֶל־הַמִּשְׁתֶּה אֲשֶׁר אֶעֱשֶׂה לָהֶם וּמָחָר

ט אֶעֱשֶׂה כִּדְבַר הַמֶּלֶךְ: וַיֵּצֵא הָמָן בַּיּוֹם הַהוּא שָׂמֵחַ וְטוֹב
לֵב וְכִרְאוֹת הָמָן אֶת־מָרְדֳּכַי בְּשַׁעַר הַמֶּלֶךְ וְלֹא־קָם

י וְלֹא־זָע מִמֶּנּוּ וַיִּמָּלֵא הָמָן עַל־מָרְדֳּכַי חֵמָה: וַיִּתְאַפַּק
הָמָן וַיָּבוֹא אֶל־בֵּיתוֹ וַיִּשְׁלַח וַיָּבֵא אֶת־אֹהֲבָיו וְאֶת־זֶרֶשׁ

יא אִשְׁתּוֹ: וַיְסַפֵּר לָהֶם הָמָן אֶת־כְּבוֹד עָשְׁרוֹ וְרֹב בָּנָיו וְאֵת
כָּל־אֲשֶׁר גִּדְּלוֹ הַמֶּלֶךְ וְאֵת אֲשֶׁר נִשְּׂאוֹ עַל־הַשָּׂרִים וְעַבְדֵי

יב הַמֶּלֶךְ: וַיֹּאמֶר הָמָן אַף לֹא־הֵבִיאָה אֶסְתֵּר הַמַּלְכָּה

every time I see that Jew Mordecai sitting in the palace gate." [14]Then his wife Zeresh and all his friends said to him, "Let a stake be put up, fifty cubits high, and in the morning ask the king to have Mordecai impaled on it. Then you can go gaily with the king to the feast."

The proposal pleased Haman, and he had the stake put up.

6 [1]That night, sleep deserted the king, and he ordered the book of records, the annals, to be brought; and it was read to the king. [2]There it was found written that Mordecai had denounced Bigthana and Teresh, two of the king's eunuchs who guarded the threshold, who had plotted to do away with King Ahasuerus. [3]"What honor or advancement has been conferred on Mordecai for this?" the king inquired. "Nothing at all has been done for him," replied the king's servants who were in attendance on him. [4]"Who is in the court?" the king asked. For Haman had just entered the outer court of the royal palace, to speak to the king about having Mordecai impaled on the stake he had prepared for him. [5]"It is Haman standing in the court," the king's servants answered him. "Let him enter," said the king. [6]Haman entered, and the king asked him, "What should be done for a man whom the king desires to honor?" Haman said to himself, "Whom would the king desire to honor more than me?" [7]So Haman said to the king, "For the man whom the king desires to honor, [8]let royal garb which the king has worn be brought, and a horse on which the king has ridden and on whose head a royal diadem has been set; [9]and let the attire and the horse be put in the charge of one of the king's noble courtiers. And let the man whom the king desires to honor be attired and paraded on the horse through the city square, while they proclaim before him: This is what is done for the man whom the king desires to honor!" [10]"Quick, then!" said the king to Haman. "Get the garb and the horse, as you have said, and do this to Mordecai the Jew, who sits in the king's gate. Omit nothing of all you have proposed." [11]So Haman took the garb and the horse and arrayed Mordecai and paraded him through the city square; and he proclaimed before him: This is what is done for the man whom the king desires to honor!

עִם־הַמֶּלֶךְ אֶל־הַמִּשְׁתֶּה אֲשֶׁר־עָשָׂתָה כִּי אִם־אוֹתִי

יג וְגַם־לְמָחָר אֲנִי קָרוּא־לָהּ עִם־הַמֶּלֶךְ: וְכָל־זֶה אֵינֶנּוּ שֹׁוֶה
לִי בְּכָל־עֵת אֲשֶׁר אֲנִי רֹאֶה אֶת־מָרְדֳּכַי הַיְּהוּדִי יוֹשֵׁב

יד בְּשַׁעַר הַמֶּלֶךְ: וַתֹּאמֶר לוֹ זֶרֶשׁ אִשְׁתּוֹ וְכָל־אֹהֲבָיו יַעֲשׂוּ־עֵץ
גָּבֹהַּ חֲמִשִּׁים אַמָּה וּבַבֹּקֶר ׀ אֱמֹר לַמֶּלֶךְ וְיִתְלוּ אֶת־מָרְדֳּכַי
עָלָיו וּבֹא עִם־הַמֶּלֶךְ אֶל־הַמִּשְׁתֶּה שָׂמֵחַ וַיִּיטַב הַדָּבָר לִפְנֵי

ו א הָמָן וַיַּעַשׂ הָעֵץ: בַּלַּיְלָה הַהוּא נָדְדָה שְׁנַת הַמֶּלֶךְ
וַיֹּאמֶר לְהָבִיא אֶת־סֵפֶר הַזִּכְרֹנוֹת דִּבְרֵי הַיָּמִים וַיִּהְיוּ

ב נִקְרָאִים לִפְנֵי הַמֶּלֶךְ: וַיִּמָּצֵא כָתוּב אֲשֶׁר הִגִּיד מָרְדֳּכַי
עַל־בִּגְתָנָא וָתֶרֶשׁ שְׁנֵי סָרִיסֵי הַמֶּלֶךְ מִשֹּׁמְרֵי הַסַּף אֲשֶׁר

ג בִּקְשׁוּ לִשְׁלֹחַ יָד בַּמֶּלֶךְ אֲחַשְׁוֵרוֹשׁ: וַיֹּאמֶר הַמֶּלֶךְ
מַה־נַּעֲשָׂה יְקָר וּגְדוּלָּה לְמָרְדֳּכַי עַל־זֶה וַיֹּאמְרוּ נַעֲרֵי

ד הַמֶּלֶךְ מְשָׁרְתָיו לֹא־נַעֲשָׂה עִמּוֹ דָּבָר: וַיֹּאמֶר הַמֶּלֶךְ מִי
בֶחָצֵר וְהָמָן בָּא לַחֲצַר בֵּית־הַמֶּלֶךְ הַחִיצוֹנָה לֵאמֹר

ה לַמֶּלֶךְ לִתְלוֹת אֶת־מָרְדֳּכַי עַל־הָעֵץ אֲשֶׁר־הֵכִין לוֹ:
וַיֹּאמְרוּ נַעֲרֵי הַמֶּלֶךְ אֵלָיו הִנֵּה הָמָן עֹמֵד בֶּחָצֵר וַיֹּאמֶר

ו הַמֶּלֶךְ יָבוֹא: וַיָּבוֹא הָמָן וַיֹּאמֶר לוֹ הַמֶּלֶךְ מַה־לַעֲשׂוֹת
בָּאִישׁ אֲשֶׁר הַמֶּלֶךְ חָפֵץ בִּיקָרוֹ וַיֹּאמֶר הָמָן בְּלִבּוֹ לְמִי

ז יַחְפֹּץ הַמֶּלֶךְ לַעֲשׂוֹת יְקָר יוֹתֵר מִמֶּנִּי: וַיֹּאמֶר הָמָן

ח אֶל־הַמֶּלֶךְ אִישׁ אֲשֶׁר הַמֶּלֶךְ חָפֵץ בִּיקָרוֹ: יָבִיאוּ לְבוּשׁ
מַלְכוּת אֲשֶׁר לָבַשׁ־בּוֹ הַמֶּלֶךְ וְסוּס אֲשֶׁר רָכַב עָלָיו

ט הַמֶּלֶךְ וַאֲשֶׁר נִתַּן כֶּתֶר מַלְכוּת בְּרֹאשׁוֹ: וְנָתוֹן הַלְּבוּשׁ
וְהַסּוּס עַל־יַד־אִישׁ מִשָּׂרֵי הַמֶּלֶךְ הַפַּרְתְּמִים וְהִלְבִּישׁוּ
אֶת־הָאִישׁ אֲשֶׁר הַמֶּלֶךְ חָפֵץ בִּיקָרוֹ וְהִרְכִּיבֻהוּ עַל־הַסּוּס
בִּרְחוֹב הָעִיר וְקָרְאוּ לְפָנָיו כָּכָה יֵעָשֶׂה לָאִישׁ אֲשֶׁר הַמֶּלֶךְ

י חָפֵץ בִּיקָרוֹ: וַיֹּאמֶר הַמֶּלֶךְ לְהָמָן מַהֵר קַח אֶת־הַלְּבוּשׁ
וְאֶת־הַסּוּס כַּאֲשֶׁר דִּבַּרְתָּ וַעֲשֵׂה־כֵן לְמָרְדֳּכַי הַיְּהוּדִי

[12]Then Mordecai returned to the king's gate, while Haman hurried home, his head covered in mourning. [13]There Haman told his wife Zeresh and all his friends everything that had befallen him. His advisers and his wife Zeresh said to him, "If Mordecai, before whom you have begun to fall, is of Jewish stock, you will not overcome him; you will fall before him to your ruin."

[14]While they were still speaking with him, the king's eunuchs arrived and hurriedly brought Haman to the banquet which Esther had prepared.

7 [1]So the king and Haman came to feast with Queen Esther. [2]On the second day, the king again asked Esther at the wine feast, "What is your wish, Queen Esther? It shall be granted you. And what is your request? Even to half the kingdom, it shall be fulfilled." [3]Queen Esther replied: "If Your Majesty will do me the favor, and if it pleases Your Majesty, let my life be granted me as my wish, and my people as my request. [4]For we have been sold, my people and I, to be destroyed, massacred, and exterminated. Had we only been sold as bondmen and bond-women, I would have kept silent; for the adversary is not worthy of the king's trouble."

[5]Thereupon King Ahasuerus demanded of Queen Esther, "Who is he and where is he who dared to do this?" [6]"The adversary and enemy," replied Esther, "is this evil Haman!" And Haman cringed in terror before the king and the queen. [7]The king, in his fury, left the wine feast for the palace garden, while Haman remained to plead with Queen Esther for his life; for he saw that the king had resolved to destroy him. [8]When the king returned from the palace garden to the banquet room, Haman was lying prostrate on the couch on which Esther reclined. "Does he mean," cried the king, "to ravish the queen in my own palace?" No sooner did these words leave the king's lips than Haman's face was covered. [9]Then Harbonah, one of the eunuchs in attendance on the king, said, "What is more, a stake is standing at Haman's house, fifty cubits high, which Haman made for Mordecai – the man whose words saved the king." "Impale him on it!" the king ordered.

הַיּוֹשֵׁב בְּשַׁעַר הַמֶּלֶךְ אַל־תִּפֹּל דָּבָר מִכֹּל אֲשֶׁר דִּבַּרְתָּ:

יא וַיִּקַּח הָמָן אֶת־הַלְּבוּשׁ וְאֶת־הַסּוּס וַיַּלְבֵּשׁ אֶת־מָרְדֳּכָי וַיַּרְכִּיבֵהוּ בִּרְחוֹב הָעִיר וַיִּקְרָא לְפָנָיו כָּכָה יֵעָשֶׂה לָאִישׁ

יב אֲשֶׁר הַמֶּלֶךְ חָפֵץ בִּיקָרוֹ: וַיָּשָׁב מָרְדֳּכַי אֶל־שַׁעַר הַמֶּלֶךְ

יג וְהָמָן נִדְחַף אֶל־בֵּיתוֹ אָבֵל וַחֲפוּי רֹאשׁ: וַיְסַפֵּר הָמָן לְזֶרֶשׁ אִשְׁתּוֹ וּלְכָל־אֹהֲבָיו אֵת כָּל־אֲשֶׁר קָרָהוּ וַיֹּאמְרוּ לוֹ חֲכָמָיו וְזֶרֶשׁ אִשְׁתּוֹ אִם מִזֶּרַע הַיְּהוּדִים מָרְדֳּכַי אֲשֶׁר הַחִלּוֹתָ לִנְפֹּל לְפָנָיו לֹא־תוּכַל לוֹ כִּי־נָפוֹל תִּפּוֹל לְפָנָיו:

יד עוֹדָם מְדַבְּרִים עִמּוֹ וְסָרִיסֵי הַמֶּלֶךְ הִגִּיעוּ וַיַּבְהִלוּ לְהָבִיא

ז א אֶת־הָמָן אֶל־הַמִּשְׁתֶּה אֲשֶׁר־עָשְׂתָה אֶסְתֵּר: וַיָּבֹא

ב הַמֶּלֶךְ וְהָמָן לִשְׁתּוֹת עִם־אֶסְתֵּר הַמַּלְכָּה: וַיֹּאמֶר הַמֶּלֶךְ לְאֶסְתֵּר גַּם בַּיּוֹם הַשֵּׁנִי בְּמִשְׁתֵּה הַיַּיִן מַה־שְּׁאֵלָתֵךְ אֶסְתֵּר הַמַּלְכָּה וְתִנָּתֵן לָךְ וּמַה־בַּקָּשָׁתֵךְ עַד־חֲצִי הַמַּלְכוּת

ג וְתֵעָשׂ: וַתַּעַן אֶסְתֵּר הַמַּלְכָּה וַתֹּאמַר אִם־מָצָאתִי חֵן בְּעֵינֶיךָ הַמֶּלֶךְ וְאִם־עַל־הַמֶּלֶךְ טוֹב תִּנָּתֶן־לִי נַפְשִׁי

ד בִּשְׁאֵלָתִי וְעַמִּי בְּבַקָּשָׁתִי: כִּי נִמְכַּרְנוּ אֲנִי וְעַמִּי לְהַשְׁמִיד לַהֲרוֹג וּלְאַבֵּד וְאִלּוּ לַעֲבָדִים וְלִשְׁפָחוֹת נִמְכַּרְנוּ הֶחֱרַשְׁתִּי

ה כִּי אֵין הַצָּר שֹׁוֶה בְּנֵזֶק הַמֶּלֶךְ:   וַיֹּאמֶר הַמֶּלֶךְ אֲחַשְׁוֵרוֹשׁ וַיֹּאמֶר לְאֶסְתֵּר הַמַּלְכָּה מִי הוּא זֶה וְאֵי־זֶה

ו הוּא אֲשֶׁר־מְלָאוֹ לִבּוֹ לַעֲשׂוֹת כֵּן: וַתֹּאמֶר אֶסְתֵּר אִישׁ צַר וְאוֹיֵב הָמָן הָרָע הַזֶּה וְהָמָן נִבְעַת מִלִּפְנֵי הַמֶּלֶךְ

ז וְהַמַּלְכָּה: וְהַמֶּלֶךְ קָם בַּחֲמָתוֹ מִמִּשְׁתֵּה הַיַּיִן אֶל־גִּנַּת הַבִּיתָן וְהָמָן עָמַד לְבַקֵּשׁ עַל־נַפְשׁוֹ מֵאֶסְתֵּר הַמַּלְכָּה כִּי

ח רָאָה כִּי־כָלְתָה אֵלָיו הָרָעָה מֵאֵת הַמֶּלֶךְ: וְהַמֶּלֶךְ שָׁב מִגִּנַּת הַבִּיתָן אֶל־בֵּית | מִשְׁתֵּה הַיַּיִן וְהָמָן נֹפֵל עַל־הַמִּטָּה אֲשֶׁר אֶסְתֵּר עָלֶיהָ וַיֹּאמֶר הַמֶּלֶךְ הֲגַם לִכְבּוֹשׁ אֶת־ הַמַּלְכָּה עִמִּי בַּבָּיִת הַדָּבָר יָצָא מִפִּי הַמֶּלֶךְ וּפְנֵי הָמָן

[10]So they impaled Haman on the stake which he had put up for Mordecai, and the king's fury abated.

8 [1]That very day King Ahasuerus gave the property of Haman, the enemy of the Jews, to Queen Esther. Mordecai presented himself to the king, for Esther had revealed how he was related to her. [2]The king slipped off his ring, which he had taken back from Haman, and gave it to Mordecai; and Esther put Mordecai in charge of Haman's property.

[3]Esther spoke to the king again, falling at his feet and weeping, and beseeching him to avert the evil plotted by Haman the Agagite against the Jews. [4]The king extended the golden scepter to Esther, and Esther arose and stood before the king. [5]"If it please Your Majesty," she said, "and if I have won your favor and the proposal seems right to Your Majesty, and if I am pleasing to you – let dispatches be written countermanding those which were written by Haman son of Hammedatha the Agagite, embodying his plot to annihilate the Jews throughout the king's provinces. [6]For how can I bear to see the disaster which will befall my people! And how can I bear to see the destruction of my kindred!"

[7]Then King Ahasuerus said to Queen Esther and Mordecai the Jew, "I have given Haman's property to Esther, and he has been impaled on the stake for scheming against the Jews. [8]And you may further write with regard to the Jews as you see fit. [Write it] in the king's name and seal it with the king's signet, for an edict that has been written in the king's name and sealed with the king's signet may not be revoked."

[9]So the king's scribes were summoned at that time, on the twenty-third day of the third month, that is, the month of Sivan; and letters were written, at Mordecai's dictation, to the Jews and to the satraps, the governors and the officials of the one hundred and twenty-seven provinces from India to Ethiopia: to every province in its own script and to every people in its own language, and to the Jews in their own script and language. [10]He had them written in the name of King Ahasuerus and sealed with the king's signet. Letters were dispatched by mounted couriers,

ט חָפוּ: וַיֹּאמֶר חַרְבוֹנָה אֶחָד מִן־הַסָּרִיסִים לִפְנֵי הַמֶּלֶךְ
גַּם הִנֵּה־הָעֵץ אֲשֶׁר־עָשָׂה הָמָן לְמָרְדֳּכַי אֲשֶׁר דִּבֶּר־טוֹב
עַל־הַמֶּלֶךְ עֹמֵד בְּבֵית הָמָן גָּבֹהַּ חֲמִשִּׁים אַמָּה וַיֹּאמֶר
י הַמֶּלֶךְ תְּלֻהוּ עָלָיו: וַיִּתְלוּ אֶת־הָמָן עַל־הָעֵץ אֲשֶׁר־הֵכִין
ח לְמָרְדֳּכָי וַחֲמַת הַמֶּלֶךְ שָׁכָכָה: בַּיּוֹם הַהוּא נָתַן
א הַמֶּלֶךְ אֲחַשְׁוֵרוֹשׁ לְאֶסְתֵּר הַמַּלְכָּה אֶת־בֵּית הָמָן צֹרֵר
היהודים הַיְּהוּדִים* וּמָרְדֳּכַי בָּא לִפְנֵי הַמֶּלֶךְ כִּי־הִגִּידָה אֶסְתֵּר
ב מַה הוּא־לָהּ: וַיָּסַר הַמֶּלֶךְ אֶת־טַבַּעְתּוֹ אֲשֶׁר הֶעֱבִיר
מֵהָמָן וַיִּתְּנָהּ לְמָרְדֳּכָי וַתָּשֶׂם אֶסְתֵּר אֶת־מָרְדֳּכַי עַל־בֵּית
ג הָמָן: וַתּוֹסֶף אֶסְתֵּר וַתְּדַבֵּר לִפְנֵי הַמֶּלֶךְ וַתִּפֹּל
לִפְנֵי רַגְלָיו וַתֵּבְךְּ וַתִּתְחַנֶּן־לוֹ לְהַעֲבִיר אֶת־רָעַת הָמָן
ד הָאֲגָגִי וְאֵת מַחֲשַׁבְתּוֹ אֲשֶׁר חָשַׁב עַל־הַיְּהוּדִים: וַיּוֹשֶׁט
הַמֶּלֶךְ לְאֶסְתֵּר אֵת שַׁרְבִט הַזָּהָב וַתָּקָם אֶסְתֵּר וַתַּעֲמֹד
ה לִפְנֵי הַמֶּלֶךְ: וַתֹּאמֶר אִם־עַל־הַמֶּלֶךְ טוֹב וְאִם־מָצָאתִי
חֵן לְפָנָיו וְכָשֵׁר הַדָּבָר לִפְנֵי הַמֶּלֶךְ וְטוֹבָה אֲנִי בְּעֵינָיו יִכָּתֵב
לְהָשִׁיב אֶת־הַסְּפָרִים מַחֲשֶׁבֶת הָמָן בֶּן־הַמְּדָתָא הָאֲגָגִי
אֲשֶׁר כָּתַב לְאַבֵּד אֶת־הַיְּהוּדִים אֲשֶׁר בְּכָל־מְדִינוֹת הַמֶּלֶךְ:
ו כִּי אֵיכָכָה אוּכַל וְרָאִיתִי בָּרָעָה אֲשֶׁר־יִמְצָא אֶת־עַמִּי
ז וְאֵיכָכָה אוּכַל וְרָאִיתִי בְּאָבְדַן מוֹלַדְתִּי: וַיֹּאמֶר
הַמֶּלֶךְ אֲחַשְׁוֵרֹשׁ לְאֶסְתֵּר הַמַּלְכָּה וּלְמָרְדֳּכַי הַיְּהוּדִי הִנֵּה
בֵית־הָמָן נָתַתִּי לְאֶסְתֵּר וְאֹתוֹ תָּלוּ עַל־הָעֵץ עַל אֲשֶׁר־
ביהודים שָׁלַח יָדוֹ ביהודיים*: וְאַתֶּם כִּתְבוּ עַל־הַיְּהוּדִים כַּטּוֹב
בְּעֵינֵיכֶם בְּשֵׁם הַמֶּלֶךְ וְחִתְמוּ בְּטַבַּעַת הַמֶּלֶךְ כִּי־כְתָב
אֲשֶׁר־נִכְתָּב בְּשֵׁם־הַמֶּלֶךְ וְנַחְתּוֹם בְּטַבַּעַת הַמֶּלֶךְ אֵין
ט לְהָשִׁיב: וַיִּקָּרְאוּ סֹפְרֵי־הַמֶּלֶךְ בָּעֵת־הַהִיא בַּחֹדֶשׁ הַשְּׁלִישִׁי
הוּא־חֹדֶשׁ סִיוָן בִּשְׁלוֹשָׁה וְעֶשְׂרִים בּוֹ וַיִּכָּתֵב כְּכָל־אֲשֶׁר־
צִוָּה מָרְדֳּכַי אֶל־הַיְּהוּדִים וְאֶל הָאֲחַשְׁדַּרְפְּנִים וְהַפַּחוֹת

riding steeds used in the king's service, bred of the royal stud,[11]to this effect: The king has permitted the Jews of every city to assemble and fight for their lives; if any people or province attacks them, they may destroy, massacre, and exterminate its armed force together with women and children, and plunder their possessions – [12]on a single day in all the provinces of King Ahasuerus, namely, on the thirteenth day of the twelfth month, that is, the month of Adar. [13]The text of the document was to be issued as a law in every single province: it was to be publicly displayed to all the peoples, so that the Jews should be ready for that day to avenge themselves on their enemies.

[14]The couriers, mounted on royal steeds, went out in urgent haste at the king's command; and the decree was proclaimed in the fortress Shushan.

[15]Mordecai left the king's presence in royal robes of blue and white, with a magnificent crown of gold and a mantle of fine linen and purple wool. And the city of Shushan rang with joyous cries. [16]The Jews enjoyed light and gladness, happiness and honor. [17]And in every province and in every city, when the king's command and decree arrived, there was gladness and joy among the Jews, a feast and a holiday. And many of the people of the land professed to be Jews, for the fear of the Jews had fallen upon them.

9 [1]And so, on the thirteenth day of the twelfth month – that is, the month of Adar – when the king's command and decree were to be executed, the very day on which the enemies of the Jews had expected to get them in their power, the opposite happened, and the Jews got their enemies in their power. [2]Throughout the provinces of King Ahasuerus, the Jews mustered in their cities to attack those who sought their hurt; and no one could withstand them, for the fear of them had fallen upon all the peoples. [3]Indeed, all the officials of the provinces – the satraps, the governors, and the king's stewards – showed deference to the Jews, because the fear of Mordecai had fallen upon them. [4]For Mordecai was now powerful in the royal palace, and his fame was spreading through all

וְשָׂרֵי הַמְּדִינוֹת אֲשֶׁר ׀ מֵהֹדּוּ וְעַד־כּוּשׁ שֶׁבַע וְעֶשְׂרִים
וּמֵאָה מְדִינָה מְדִינָה וּמְדִינָה כִּכְתָבָהּ וְעַם וָעָם כִּלְשֹׁנוֹ
וְאֶל־הַיְּהוּדִים כִּכְתָבָם וְכִלְשׁוֹנָם: וַיִּכְתֹּב בְּשֵׁם הַמֶּלֶךְ

י אֲחַשְׁוֵרֹשׁ וַיַּחְתֹּם בְּטַבַּעַת הַמֶּלֶךְ וַיִּשְׁלַח סְפָרִים בְּיַד
הָרָצִים בַּסּוּסִים רֹכְבֵי הָרֶכֶשׁ הָאֲחַשְׁתְּרָנִים בְּנֵי הָרַמָּכִים:

יא אֲשֶׁר נָתַן הַמֶּלֶךְ לַיְּהוּדִים ׀ אֲשֶׁר בְּכָל־עִיר־וָעִיר לְהִקָּהֵל
וְלַעֲמֹד עַל־נַפְשָׁם לְהַשְׁמִיד וְלַהֲרֹג וּלְאַבֵּד אֶת־כָּל־חֵיל

יב עַם וּמְדִינָה הַצָּרִים אֹתָם טַף וְנָשִׁים וּשְׁלָלָם לָבוֹז: בְּיוֹם
אֶחָד בְּכָל־מְדִינוֹת הַמֶּלֶךְ אֲחַשְׁוֵרוֹשׁ בִּשְׁלוֹשָׁה עָשָׂר

יג לְחֹדֶשׁ שְׁנֵים־עָשָׂר הוּא־חֹדֶשׁ אֲדָר: פַּתְשֶׁגֶן הַכְּתָב
לְהִנָּתֵן דָּת בְּכָל־מְדִינָה וּמְדִינָה גָּלוּי לְכָל־הָעַמִּים וְלִהְיוֹת

יד הַיְּהוּדִיים* עֲתוּדִים** לַיּוֹם הַזֶּה לְהִנָּקֵם מֵאֹיְבֵיהֶם: הָרָצִים _{הַיְּהוּדִים*}
_{עֲתִידִים**}
רֹכְבֵי הָרֶכֶשׁ הָאֲחַשְׁתְּרָנִים יָצְאוּ מְבֹהָלִים וּדְחוּפִים בִּדְבַר

טו הַמֶּלֶךְ וְהַדָּת נִתְּנָה בְּשׁוּשַׁן הַבִּירָה: וּמָרְדֳּכַי יָצָא ׀ מִלִּפְנֵי

טז הַמֶּלֶךְ בִּלְבוּשׁ מַלְכוּת תְּכֵלֶת וָחוּר וַעֲטֶרֶת זָהָב גְּדוֹלָה
וְתַכְרִיךְ בּוּץ וְאַרְגָּמָן וְהָעִיר שׁוּשָׁן צָהֲלָה וְשָׂמֵחָה: לַיְּהוּדִים

יז הָיְתָה אוֹרָה וְשִׂמְחָה וְשָׂשֹׂן וִיקָר: וּבְכָל־מְדִינָה וּמְדִינָה
וּבְכָל־עִיר וָעִיר מְקוֹם אֲשֶׁר דְּבַר־הַמֶּלֶךְ וְדָתוֹ מַגִּיעַ שִׂמְחָה
וְשָׂשׂוֹן לַיְּהוּדִים מִשְׁתֶּה וְיוֹם טוֹב וְרַבִּים מֵעַמֵּי הָאָרֶץ

ט
א מִתְיַהֲדִים כִּי־נָפַל פַּחַד־הַיְּהוּדִים עֲלֵיהֶם: וּבִשְׁנֵים
עָשָׂר חֹדֶשׁ הוּא־חֹדֶשׁ אֲדָר בִּשְׁלוֹשָׁה עָשָׂר יוֹם בּוֹ אֲשֶׁר
הִגִּיעַ דְּבַר־הַמֶּלֶךְ וְדָתוֹ לְהֵעָשׂוֹת בַּיּוֹם אֲשֶׁר שִׂבְּרוּ אֹיְבֵי

ב הַיְּהוּדִים לִשְׁלוֹט בָּהֶם וְנַהֲפוֹךְ הוּא אֲשֶׁר יִשְׁלְטוּ הַיְּהוּדִים
הֵמָּה בְּשֹׂנְאֵיהֶם: נִקְהֲלוּ הַיְּהוּדִים בְּעָרֵיהֶם בְּכָל־מְדִינוֹת הַמֶּלֶךְ
אֲחַשְׁוֵרוֹשׁ לִשְׁלֹחַ יָד בִּמְבַקְשֵׁי רָעָתָם וְאִישׁ לֹא־עָמַד לִפְנֵיהֶם

ג כִּי־נָפַל פַּחְדָּם עַל־כָּל־הָעַמִּים: וְכָל־שָׂרֵי הַמְּדִינוֹת
וְהָאֲחַשְׁדַּרְפְּנִים וְהַפַּחוֹת וְעֹשֵׂי הַמְּלָאכָה אֲשֶׁר לַמֶּלֶךְ מְנַשְּׂאִים

the provinces; the man Mordecai was growing ever more powerful. ⁵So the Jews struck at their enemies with the sword, slaying and destroying; they wreaked their will upon their enemies.

⁶In the fortress Shushan the Jews killed a total of five hundred men. ⁷They also killed

Parshandatha,

Dalphon,

Aspatha,

⁸Poratha,

Adalia,

Aridatha,

⁹Parmashta,

Arisai,

Aridai,

and Vaizatha,

¹⁰the ten sons of Haman son of Hammedatha, the foe of the Jews. But they did not lay hands on the spoil. ¹¹When the number of those slain in the fortress Shushan was reported on that same day to the king, ¹²the king said to Queen Esther, "In the fortress Shushan alone the Jews have killed a total of five hundred men, as well as the ten sons of Haman. What then must they have done in the provinces of the realm! What is your wish now? It shall be granted you. And what else is your request? It shall be fulfilled." ¹³"If it please Your Majesty," Esther replied, "let the Jews in Shushan be permitted to act tomorrow also as they did today; and let Haman's ten sons be impaled on the stake." ¹⁴The king ordered that this should be done, and the decree was proclaimed in Shushan. Haman's ten sons were impaled: ¹⁵and the Jews in Shushan mustered again on the fourteenth day of Adar and slew three hundred men in Shushan. But they did not lay hands on the spoil.

¹⁶The rest of the Jews, those in the king's provinces, likewise mustered and fought for their lives. They disposed of their enemies, killing seventy-five thousand of their foes; but they did not lay hands on the spoil. ¹⁷That was on the thirteenth day of the month of Adar; and they rested on the

ד אֶת־הַיְּהוּדִ֔ים כִּי־נָפַ֥ל פַּֽחַד־מָרְדֳּכַ֖י עֲלֵיהֶֽם: כִּֽי־גָד֤וֹל מָרְדֳּכַי֙
בְּבֵ֣ית הַמֶּ֔לֶךְ וְשׇׁמְע֖וֹ הוֹלֵ֣ךְ בְּכׇל־הַמְּדִינ֑וֹת כִּֽי־הָאִ֥ישׁ מׇרְדֳּכַ֖י הוֹלֵ֥ךְ
ה וְגָדֽוֹל: וַיַּכּ֤וּ הַיְּהוּדִים֙ בְּכׇל־אֹ֣יְבֵיהֶ֔ם מַכַּת־חֶ֥רֶב וְהֶ֖רֶג וְאַבְדָ֑ן וַיַּעֲשׂ֥וּ
ו בְשֹׂנְאֵיהֶ֖ם כִּרְצוֹנָֽם: וּבְשׁוּשַׁ֣ן הַבִּירָ֗ה הָרְג֤וּ הַיְּהוּדִים֙ וְאַבֵּ֔ד

ז חֲמֵ֥שׁ מֵא֖וֹת אִֽישׁ: | וְאֵ֣ת ׀
פַּרְשַׁ֨נְדָּ֜תָא | וְאֵ֣ת ׀
דַּֽלְפ֥וֹן | וְאֵ֣ת ׀
ח אַסְפָּ֖תָא: | וְאֵ֣ת ׀
פּוֹרָ֛תָא | וְאֵ֣ת ׀
אֲדַלְיָ֖א | וְאֵ֣ת ׀
ט אֲרִֽידָ֑תָא: | וְאֵ֣ת ׀
פַּרְמַ֖שְׁתָּא | וְאֵ֣ת ׀
אֲרִיסַ֖י | וְאֵ֣ת ׀
אֲרִדַ֖י | וְאֵ֣ת ׀
י וַיְזָֽתָא: | עֲשֶׂ֗רֶת

בְּנֵ֨י הָמָ֧ן בֶּֽן־הַמְּדָ֛תָא צֹרֵ֥ר הַיְּהוּדִ֖ים הָרָ֑גוּ וּבַ֨בִּזָּ֔ה לֹ֥א
יא שָׁלְח֖וּ אֶת־יָדָֽם: בַּיּ֣וֹם הַה֗וּא בָּ֣א מִסְפַּ֧ר הַהֲרוּגִ֛ים בְּשׁוּשַׁ֥ן
יב הַבִּירָ֖ה לִפְנֵ֣י הַמֶּֽלֶךְ: וַיֹּ֨אמֶר הַמֶּ֜לֶךְ לְאֶסְתֵּ֣ר הַמַּלְכָּ֗ה
בְּשׁוּשַׁ֣ן הַבִּירָ֡ה הָרְגוּ֩ הַיְּהוּדִ֨ים וְאַבֵּ֜ד חֲמֵ֧שׁ מֵא֣וֹת אִ֗ישׁ
וְאֵת֙ עֲשֶׂ֣רֶת בְּנֵֽי־הָמָ֔ן בִּשְׁאָ֛ר מְדִינ֥וֹת הַמֶּ֖לֶךְ מֶ֣ה עָשׂ֑וּ
יג וּמַה־שְּׁאֵֽלָתֵךְ֙ וְיִנָּ֣תֵֽן לָ֔ךְ וּמַה־בַּקָּשָׁתֵ֥ךְ ע֖וֹד וְתֵעָֽשׂ: וַתֹּ֤אמֶר
אֶסְתֵּר֙ אִם־עַל־הַמֶּ֣לֶךְ ט֔וֹב יִנָּתֵ֣ן גַּם־מָחָ֗ר לַיְּהוּדִים֙ אֲשֶׁ֣ר
בְּשׁוּשָׁ֔ן לַעֲשׂ֖וֹת כְּדָ֣ת הַיּ֑וֹם וְאֵ֛ת עֲשֶׂ֥רֶת בְּנֵֽי־הָמָ֖ן יִתְל֥וּ
יד עַל־הָעֵֽץ: וַיֹּ֤אמֶר הַמֶּ֙לֶךְ֙ לְהֵֽעָשׂ֣וֹת כֵּ֔ן וַתִּנָּתֵ֥ן דָּ֖ת בְּשׁוּשָׁ֑ן
טו וְאֵ֛ת עֲשֶׂ֥רֶת בְּנֵֽי־הָמָ֖ן תָּלֽוּ: וַיִּקָּהֲל֞וּ הַיְּהוּדִים* אֲשֶׁ֣ר־בְּשׁוּשָׁ֗ן
גַּ֠ם בְּי֣וֹם אַרְבָּעָ֤ה עָשָׂר֙ לְחֹ֣דֶשׁ אֲדָ֔ר וַיַּֽהַרְג֣וּ בְשׁוּשָׁ֔ן שְׁלֹ֥שׁ הַיְּהוּדִים
טז מֵא֖וֹת אִ֑ישׁ וּבַ֨בִּזָּ֔ה לֹ֥א שָׁלְח֖וּ אֶת־יָדָֽם: וּשְׁאָ֣ר הַיְּהוּדִ֡ים

fourteenth day and made it a day of feasting and merrymaking. [18](But the Jews in Shushan mustered on both the thirteenth and fourteenth days, and so rested on the fifteenth, and made it a day of feasting and merrymaking.) [19]That is why village Jews, who live in unwalled towns, observe the fourteenth day of the month of Adar and make it a day of merrymaking and feasting, and as a holiday and an occasion for sending gifts to one another.

[20]Mordecai recorded these events. And he sent dispatches to all the Jews throughout the provinces of King Ahasuerus, near and far, [21]charging them to observe the fourteenth and fifteenth days of Adar, every year – [22]the same days on which the Jews enjoyed relief from their foes and the same month which had been transformed for them from one of grief and mourning to one of festive joy. They were to observe them as days of feasting and merrymaking, and as an occasion for sending gifts to one another and presents to the poor. [23]The Jews accordingly assumed as an obligation that which they had begun to practice and which Mordecai prescribed for them.

[24]For Haman son of Hammedatha the Agagite, the foe of all the Jews, had plotted to destroy the Jews, and had cast pur – that is, the lot – with intent to crush and exterminate them. [25]But when [Esther] came before the king, he commanded: "With the promulgation of this decree, let the evil plot, which he devised against the Jews, recoil on his own head!" So they impaled him and his sons on the stake. [26]For that reason these days were named Purim, after pur. In view, then, of all the instructions in the said letter and of what they had experienced in that matter and what had befallen them, [27]the Jews undertook and irrevocably obligated themselves and their descendants, and all who might join them, to observe these two days in the manner prescribed and at the proper time each year. [28]Consequently, these days are recalled and observed in every generation: by every family, every province, and every city. And these days of Purim shall never cease among the Jews, and the memory of them shall never perish among their descendants.

[29]Then Queen Esther daughter of Abihail wrote a second letter of

אֲשֶׁר בִּמְדִינוֹת הַמֶּלֶךְ נִקְהֲלוּ ׀ וְעָמֹד עַל־נַפְשָׁם וְנוֹחַ
מֵאֹיְבֵיהֶם וְהָרֹג בְּשֹׂנְאֵיהֶם חֲמִשָּׁה וְשִׁבְעִים אָלֶף וּבַבִּזָּה
יז לֹא שָׁלְחוּ אֶת־יָדָם: בְּיוֹם־שְׁלוֹשָׁה עָשָׂר לְחֹדֶשׁ אֲדָר
וְנוֹחַ בְּאַרְבָּעָה עָשָׂר בּוֹ וְעָשֹׂה אֹתוֹ יוֹם מִשְׁתֶּה וְשִׂמְחָה:
יח וְהַיְּהוּדִיים* אֲשֶׁר־בְּשׁוּשָׁן נִקְהֲלוּ בִּשְׁלוֹשָׁה עָשָׂר בּוֹ וְהַיְּהוּדִים
וּבְאַרְבָּעָה עָשָׂר בּוֹ וְנוֹחַ בַּחֲמִשָּׁה עָשָׂר בּוֹ וְעָשֹׂה אֹתוֹ
יט יוֹם מִשְׁתֶּה וְשִׂמְחָה: עַל־כֵּן הַיְּהוּדִים הַפְּרוֹזִים* הַיֹּשְׁבִים הַפְּרָזִים
בְּעָרֵי הַפְּרָזוֹת עֹשִׂים אֵת יוֹם אַרְבָּעָה עָשָׂר לְחֹדֶשׁ אֲדָר
שִׂמְחָה וּמִשְׁתֶּה וְיוֹם טוֹב וּמִשְׁלֹחַ מָנוֹת אִישׁ לְרֵעֵהוּ:
כ וַיִּכְתֹּב מָרְדֳּכַי אֶת־הַדְּבָרִים הָאֵלֶּה וַיִּשְׁלַח סְפָרִים
אֶל־כָּל־הַיְּהוּדִים אֲשֶׁר בְּכָל־מְדִינוֹת הַמֶּלֶךְ אֲחַשְׁוֵרוֹשׁ
כא הַקְּרוֹבִים וְהָרְחוֹקִים: לְקַיֵּם עֲלֵיהֶם לִהְיוֹת עֹשִׂים אֵת יוֹם
אַרְבָּעָה עָשָׂר לְחֹדֶשׁ אֲדָר וְאֵת יוֹם־חֲמִשָּׁה עָשָׂר בּוֹ
כב בְּכָל־שָׁנָה וְשָׁנָה: כַּיָּמִים אֲשֶׁר־נָחוּ בָהֶם הַיְּהוּדִים
מֵאֹיְבֵיהֶם וְהַחֹדֶשׁ אֲשֶׁר נֶהְפַּךְ לָהֶם מִיָּגוֹן לְשִׂמְחָה
וּמֵאֵבֶל לְיוֹם טוֹב לַעֲשׂוֹת אוֹתָם יְמֵי מִשְׁתֶּה וְשִׂמְחָה
כג וּמִשְׁלֹחַ מָנוֹת אִישׁ לְרֵעֵהוּ וּמַתָּנוֹת לָאֶבְיֹנִים: וְקִבֵּל
הַיְּהוּדִים אֵת אֲשֶׁר־הֵחֵלּוּ לַעֲשׂוֹת וְאֵת אֲשֶׁר־כָּתַב
כד מָרְדֳּכַי אֲלֵיהֶם: כִּי הָמָן בֶּן־הַמְּדָתָא הָאֲגָגִי צֹרֵר
כָּל־הַיְּהוּדִים חָשַׁב עַל־הַיְּהוּדִים לְאַבְּדָם וְהִפִּל פּוּר הוּא
כה הַגּוֹרָל לְהֻמָּם וּלְאַבְּדָם: וּבְבֹאָהּ לִפְנֵי הַמֶּלֶךְ אָמַר
עִם־הַסֵּפֶר יָשׁוּב מַחֲשַׁבְתּוֹ הָרָעָה אֲשֶׁר־חָשַׁב עַל־
כו הַיְּהוּדִים עַל־רֹאשׁוֹ וְתָלוּ אֹתוֹ וְאֶת־בָּנָיו עַל־הָעֵץ: עַל־כֵּן
קָרְאוּ לַיָּמִים הָאֵלֶּה פוּרִים עַל־שֵׁם הַפּוּר עַל־כֵּן עַל־כָּל־
דִּבְרֵי הָאִגֶּרֶת הַזֹּאת וּמָה־רָאוּ עַל־כָּכָה וּמָה הִגִּיעַ
כז אֲלֵיהֶם: קִיְּמוּ וְקִבֵּל הַיְּהוּדִים* ׀ עֲלֵיהֶם וְעַל־זַרְעָם וְעַל
כָּל־הַנִּלְוִים עֲלֵיהֶם וְלֹא יַעֲבוֹר לִהְיוֹת עֹשִׂים אֵת־שְׁנֵי

Purim for the purpose of confirming with full authority the aforementioned one of Mordecai the Jew. [30]Dispatches were sent to all the Jews in the hundred and twenty-seven provinces of the realm of Ahasuerus with an ordinance of "equity and honesty:" [31]These days of Purim shall be observed at their proper time, as Mordecai the Jew – and now Queen Esther – has obligated them to do, and just as they have assumed for themselves and their descendants the obligation of the fasts with their lamentations.

[32]And Esther's ordinance validating these observances of Purim was recorded in a scroll.

10
[1]King Ahasuerus imposed tribute on the mainland and the islands. [2]All his mighty and powerful acts, and a full account of the greatness to which the king advanced Mordecai, are recorded in the Annals of the Kings of Media and Persia. [3]For Mordecai the Jew ranked next to King Ahasuerus and was highly regarded by the Jews and popular with the multitude of his brethren; he sought the good of his people and interceded for the welfare of all his kindred.

כח הַיָּמִים הָאֵלֶּה כְּכְתָבָם וְכִזְמַנָּם בְּכָל־שָׁנָה וְשָׁנָה: וְהַיָּמִים
הָאֵלֶּה נִזְכָּרִים וְנַעֲשִׂים בְּכָל־דּוֹר וָדוֹר מִשְׁפָּחָה וּמִשְׁפָּחָה
מְדִינָה וּמְדִינָה וְעִיר וָעִיר וִימֵי הַפֻּרִים הָאֵלֶּה לֹא יַעַבְרוּ
מִתּוֹךְ הַיְּהוּדִים וְזִכְרָם לֹא־יָסוּף מִזַּרְעָם: כט וַתִּכְתֹּב
אֶסְתֵּר הַמַּלְכָּה בַת־אֲבִיחַיִל וּמָרְדֳּכַי הַיְּהוּדִי אֶת־כָּל־
ל תֹּקֶף לְקַיֵּם אֵת אִגֶּרֶת הַפֻּרִים הַזֹּאת הַשֵּׁנִית: וַיִּשְׁלַח
סְפָרִים אֶל־כָּל־הַיְּהוּדִים אֶל־שֶׁבַע וְעֶשְׂרִים וּמֵאָה מְדִינָה
לא מַלְכוּת אֲחַשְׁוֵרוֹשׁ דִּבְרֵי שָׁלוֹם וֶאֱמֶת: לְקַיֵּם אֶת־יְמֵי
הַפֻּרִים הָאֵלֶּה בִּזְמַנֵּיהֶם כַּאֲשֶׁר קִיַּם עֲלֵיהֶם מָרְדֳּכַי
הַיְּהוּדִי וְאֶסְתֵּר הַמַּלְכָּה וְכַאֲשֶׁר קִיְּמוּ עַל־נַפְשָׁם וְעַל־
לב זַרְעָם דִּבְרֵי הַצּוֹמוֹת וְזַעֲקָתָם: וּמַאֲמַר אֶסְתֵּר קִיַּם דִּבְרֵי
א הַפֻּרִים הָאֵלֶּה וְנִכְתָּב בַּסֵּפֶר: וַיָּשֶׂם הַמֶּלֶךְ ❜
ב אֲחַשֵׁרֹשׁ* מַס עַל־הָאָרֶץ וְאִיֵּי הַיָּם: וְכָל־מַעֲשֵׂה תָקְפּוֹ אֲחַשְׁוֵרוֹשׁ
וּגְבוּרָתוֹ וּפָרָשַׁת גְּדֻלַּת מָרְדֳּכַי אֲשֶׁר גִּדְּלוֹ הַמֶּלֶךְ
הֲלוֹא־הֵם כְּתוּבִים עַל־סֵפֶר דִּבְרֵי הַיָּמִים לְמַלְכֵי מָדַי
ג וּפָרָס: כִּי ׀ מָרְדֳּכַי הַיְּהוּדִי מִשְׁנֶה לַמֶּלֶךְ אֲחַשְׁוֵרוֹשׁ וְגָדוֹל
לַיְּהוּדִים וְרָצוּי לְרֹב אֶחָיו דֹּרֵשׁ טוֹב לְעַמּוֹ וְדֹבֵר שָׁלוֹם
לְכָל־זַרְעוֹ:

☙ Esther ☙

T he story of Esther and Mordecai at the court of the Persian king Ahasuerus is so neatly constructed and so full of coincidence and happy accidents that most readers will declare it to be improbable and unhistorical. This position seems to be the general verdict of scholars, although they acknowledge that the Book contains considerable authentic detail of the Persian Empire and its royal court.

For example, a very full and fair review is given by Carey Moore in his "Esther" (Moore 1971) and his entry under Esther in the Anchor Bible Dictionary (Moore 1992). Moore is a pupil of the great orientalist, W. F. Albright, and he marshals all the right arguments, coming to the conclusion that Esther is an historical novel (1992, II, 639). He acknowledges such accuracies as the historical figure of Xerxes (Ahasuerus), the seven princely advisors to the king, the efficient postal service and the use of Persian terms for nobles (*partemim*), decree (*pathshegen*) and so on. But he questions many other details. The number of satrapies should be 20 and not 127; giving the Jews nearly twelve months' notice of their fate is not credible; feasting for 180 days is impossible. Above all, how can one claim that the king's decree is irrevocable once it has been issued (Esther 8:8)? It does not accord with the historical facts and it is no way to run a country. Moore also sees little relevance in the short concluding chapter on the taxes levied by the king (Moore 1971, 98).

Another modern author (Levenson 1997) raises further problems. He sees the use of Persian terms merely as a device to give the book veracity and no proof of its authenticity. He questions the nature of an all-powerful monarch who cannot even control his own wife Vashti; he asks why there is no mention of Esther's marriage to the king, no mention of the Passover which occurs in the month of Haman's decree (Nisan) and no mention at all of the land of Israel. He thinks the short concluding chapter is out of place and that it appears to be spliced on from another narrative (ibid. 132). All in all, Levenson supports the general idea that the Book lacks historicity, pointing out its "gross lack of historical verisimilitude" (ibid.14) and observing, "Esther herself is even more of a historical improbability" (ibid. 24).

On the one hand it is clear that the problems outlined by these writers are all legitimate ones, but on the other hand one has to ask why, if this is just a fairy tale, should the author introduce such difficulties or why did the editor, if indeed there was one, not resolve them in his compilation?

Elias Bickerman (1967) takes a different approach to the work. In addition to many of the details mentioned above he cites comments from the Midrash and the Talmud. His conclusions are rather different from those of Moore and Levenson. He is of a mind that the author of Esther has combined two related accounts, one the story of Mordecai, the other the story of Esther, and made them into one coherent narrative. In this way he is able to explain a number of the difficulties and the "jumps" in the story, such as the beginning of Chapter 3, when the scene diverges from the rise of Esther to the rise of Haman; and Chapter 10, when the romance seems to end and the account reverts to a mundane recital of royal taxation. Bickerman is not alone in this thesis (as he is the first to acknowledge) and another scholar (Bardtke 1973) has postulated a triple source consisting of the separate tales of Vashti, Mordecai and Esther. However, such analyses destroy the integrity of the narrative and if we can explain the difficulties in a rational way, it becomes unnecessary to carve up the text. A logical explanation would also demonstrate the essential unity, and indeed beauty, of a fine piece of descriptive history.

ESTHER IN THE APOCRYPHA

Moore, Levenson and Bickerman all mention the Apocryphal Book of Esther, which makes considerable additions to the canonical work. Unlike other books of the Apocrypha, it is not a self-contained narrative but consists of passages that are used to top and tail the original version. It also makes some judicious alterations to the main text. The account is in five sections, which are fitted between sections of our Book of Esther. There is general agreement on the following order:

1. A prologue, describing the dream of Mardochaeus (Mordecai); placed before Chap. 1:1.
2. The letter sent by Artaxerxes praising Haman's plan; placed between Chap. 3:13 and 14.
3. The prayer of Mardochaeus to save the Jews; placed after Chap. 4:17 and continuing with 5:3 (5:1,2 are omitted).
4. The letter of Artaxerxes permitting the Jews to defend themselves; placed between Chap. 8:12 and 13.
5. An epilogue, in which Mardochaeus recalls his original dream of two dragons (Haman and Mardochaeus) fighting and casting lots for the future of Israel, and a river (Esther) welling up to save Israel with God's help, saying now it has all come true; placed at the end, after Chap. 10:3.

There is an end piece that dates the expanded version:

In the fourth year of the reign of Ptolemy and Cleopatra, Dositheus, who said that he was a levitical priest, and

Ptolemaeus his son, brought the foregoing letter about Purim, which they said was authentic and had been translated by Lysimachus, son of Ptolemaeus, a resident in Jerusalem (Esther, Apocrypha, 133).

This coda tells us that the text came from Jerusalem, was translated into Greek by Lysimachus and brought by Dositheus and his son to the rulers in Alexandria. It may refer to a well-known Jewish official, Dositheus son of Drimylos, secretary to Ptolemy III Euergetes and his queen Arsinoe II (the name "Cleopatra" is adopted for many Egyptian consorts) that would place this version at the rather early date of about 230 BCE. It is, however, unlikely to refer to this famous Dositheus, "who had renounced his ancestral faith" (Modrzejewski 1995, 56). Scholars generally have tended to place it later, at c.105 BCE in the time of Ptolemy X Alexander and his queen Cleopatra III (Bickerman 1967, 233) or in either 114 or 77 BCE (Moore 1992, II, 632). Whichever it is, it is clear that the author (or translator) Lysimachus has tried to interpret the original book to make it more convincing and more palatable to Jewish taste. For instance he introduces the notion of salvation by God (who is nowhere mentioned in our Book) and in his repetition of Esther 2:20, he writes that:

Esther had not disclosed her country – such were the instructions of Mardochaeus; but she was to fear God and keep His commandments just as she had done when she was with him. So Esther made no change in her way of life.

This is clearly a sop to Jewish taste; the Jews would worry about how Esther was conducting herself in the king's harem.

However, Lysimachus takes Ahasuerus to be Artaxerxes, which does not fit the details of our Book in relation to Persian history, as we shall demonstrate below; and he adds other details such as inserting the date of Adar, the thirteenth, as the day on which the lot fell to destroy all the Jews. This date is *not* mentioned in Esther, which only says that, "the *pur* (lot) was cast before Haman from day to day and from month to month, to the twelfth month, the month of Adar" (3:7). Significantly (as we shall see), no day of the month is mentioned in the Hebrew. The Septuagint adds the date of the fourteenth, quite gratuitously and mistakenly.

Lysimachus also changes Chapter 10 which, in Esther, states that Ahasuerus "levied a tax on the land and the islands of the sea" (10:1). He changes that to "the king made decrees for the Empire by land and sea," which softens the text, makes it more comprehensible and acceptable to public opinion, but destroys the real meaning. Similarly, the introduction of a dream sequence at the beginning and its apparent fulfillment at the end enables Mordecai to cast the whole story in a religious mode, suitably resolved with the help of God.

However, the effect of all the additions and alterations made in the Apocryphal version only tend to obscure the true meaning of the text. They demonstrate how texts can be distorted by pious intervention and it is our opinion that in this case they only serve to undermine the real events of the story.

WHO WAS THE REAL ESTHER?

Before getting down to our exposition, we have to look briefly at the early Jewish attitude to Esther. Whatever its rights or wrongs, the Greek version of the Apocrypha was presumably accepted by the Jews of Alexandria, who flourished until the terrible pogroms of 115-117 CE in that city. In Palestine the situation was different. It is a well-known fact that, of all the books of the *Tanakh* (Hebrew Bible), Esther is the only one that does not get a mention in any of the Dead Sea Scrolls. This may just be an accident of preservation though it does seem to indicate that at least the Dead Sea Sect did not have it in their canon. As we have already seen, several possible objections to Esther come to mind. The Book is secular in nature without any overt reference to God. It describes how a Jewish girl becomes wife to a heathen king, with the active consent of her guardian cousin, who is shown to be a staunchly observant Jew. It describes the events of a full year without mentioning the restrictions imposed by the festivals, particularly the Passover, which occurs a few days after the issue of Haman's decree on 13th Nisan. These strictures may be summed up in the comment of the Talmudic Rabbis that when, at the end of Esther, we read that Mordecai was "great among the Jews and acceptable to the *majority* of his brothers" (10:3) it means some of the Sanhedrin did not accept him because he had neglected the Torah (B. *Megillah* 16B).

Exactly when the book of Esther was accepted into the canon of the *Tanakh* is not clear. There seems to have been some argument about it as late as the third century CE, when Rav Judah of Pumbeditha claimed that Esther "does not make the hands unclean" (that is, it is not so holy that it cannot be touched) even though his teacher Samuel had declared that it was composed under divine inspiration (B. *Megillah* 7A). Indeed, one hundred years before Samuel, Rabbi Akiva and his contemporaries had declared it to be written under divine guidance (ibid.), though the fact that they were still discussing it in the second century CE suggests it was not included in the canon agreed at the Sanhedrin of Jabneh, shortly after the destruction of the second Temple in 70 CE. It is, however, included (without comment) in the list of Hagiographa (*Kethubim* or Writings) laid down by the Babylonian Talmud (B. *Baba Bathra* 14B), and the Rabbis of the third century CE were already vying with each other in their opening remarks to a discourse on the Book of Esther (B. *Megillah* 10B). Today the Book is accepted by orthodox Jewry as divinely inspired but, unlike the scroll of the Torah, it is permissible to touch the parchment, following Rav Judah, that "it does not make the hands unclean."

Seen from another angle, we note that the festival of Purim is already mentioned in the coda to the Apocryphal Book (see above) and there is an independent mention of the festival date in the Second Book of Maccabees:

> It was unanimously decreed that this day (the Maccabean victory over Nicanor) should never pass unnoticed...it is the thirteenth day of the twelfth month, called Adar in Aramaic, the day before *Mordecai's Day* (2 Macc.15:36).

According to the *Cambridge Bible Commentary*, whose translation this is, the original date of the victory over Nicanor fell on March 17, 160 BCE (Bartlett 1973, 343), while the Second Book of Maccabees was written down in 124 BCE (ibid. 220). It is perhaps significant that Second Maccabees is addressed to the Jews of Egypt (2 Macc.1:1) as is the Apocryphal Book of Esther, and that these are our two earliest datable sources of the story of Esther and Mordecai.

THE ESTHER STORY

The story is simple and intriguing. In his third year, the great king Ahasuerus of Persia, ruling over one hundred and twenty seven provinces, makes a half-year long feast in Shushan for all his subjects and finally orders his queen Vashti to appear (presumably naked) before the guests. She refuses and is banished. The courtiers advise that a new queen be selected and eventually, in the king's seventh year, a Jewish orphan girl Hadassah, also called Esther, is chosen. Her cousin and guardian, Mordecai, instructs her not to reveal her Jewish origin. Meanwhile, this Mordecai who, as an important functionary, sits in the King's gate, uncovers a plot by two eunuchs (courtiers) to murder the king. Esther reports the matter to the king in Mordecai's name and the plotters are hanged.

In the twelfth year of his reign, Ahasuerus promotes Haman to be chief minister and all bow to him except Mordecai the Jew. This incenses Haman, who vows to destroy the Jews and he makes an agreement to that end with the king. The decree is issued on 13th Nisan, the first month, to take effect in Adar, the last month of the year. Haman offers the king ten thousand silver talents to conclude the matter; the orders are issued by express messenger to all the provinces, and the king and Haman drink together to seal their handiwork. The people of Shushan are astonished when they hear the decree.

Mordecai, hearing of the evil order, urges Esther to petition the king. She is reluctant but agrees to do so if the Jews will fast on her behalf for three days. She then approaches Ahasuerus who welcomes her and agrees to drink with her the next day, together with Haman. At the party, Esther will only repeat her request to the king and Haman to come again the next day. Haman goes off happily but is upset when he sees Mordecai again refusing to bow to him, so as soon as he gets home he and his advisers build a gallows on which to hang the Jew.

THE KING'S FATEFUL INSOMNIA

That night the king cannot sleep and the book of the royal chronicles is read to him. It is the section dealing with Mordecai's exposure of the two plotters, and when the king hears that Mordecai has not been rewarded, he gives orders to summon the first courtier to appear that morning to suggest an appropriate honor. This happens to be Haman coming to ask the king's permission to hang Mordecai. Thinking he will be the recipient of the reward, Haman advises the king to let the man be clothed like the king and paraded through the streets on the king's horse.

The king agrees and orders Haman to perform these honors for Mordecai, which Haman is forced to do. Crestfallen, Haman goes home and is discussing how to deal with the Jews, when he is summoned to the second banquet to be held in the queen's chamber, with the king also present. This time Esther reveals her Jewish origins and accuses Haman of trying to destroy her people. Furious, the king storms out into the garden to cool off, and on his return, finding Haman pleading for his life at the queen's couch, he accuses him of attempted rape. Haman is led off to be hanged on the gallows he had just prepared for Mordecai.

The king passes on Haman's household and estate to Esther and Mordecai, who takes Haman's place as chief minister. Haman's decree cannot be reversed, since it bore the king's seal, but the king issues a new one on 23rd Sivan (the third month) allowing the Jews to stand and defend themselves on the fateful 13th Adar (the twelfth month), when they are due to be destroyed. Having disposed of Haman, there is great rejoicing amongst the Jews, and many other citizens join their side.

At the appointed date, the Jews, with the help of the Persian governors, defend themselves against their enemies; they hang Haman's ten sons and kill eight hundred others in Shushan and its Castle. In the provinces they kill 75,000 enemies in one day, whereas in Shushan itself they continue the fight for another day. Thus, in the provinces they celebrate Purim on 14th Adar and in Shushan on the 15th. This whole story was written down by Esther and Mordecai, instructing Jews everywhere to celebrate the festival of Purim. Finally Ahasuerus imposes a tax over all his lands; and these matters are all recorded in the annals of the Medes and the Persians.

THE EVIL TAX

After summarizing the story, it is appropriate to start our explanation at the end for, as we have seen above, neither the modern critics, nor the ancient Apocryphal version, accept Chapter 10 at face value. The question it raises is, why does the king impose a tax on all his lands, or rather, seeing this is a normal thing that all kings have to do, why is it mentioned here at the end of such a romantic tale? Why is such a sordid detail of taxation used to conclude the brilliant tale of a scheming minister and a vacillating king brought low by a beautiful Jewess? With this query in mind, we should now look at the context of the book as a whole and we shall see that it revolves entirely around the whole question of taxation.

Fig. 1 *Cuneiform Lintol of Xerxes at Persepolis. The inscription reads "Xerxes, the great king, king of kings, the son of Darius the king, an Achaemenian". The script reads from left to right and the first word in the first line is Cha-sha-va-ara-sha-a or Achashaverash (Xerxes) and the second word in the third line reads Da-a-ra-ya-va-ha-u-sha or Daryavesh (Heb.) being Darius (from Walker 1987, 50).*

The king's name is Ahasuerus, in Hebrew *Aḥashverosh*, which is very close to the Persian name of the monarch *Chashavarasha*, and much nearer to it than the Greek equivalent, Xerxes. The name is inscribed over the doorways of the palace at Persepolis ("city of the Persians") founded by Xerxes's father Darius I (see fig. 1). Darius had built up the great Persian Empire of numerous provinces, as recorded in the histories of Herodotus of Halicarnassus, who was a keen eyewitness of the events of the fifth century BCE. Herodotus was a Greek citizen and an observant visitor to both Egypt and Persia. He recorded many of the local customs and events of those countries and noted that the Persian Empire consisted of twenty provinces (The Histories III, 89). These were divided further into satrapies, some of which were further subdivided, as for instance in the case of Egypt, which was under one satrap (ruler) but was divided into nomes (districts), each with its own governor (Cook 1983, 173). So there could well have been 127 states (Heb. *medinoth*) as claimed by the Book of Esther, with Ahasuerus reigning "from Hodu (India) to Kush (Nubia) " (Esther 1:1). We have a cuneiform tablet from Persepolis that states:

Thus speaks king Xerxes: these are the countries - in addition to Persia - over which I am King ... Media, Elam, Arachosia, Urartu, Drangiana, Parthia, Haria, Bactria, Sogdia, Chorasimia, Babylonia Assyria, Sattagydia, Sardis, Egypt, the Ionians ... Maka, Arabia, Gandara, India, Cappadocia, Da'an, the Amyrigian Cimmerians, the Cimmerarians of pointed caps, the Skudra, the Akupish, Libya, Banneshu and Kush (Pritchard 1955, 316).

This is a list of thirty countries, which will have been sub-divided into smaller states, but it clearly includes the two outlying countries of India to the east and Kush (Nubia) to the west, exactly as in Esther 1:1.

The meaning of the Hebrew word *medinah* (plural – *medinoth*) is neither country nor province; we therefore translate it literally as "state." Some doubt must remain about the exact definition of countries, satrapies and provinces, but it is clear that there was a difference of rank between the satrap (*aḥashtarpen*) and the governor (*pasha*) who are mentioned separately in Esther (3:12) as well as in Ezra (8:36) and Daniel (3:2). Without doubt, the Persian King commanded the greatest of empires up to the time of Alexander (see fig. 2).

Darius bequeathed the great kingdom to his son Xerxes (see fig. 3) in 486 BCE; and historically, he left his son several major problems unresolved. Darius, his army and his fleet, had been defeated and humiliated in Greece in 491, and in Egypt, a revolt against Persia was brewing. The latter situation needed urgent attention, so Xerxes was forced to spend the first two years of his reign in ruthless suppression of the Egyptian uprising (Cook 1983, 99). The matter of Greece was more complicated, and geographically more distant, so vengeance for his father's defeat had to wait until the fifth year of his reign. But eventually, after much planning and some prevarication, Xerxes set out from Susa (*Shush* in Persian) in 481 BCE, for an extended and costly war against the Greek states. He crossed the

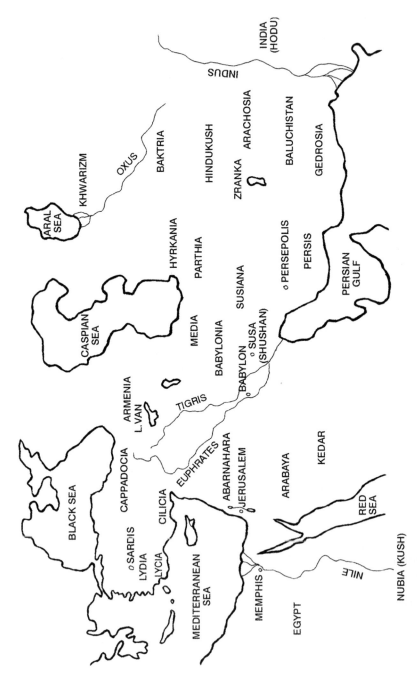

Fig. 2 *Map of the Persian Empire under Xerxes.*

Hellespont on the world's first pontoon bridges (Herodotus VII, 36) and went on to capture and burn Athens, but he was eventually defeated at sea at Salamis and at the land battle of Plataea in 479 BCE (Briant 1996, 545).

Fig. 3 *Crown Prince Xerxes in attendance on his father Darius I (part of a carving from the Treasury at Persepolis, now in the Oriental Institute of Chicago University).*

Thus, he had spent two expensive years many miles away from his homeland of Persia and achieved nothing, except to demonstrate that the great Persian Army was no longer invincible. The campaign against Egypt in the first years of his reign, mounted away from home, had also been costly, but at least it was successful and ensured that the Persian Empire continued to extend from India through Egypt to Nubia. These expensive wars convinced Xerxes to stay at home for the remaining fourteen years of his reign and concentrate on building palaces and collecting concubines:

> Discouraged and bitter, Xerxes gave up all attempts at conquest. He spent his final days building and improving his glorious palaces. Drained by years of crippling and useless war, his subjects were now milked of money and labor to complete these monuments to the royal vanity (Collins 1974, 148).

There were further skirmishes with Greece in 469 BCE at Pamphylia (southern Turkey) but these were conducted by the sons of Xerxes, and only resulted in further losses (Cook 1983, 126).

▥ THE SPLENDID FEAST OF AHASUERUS

The wars of Xerxes fit in well with the story of Ahasuerus in the Book of Esther. The great feast that he makes for his subjects in his third year (Esther 1:3) comes after his successful two-year campaign into Egypt in the years 486 to 484 BCE. It explains why he did not throw the great party in his first year, as one would have expected. The feast was held two years before his fateful assault on the Greeks and would underline what Herodotus tells us (VII, 8) – that Xerxes held extensive and elaborate consultations before making his decision to attack. Presumably he invited the representatives of all the provinces to the great feast to ensure their loyalty in the coming war. If the twenty provincial governors (satraps, nobles) came one after the other, it could well take 180 days (Esther 1:4) to entertain them all, for no doubt negotiations took place with each of them before each feast.

The second more modest party of seven days (1:5) for the people of the Castle of Shushan, would have been for his close advisors, to assess the loyalty of the provinces and to plan the war in detail. That may be why at this final sitting we are told the curious detail that no one was forced to imbibe (1:8). Nevertheless Ahasuerus himself was drinking, and in his cups he instructed his seven eunuchs to summon Vashti, the queen (1:10). Presumably the king had seven eunuch-chamberlains in the same way as he had seven close advisors (1:14). Vashti refuses to appear for reasons that are not explained, but probably because it was not dignified for the queen to attend the final drinking bouts, when things tended to get out of hand. It was left to the concubines to join the men on those occasions and so, by summoning Vashti at this stage, Ahasuerus was demoting her to a lower rank (Bickerman 1967, 185). So much is clear from Belshazzar's feast, where the concubines and courtesans attend the drinking bout (Daniel 5:2, 3) whereas the queen only comes in at the emergency caused by Belshazzar's fear of the writing on the wall (ibid. 5:10).

After Vashti's refusal, the king's seven close advisors, those "who saw the face of the king" are called (Esther 1:14). The Book of Ezra (7:14) claims that the Persian kings had seven close companions who had permanent access to the king. Jeremiah (52:25) mentions that the Babylonians took away "the seven men who saw the face of the king" when they sacked Jerusalem. In Herodotus the number is also seven, based on the seven noble families, who brought Darius to the throne (Herodotus III, 77) and, according to Xenophon, Cyrus the younger (c. 400 BCE) summoned the seven noblest Persians in his train to a court-martial (Cook 1983, 145).

After the demotion (not necessarily death) of Vashti, Ahasuerus is advised to select a new queen, but that happens some years later because Esther only comes into the title in the king's seventh year (Esther 2:16) that is, in 479 BCE. Why has it taken four years to select a queen since the fall of Vashti at the banquet of the third year? It is clear from the history of Xerxes that the king spent two years preparing for battle and then another two years at war with Greece. It was only after these events in his seventh year that he could concentrate on selecting a new queen, probably needing one to comfort him after his ignominious defeat by the Greeks.

It was really only then that Ahasuerus could devote himself to domestic policy, and to seeing that he had a fitting consort on the throne. Presumably it was while the king and the army were away in Greece and Asia Minor that the maidens were being prepared by eunuchs over a period of twelve months with their perfumes and ointments; and thus, indeed, there was no hurry to bring them to the monarch (2:12). Only after the war does Ahasuerus settle down and hold another party, this time a feast for Esther's coronation (2:18).

So far, the known events of Xerxes's reign and the dates given in the Book of Esther dovetail accurately (see fig. 4). We could add that the first verse of Chapter 2: "After these things when the anger of king Ahasuerus had subsided," refers to his anger at the failure of his Greek expeditions rather than at the disobedience of Vashti, which may not have concerned him that much.

🪶 THE RISE OF HAMAN

The next dated event is the rise of Haman, in the king's twelfth year (3:7), which is some five years after Esther's promotion. Critics have queried this delay, but it is quite plausible, although it presupposes that Esther kept her racial affiliation to herself all this time. If our narrator is so keen to show the promotion of Haman in the king's favor, why does it take Haman five years to reach the top? We see that Haman is not named as one of the inner circle of the seven close advisors to the king (1:14) and so, at the most, he would be considered to be eighth in line after the king and those nobles. This is significant for our dating.

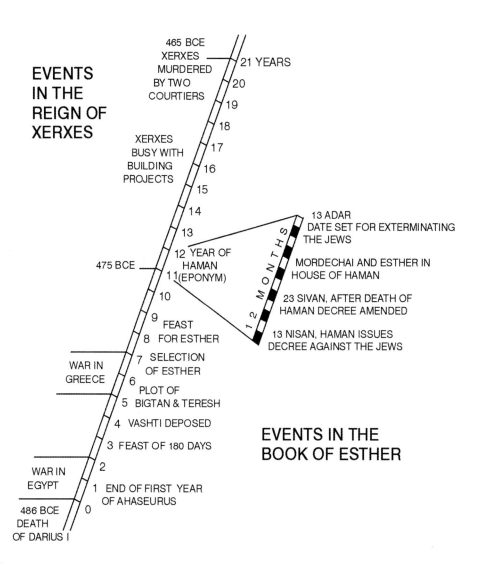

Fig. 4 *Time Chart of the Book of Esther, compared to the historical reign of Xerxes.*

It is known that the Assyrian kingdom had a system of eponymous or "limmu" (named) years where ministers took it in turn to be
"first among equals" for each year (Saggs 1984, 273). The king would
take the first year, and his nobles would cast lots for the privilege in
subsequent years. Tablets to this effect are recorded in Assyria
(Oppenheim 1977, 99; Hallo 1983, 27) and it is quite possible that
the Persians used a similar system, since they took over so many of
their predecessor's customs and laws.

In years of war, the king would probably retain overall control, so in
his twelfth year, having had four years of war (two in Egypt, two in Greece)
Persia would now be in its eighth year of "eponym." If the seven nobles
had had their year, it was now open to another courtier, one immediately below the first rank, to try his luck, and so it was only in this
twelfth year that Haman had a chance to gain this privilege. But presumably, because he was not the only candidate of the second rank to
try for first minister, it would be up to the "casting of lots" to see who
would get the prize. It may well be possible that Mordecai was also in
line to try for the honor of eponym at this time. He did, after all, sit in
the King's gate (Esther 2:19).

This matter of choosing the chief minister by lot seems to be the
actual meaning behind the verse:

> In the first month, which is the month of Nisan, in the twelfth
> year of king Ahasuerus, they cast *pur*, that is, the lot, before
> (for) Haman from day to day, and from month to month, to
> the twelfth month, which is the month Adar (3:7).

Conventionally this is taken to mean that Haman's advisors cast
the lot (Heb. *goral*) to settle on a date for the destruction of the Jews,
and finally they settled on 13th Adar. But this cannot be so, since the
date of the 13th is never mentioned here, although it is the day mentioned in the fateful decree (3:13). The verse only says that the *pur*

was cast from day to day and from month to month to confirm (that this was the year of) Haman, for every day and every month of that year, the twelfth year of Ahasuerus. So much is clear from the find of a *pur* in the basement of the Yale Institute of Archaeology (Hallo 1983, 19), as we shall now see.

The word *pur* has caused endless trouble and it is briefly explained in the verse itself, "the *pur* was cast, that is the *goral*" (3:7). Now *goral* is a good Hebrew word for "lot," so casting the *pur* meant casting the lot, but what exactly is a *pur*? It seems that one was found in 1934 in the Yale Babylonian collection at New Haven, USA and

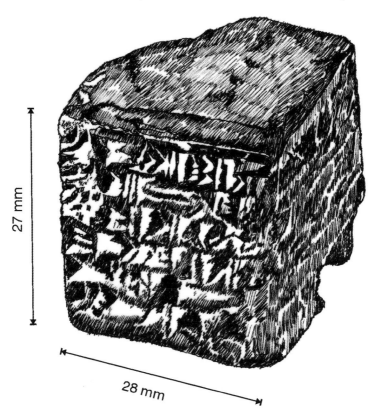

Fig. 5 *The* Puru *or "lot" of Iahali, a high official in the Court of Shalmaneser III of Assyria (858-824 BCE), now in the Yale Babylonian Collection (from Hallo 1983, 19).*

indeed it turned out to be a small die, a cube of just over one inch (27 x 27 x 28mm) covered in cuneiform script on four sides (fig. 5), telling us it was the lot of a man called Iahali, senior minister of Shalmaneser III of Assyria (858-824 BCE). This *pur* or "lot" served in the annual selection of the "eponym official" for the year (Hallo 1983, 20). It was believed that the events of the year were predetermined on New Year's Day, after which the eponym (the one giving his name to the year) was inaugurated into office. This *pur* of Iahali is from a period well before our story, but our verse shows the Persians had adopted the *pur* system of electing by lot a chief minister for each year, starting from the first month of the year. Now it was Haman who was selected by *pur* for the year starting from the first month, Nisan, the month of spring. It is possible that, as in Babylon, the festivities of the New Year lasted for eleven days (Oates 1986, 175) so the casting of the *pur* was on 12th Nisan and Haman's decrees were written on the 13th (Esther 3:12). This was not the date chosen by the "lot," it was just the first convenient date after the New Year festivities.

So far we have been able to explain the whole story in terms compatible with the Persian monarch and his court, his history and their customs, as far as they are known to us from Herodotus and other external sources. Now, however, we come to two great stumbling blocks. For the payment of ten thousand silver talents Haman obtains from the king the right to kill "a certain people scattered and dispersed amongst the peoples in all the states of your kingdom" (Esther 3:8). How can it be that Ahasuerus hands out the power of life and death over his subjects, even for such a large bribe and even to the chief minister for the year? For when it comes to the life of a single Jew, Mordecai, whom Haman wants to hang, he must ask permission from the king before he is able to execute him (5:14 and 6:4). We find again and again that the right of capital punishment is vested in the king, and only the king (Herodotus VII, 39; IX, 113). Furthermore, if Haman intends to destroy the Jews, why does he give them eleven months' notice of the event? The decree goes out on 13th Nisan (the first month) and the fateful day is set for 13th Adar, eleven months later (Esther 3:12, 13). It cannot be that the messengers were slow to cover the 127 states for we know the Persian post was the best in the world. Herodotus tells us (VIII, 98) that:

> There is nothing in the world which travels faster than these Persian couriers. The whole idea is a Persian invention, and works like this: riders are stationed along the road, equal in number to the number of days the journey takes – a man and a horse for each day. Nothing stops these couriers from covering their allotted stage in the quickest possible time – neither snow, rain, heat, nor darkness. The first, at the end of his stage, passes the dispatch to the second, the second to the third, and so on along the line, as in the Greek torch-race which is held in honor of Hephaestus. The Persian word for this form of post is *angarium*.

This speed of communication was one of the main factors that enabled the administrative center at Susa (Roaf 1990, 204) to hold together the vast Persian Empire. A similar system of couriers had enabled the former Assyrian Empire to extend to the borders of Egypt (but not beyond) because a courier could take a message to the borders of Sinai and get a reply back to the capital Nineveh within a week (Saggs 1984, 196).

In the matter of Haman's decree there could have been no delay, since "the runners went out in haste at the king's command" (Esther 3:15). In any case everyone knew about it in Shushan the Castle immediately (3:15) and the whole Empire must have known about it at least before 23rd Sivan (two months later), when the countermand, allowing the Jews to defend themselves, was issued (8:9). If the Jews were given eleven months' notice (or even only nine months) of their imminent destruction, would they not have fled the empire, to Greece for example, or at least organized themselves better in fortified enclaves? Why did the Jews not petition the king, or indeed offer him greater bribes? That would have been the most likely scenario. If the story is to remain credible we have to find an explanation, for many in the past have raised this question (Voltaire 1878, 474,475; Driver 1891, 453) and consequently declared Esther to be a fable. But there is a rational explanation.

꧁ HAMAN THE TAX-FARMER

Consider Haman's inducement to Ahasuerus. He offers him ten thousand talents of silver to be put into the royal coffers. He does not necessarily give it to the king straight away; he just offers to deposit the sum into the Treasury if the king will approve his plan to destroy the Jews. He says:

> If it is to the king's good, let it be written to destroy them, and
> I will weigh ten thousand circles (talents) of silver by the hands
> of the king's agents to bring into the treasuries of the king
> (Esther 3:9).

There is a further telling sentence, when Ahasuerus agrees to Haman's request and says:

> The silver is given to you, and the people, to do with them as
> is right in your eyes (3:11).

This sentence has caused a lot of grief because it looks as if the king gives Haman permission to get rid of the Jews and to keep the money. But such an interpretation is unwarranted and goes against reason and against the text as it stands. What Ahasuerus is in fact saying is that "the silver" goes to Haman and he has the right to collect it from those people as he thinks fit. But that silver is not the ten thousand talents, which Haman has contracted to put into the Treasury; that silver is the money that he, Haman, can extract from those people, and that is the silver that he can keep for himself.

The figure of ten thousand silver talents is not an arbitrary one. We see from Herodotus (III, 95) that the annual revenue of the Empire, under Darius, father of Xerxes, was 14,560 Euboean (silver) talents, excluding gifts in kind such as horses and slaves. Herodotus calculates the annual budget by listing the contribution made by each of twenty groups of states or provinces and he points out that Persia itself, as the mother country, pays no tribute (III, 97). Now it seems that the tribute (or taxes) was collected by the satraps in each satrapy and it was their responsibility to forward it to the central authority at Susa (Cook 1983, 85; Kuhrt 1996, 690).

Haman is offering the king ten thousand talents, or two-thirds of the annual tribute, a very considerable sum but not an impossible one. The annual tribute of 14,560 silver talents has been calculated as equivalent to "87,360,000 Athenian top day-wages" in Herodotus's day (Herodotus 1972, 37). Assuming a working year of 250 days and an annual salary today of £30,000 for a good craftsman, that would work out at about 1,050 million pounds sterling or 1,600 million US dollars. Elsewhere Herodotus had pointed out (VI, 136) that 50 silver talents was a very severe fine and burden on a great estate, and on the above calculation that would be about £3.5 million or over $5 million, which would indeed be a serious imposition of say, death duties, on a stately home. As we then see, Haman has promised a very large sum, but he is not necessarily obliged to pay it immediately. He is in fact agreeing to act as a tax farmer who buys the right to raise the tribute by promising a fixed sum to the Treasury.

Is Haman agreeing to collect the whole of the annual Empire

tribute? This is unlikely, since that was the responsibility of the individual satraps. Rather it would be that Haman, having become chief minister, is undertaking to replenish the state coffers, depleted by years of war. He cannot raise taxes from the king's war-weary and impoverished subjects, but hits on a new scheme. His dastardly plan, the new element that he cunningly introduces, is to extract the money for the king solely from the Jews. He describes it thus:

> There is one people scattered and spread among the peoples in all the states of your kingdom, and their laws are different from those of other people; the laws of the king they do not follow, and it is not in the king's interest to harbor them (Esther 3:8).

This, in rational guise, is the classic cry of the political racist and anti-Semite: this group of people is different from us and we can deal with them in a way different from ours. Haman makes a bargain with the king: if they do not pay up, they will be put to death. For this privilege Haman promises that ten thousand silver talents of tribute will go to the Treasury. Anything collected over and above that sum he presumably will keep and, if it is less, then Haman will bear the difference. But since the agreement is that the Jews' property is to be confiscated after their death (3:13) there is unlikely to be any shortfall. In essence, Haman is offering to act as royal tax-farmer, but with two original conditions. Firstly, the tax is to apply only to the Jews, and secondly, the penalty for non-payment will be death. To this the king readily agrees, saying: Yes, take the money from them and extract it from those people as best you can (3:11). As for the promised ten thousand silver talents, Haman would deposit them in the Treasury coffers in due course.

We know of a similar case when a Hellenized Jew, Joseph the Tobiad, became tax-farmer to Ptolemy V Epiphanes (204-181 BCE) of Egypt, who also ruled over Palestine for a few years. When Joseph the

Tobiad found that the Jews of Ashkelon were not paying up, the historian Josephus tells us:

> He arrested some twenty of their principal men and put them to death, and sent their property, altogether worth a thousand talents, to the king… thereupon Ptolemy, who admired his spirit and commended his actions, permitted him to do whatever he wished (Antiquities XII, 180,182).

Although over two hundred years later and in a different land, this example illustrates how Ahasuerus, desperate for funds, might have allowed Haman to exercise the death penalty as a punishment for refusal to pay the tribute.

A special tax on the Jews would explain another difficulty. The decree goes out in the month of Nisan, to be implemented in the month of Adar, eleven months later. Haman is in fact giving the Jews the maximum time to pay up. Since he is chief minister for just one year, the eponym year, he will have to deposit the tax into the Treasury before the end of Adar, the last month of the year, when his term comes to an end.

Another element will also have come into play in this situation. It is unlikely that Jews were allowed to own land outside their own homeland and therefore this tax was a poll tax, which could easily be distinguished from a land or produce tax on the indigenous population. A similar situation obtained later under the Sassanids where locals paid the *kharag* or land tax and the Jews and Christians, who had no landed property, paid the *gezit*, or poll tax (Huart 1927, 156). Since the normal tribute was a land and property tax it would be up to the satraps to collect it, each from his own satrapy. The poll tax on the Jews was a different matter and, being a novel area of tribute, it could well have been the responsibility of the chief minister, Haman.

It may be idle to speculate too far on exact monetary equivalents but obviously Haman is attempting to collect, say 15,000 talents, of which two-thirds will go to the royal coffers. It is impossible to say how many identifiable Jews there may have been in the Persian Empire, but a wild guess might be two hundred thousand at the most. As a comparison, a recent figure for the population of *Yehud*, the Persian province in Israel, in the fifth to fourth centuries BCE, is put at 30,000 (Finkelstein and Silberman 2001, 308). Thus Haman was looking for 0.075 talents of silver for every man, woman and child. That would be equivalent to some £5,000 or $8,000 per head at today's figures (as calculated above), which was obviously an excessive and exorbitant sum. I mention these figures, which are quite speculative, only to illustrate that the sum of 10,000 talents is a realistic figure; that the tax on the Jews would be most oppressive but not enough, perhaps, to send them all into exile, and that the real sting in the tail is the threat of death. This threat would have applied to those thousands of Jews who were unable to pay up on time.

EMERGENCY MEASURES

It is unlikely that the complete details of the new tax would have been published throughout the empire, but the immediate royal court, situated in Shushan the Castle (*Habirah*) would have known the terms and conditions. Shushan the City (*Ha'ir*) was not so closely linked to the palace but nevertheless got wind of it and was confused (Heb. *navokhah*, 3:15). Mordecai, however, who lived in Shushan the Castle (2:5), knows all about it immediately and broadcasts it as far and wide as he can (4:1). He knows that Haman is using the promise of silver to destroy the Jews (4:7). Mordecai perceives that emergency measures are now necessary and pleads with Esther to petition the king. She is desperately reluctant to do so, because she fears that to ask for an audience may lead to her death (4:11). Esther is right; Xerxes will not allow anyone to approach him directly, except his inner council of seven "who see the face of the King" (1:14). It is quite likely that Esther is no longer in favor, because she tells Mordecai she has not seen the king for thirty days (4:11). Could it be that she has been demoted temporarily to the status of concubine? After all, after five years of marriage we do not hear that she has given the king a male heir, although in the Midrash R. Judah ben R. Shimon claims "the last Darius" was the son of Esther by Ahasuerus (*MR.* Esther VIII, 3). This would have been Darius II who reigned in 423-405 BCE. Be that as it may, no mention of this occurs in the Book.

On the other hand Herodotus states clearly that the queen at the time in question is one Amestris, a rather unpleasant character. She, in her old age, buried fourteen boys alive as an offering to the god of the underworld in the hope that he would accept them instead of herself (Herodotus VII, 114). Furthermore, Xerxes was afraid of this queen (IX, 111) and this scenario does not sound like the Esther of our Book. In the present case it is quite possible that Esther had suffered some loss of status and was genuinely afraid to approach the moody and erratic king. Another possibility may have been that the king, having several palaces, had a harem in each. His wife Amestris would have been in Persepolis, the chief palace. Shushan, or Susa, was the administrative capital of the Empire; it is quite likely that the king moved there for only temporary periods and it was there that Esther was installed in the palace. Polygamy was the norm among the Persian kings and although they had agreed, after Darius I, to marry only within the seven prominent families, they did not keep to this rule (Kuhrt 1996, 683, 687). It was also normal for the king to take local women as concubines (ibid. 696,7).

On learning of the danger to the Jews, Esther overcomes her fears and trepidation and agrees to approach the king. What would be his reaction? The Jewish commentators are divided concerning Ahasuerus – whether he was a clever king or a fool (Ḥakham 1973, 42 n. 4, and B. *Megillah* 11A) and it is true that his actions in the Book of Esther display both qualities. Since he managed to reign over a vast empire for twenty years he must at least have possessed considerable cunning. But at the same time he was quixotic, extravagant and violent-tempered, according to Herodotus. When his friend Pythius, who had done him many favors and four of whose sons were serving in the army, asks for his eldest son to be excused military service, Xerxes flies into a rage and has the son cut in half and exhibited before the whole army (Herodotus VII, 39).

No wonder Esther feared to approach the king; and she had no option but to go straight into the throne room from the harem or the royal quarters. There was no way she could go into the public courtyard first, which acted as an antechamber; that was a physical impossibility for her owing to the layout of the palace (see fig. 7). Even if that had been possible, she would have had to take the risk of first confiding her business to one of the eunuchs, which would have been risky, as she was still concealing her Jewish background. Nevertheless she takes her life in her hands and approaches Ahasuerus.

Luckily he welcomes Esther by extending his scepter to her, even offering her "half the kingdom, and it shall be given to you" (Esther 5:3). This extravagant gesture is typical of the king. When Xerxes wanted his robe back from a lady friend, in case his wife found out about it, he offered the girl "cities, gold in unlimited quantities, and an army – a thoroughly Persian gift – under her sole command" (Herodotus IX, 109). The lady in question only wants to keep the robe, given to Xerxes by his wife, and having made his promise, he has to keep it but the gift leads to terrible consequences. It reminds one of a similar situation between King Herod and Salome, when he offers her a reward for her dance, using the words "whatever thou shalt ask of me, I will give it thee, unto half of my kingdom" (Gospel of Mark 6:23), an exact echo of Ahasuerus's offer to Esther. There, Salome's request for the head of John the Baptist leads to disaster. Not so with Esther's reply. Her only request is to ask the king to attend a banquet (Heb. *mishteh*) later that day, together with his chief minister Haman (Esther 5:4).

🔖 ESTHER'S FIRST BANQUET

It is clear that Esther is now restored to the king's favor, but once Ahasuerus and Haman are at the "drinking of wine" (*mishteh hayayin*, 5:6) with Esther, she asks nothing further than that Ahasuerus and Haman come again the next day, when she will reveal her intentions (5:8).

Why should the king and Haman, both no doubt busy men, put up with this procrastination? Again Herodotus may have the answer. He tells us that if the Persians have an important decision to make, they discuss it when drunk and "the following day the master of the house.... submits their decision for reconsideration when they are sober" or sometimes it is the other way round (Herodotus I, 133). In this instance it is the mistress of the house, Esther, who delays her decision and it could well be that Ahasuerus and Haman at the first "drinking of wine" see no need to persuade Esther, who after all starts her petition by saying "my request and my plea are.... " and then breaks off in mid sentence (5:7). They did not press her, because there would be the inevitable second round with perhaps less liquid refreshment. The second time round it is still at "the drinking of wine" (7:2) but we can be sure the king is now going to press his question more vigorously.

In between these sessions we have the climactic night scene, around which the whole story revolves, when the scribes read the royal chronicles to the king. It is unlikely that Xerxes himself was able to write or read (Cook 1983, 133). The king learns how Mordecai saved his life by thwarting the plot of the two eunuch doorkeepers, Bigtan and Teresh (Esther 2:21) and he decides that Mordecai must be rewarded. The eunuchs' plot is a typical one and may reflect the fact that Xerxes's reign is eventually brought to an end when he is murdered in his own palace by his grand vizier and two eunuchs (Roaf 1990, 213) Artabanus and Aspamitres (Collins 1974, 148). Coming in between the two Esther banquets, this night or early morning scene is the turning point of the whole story and, as Levenson rightly points out, it gives the book a "chiastic structure" (Levenson 1997, 8) in which the events of the first half, mainly negative in nature, are reflected symmetrically in the second half by similar events of a positive nature (see fig. 6).

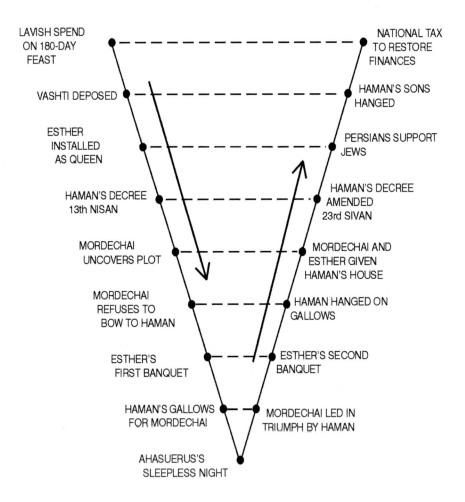

Fig. 6 *Diagram of the chiastic structure of Esther, showing events in the second half of the Book reflecting those in the first, the turning point being the king's sleepless night, after which events begin to go against Haman (adapted from Levenson 1997, 8).*

In the meanwhile Haman, having again seen Mordecai refuse to bow to him (Esther 5:9) as he left Esther's first banquet, resolves to punish Mordecai himself. On the advice of his wife Zeresh and his courtiers, he prepares a gallows on which to hang his victim (5:14). Previously Haman had decided to pursue the Jews as a whole and not Mordecai in particular (3:6), but now he is concentrating solely on killing Mordecai. This shows that the punishment he is preparing for the Jews as a whole is not one of total destruction; but as for Mordecai himself, he is to be eliminated. His crime, not bowing to Haman, was punishable, since it was the king's command to do so (3:2).

This action of bowing down to another human being is not against Jewish law. The Hebrew Bible gives several examples of bowing down especially where a king or his representative is concerned. His brothers bow down to the ground to Joseph (Gen. 50:18); the outlawed David bows to Saul (I Sam. 24:9); the woman of Tekoah, presenting his son Absalom, falls on her face to King David (2 Sam. 14:4) and Bathsheba, pleading on behalf of her son Solomon, bows to David (I Kgs. 1:16). Jewish commentators therefore find it hard to understand Mordecai's refusal to bow to Haman, and have to suggest that it was because Haman wore an idol at his neck:

> When Ahasuerus ordered that all should bow down to Haman, the latter fixed an idolatrous image on his breast for the purpose of making all bow down to an idol (*MR.* Esther VI, 2).

That could be an unnecessary interpretation; it seems more likely that this refusal to bow to Haman had a personal motive. It could well be that Mordecai, who after all lived in Shushan the Castle (Esther 2:5) and sat in the King's gate (2:19) had been a rival for the eponym year with Haman and had lost only by a throw of the die. To have to bow to another in Persian society implied a considerable difference in rank (Herodotus I, 134). Mordecai would have been unwilling to defer to Haman, who lived not in the Castle but only in Shushan the City, seeing that he always had to pass Mordecai at the gate on his way to and from the palace (Esther 5:9). Whatever the reason, the rivalry between Haman and Mordecai was obviously a deep and personal one conducted with bitterness on both sides.

THE BEGINNING OF THE END FOR HAMAN

Now that the king has to decide on the reward to be given to Mordecai, he looks to a courtier for advice. Haman, being on hand to tell the king he wants to hang Mordecai (which he gets no chance to do because the king has to speak first), gives advice that reveals his true ambition. He suggests that the reward for saving the king's life, which he imagines he has done by offering to collect the tribute, should be to wear the royal apparel and ride the royal horse (6:8,9). The advice shows Haman's true intent; he sees himself in the role of the king and no doubt Ahasuerus catches this whiff of lèse-majesté and stores it away for retribution at a later date. This day it is enough that Haman is humiliated by having to reward Mordecai with his own pipe dream (6:11).

The Talmud is happy to expand on Haman's loss of face and dignity. It tells us that Mordecai decided that he needed a wash and shave before parading in the king's clothes. Since all the bathhouses and barbers were still closed, Haman was forced to wash and shave him, saying, "the man esteemed above all others by the king has now to become a bath attendant and barber." Haman was also forced to stoop down and lift Mordecai onto the horse, in ironic contrast to Mordecai refusing to bow down to Haman. The final indignity came during the parade when Haman's daughter, thinking it was Mordecai being forced to lead her father on the horse, emptied a chamber pot onto his head. "He looked up and when she saw it was her father, she fell off the roof and died" (B. *Megillah* 16A).

The name Haman is of unknown origin. The Book gives his father as Hamdatha the Agagite, which may or may not link him to
Agag, king of Amalek (I Sam. 15:8). That would produce a nice symmetry between Haman of Agagite descent and Mordecai "the son of
Jair, the son of Shimei, the son of Kish, a Benjaminite" (Esther 2:5).
King Saul, the Benjaminite, was a son of Kish (I Sam. 9:1,2) and mortal enemy of Amalek and Agag (I Sam.15:7,8). Whether we can equate
one Kish with the other and one Agag with the other is doubtful, but
at least our passage shows that Haman was not a native Persian. He
was a foreigner, probably from the west, who had adopted a name very
similar to the eponymous founder of the Achaemanid Empire, the
dynastic name given to the Persian kings, Cyrus, Cambyses, Darius
and Xerxes and their descendants down to the time of Alexander the
Great. The foundation of the Persian dynasty is traced back to c. 700
BCE to one Achaemanes whose name in old Persian would be
Hakhamanish (Frye 1976, 298), the core of which is *Khaman*, sometimes pronounced Haman. Could it be that Haman, foreigner, upstart
and potential usurper, had deliberately chosen a name to reflect the
origins of the Empire, making himself more Persian than the Persians?
His father's name Hamdatha, however, could be a Persian one meaning "given to the moon" (BDB, 241), although "Agagite" would still
designate him as of foreign extraction.

It is indeed doubtful whether Agagite can be equated to Agag of
Amalek, since the whole tribe, which had not been wiped out by Saul,
was later eliminated at the time of Hezekiah, according to the first Book
of Chronicles (4:43). In any case, the Midrash overcomes any problem
by claiming, to its own satisfaction, that on the night before his execu-
tion by Samuel (I Sam. 15:32), Agag slept with his wife and their resulting
child became the ancestor of Haman the Agagite (Ginzberg 1968, VI,
234). It is perhaps noteworthy that the Greek Apocrypha of Esther names
him as "Haman son of Hamadathus, the Bugaean (or Macedonian),"
which designates him clearly as a foreigner and a Greek; the Greeks

being sometime enemies of the Jews of Alexandria (Modrzejewski 1995, 140). Haman's wife Zeresh (Esther 5:10) had a good Persian name meaning gold or "the golden one" (BDB, 284). If he was a foreigner, Haman at least had the good sense to marry a local girl.

On the subject of names, Mordecai is clearly an assimilationist name based on the Babylonian god Marduk, and it is borne by one of the Jews returning from Babylon with Zerubbabel (Ezra 2:2). The returnee Mordecai would have gone back to Jerusalem some fifty years before the reign of Xerxes, and his name shows that, as with the Jewish leader Zerubbabel himself, the Jews had adopted Babylonian names within a short time. In spite of this attestation of the name Mordecai, commentators doubted that a pious Jew would bear this name or that such a name even existed in the Persian records (Grayzel 1949, 3).

It is however now clear that the name *Marduka* occurs five times on tablets from Persia. One *Marduka* was an accountant who inspected Susa during the last years of Darius I or the early years of Xerxes. His name is given in Aramaic. The other instances are on tablets from Persepolis with the name in Elamite. These tablets "are dated between 505 and 499, with the name *Marduka* or *Marduku*, which may refer to up to four individuals" (Yamauchi 1990, 235). The tablets are contemporary with the reign of Darius I but we know that the posts occupied by civil servants often extended into succeeding reigns.

It should come as no surprise that a Jew would occupy a position of high trust in the kingdom, as Mordecai eventually did (Esther 8:2). Even before his elevation he "was sitting in the King's gate" (2:21) which indicates some senior position in the royal court. As is clear from his reporting the treachery of Bigtan and Teresh (2:22) his loyalty to the crown was complete. Why should a Jew show such allegiance and why should he be chosen to hold high office? One commentator has put it well:

A Jewish counselor can be trusted by the ruler more than any other. He certainly lacks the power base from which to stage a take-over. So to have a Jew in charge of the administration is best (Daube 1995, 5).

Perhaps, having made one mistake with Haman, Ahasuerus thought it better to trust a Jew than any of his closest advisers, those seven courtiers "that served the face of the king" (Esther 1:10).

If Mordecai had a Jewish name, we do not know it, but Esther still retained the Jewish name of Hadassah or "myrtle" (2:7), while her Persian name was based on the Babylonian goddess Ishtar, as even the Talmud acknowledges (B. *Megillah* 13A). The use by the Jews of names based on local gods does not necessarily imply total assimilation, but the fact that Esther stayed in the king's palace, whether as queen or concubine, for several years before revealing her true identity, must imply that she and her cousin-guardian Mordecai were sufficiently assimilated to tolerate the situation. She was there after all for five years before the Hamanic decree. It must be that Mordecai had some inkling of the rise of an anti-Jewish element in Shushan the Castle and thought it essential to retain a close ally in the king's entourage. As he later says to Esther "and who knows if (not) for such a time as this you have attained royal status?" (4:14). Mordecai may have foreseen the development of some form of anti-Jewish sentiment when he realized that his rival Haman could one day become the eponym chief minister.

Esther's position as king's consort was clearly an equivocal one. There is no suggestion of reluctance on her part to join the maidens destined for the king's bed, and seeing that Ahasuerus "loved Esther more than all the women and she raised favor and compassion before him" (2:17) she must have co-operated favorably with him; though some Jewish commentators claim she went unwillingly to the king, as it says "Esther was *taken* to the king" (2:16) meaning she was taken by force (Ḥakham 1973, 18). Curiously enough, the famous sage, Rav (*Abba Arikha*) of Babylon, of the third century CE, holds that she was intimate both with Mordecai and with the king, claiming that "she used to rise from the lap of Ahasuerus and bathe and sit in the lap of Mordecai" (B. *Megillah* 13B), while Rabbi Meir, of the second century CE, even says she was Mordecai's wife (ibid. 13A). These opinions emphasize the fact that some Rabbinic sages were not happy with her behavior, or with that of Mordecai.

As we have seen, the Apocryphal version adds, after Esther's first encounter with the king, that Mordecai's instructions to her were:

> She was to fear God and keep His commandments just as she
> had done when she was with him. So Esther made no change
> in her way of life (Esther, Apocrypha, adds. to 2:20).

Our Book, however, does not seek to gloss over circumstances that appear contrary to the orthodox norm. Daube criticizes the attitude that the end justifies the means and is horrified at Esther's submission to Ahasuerus, with the connivance of Mordecai. He equates her position to that of Dinah, raped by Shechem, son of Hamor (Gen. 34:2); Rahab, the prostitute of Jericho, who saved her family by sheltering the two Israelite spies (Josh. 2:1) and even the rape of Tamar by her half-brother Amnon (2 Sam. 13:12), concluding that "thus should not be done in Israel" (Daube 1995, 60). Nevertheless it *was* done by Ahasuerus, Mordecai and Esther and is not even questioned in the Book. The rationale was the threat to the Jews, and that Esther should be in a position to influence the king in their favor.

A TOLERANT MEGA-EMPIRE

There is no evidence that the general attitude of the Persian Empire was in any way anti-Jewish. Certainly local religions were tolerated (Kuhrt 1995, 699). Nor could there have been state xenophobia in an Empire that encompassed so many nationalities and races, although it may have been that the central powers in Persia considered themselves to be superior to their colonies. There was certainly great animosity towards the Greeks who had inflicted crushing defeats on the Empire and no doubt there was an ambivalent attitude to Ionia, the coast of Anatolia, which wavered between allegiance to Greece and Persia (Cook 1973, 93-96). None of this, however, involved the Jews. The inhabitants of the Land of Israel lived peaceably in the province of *Yehud* (Judaea), one of the Persian states, and had the support of the Persian emperors when it came to the rebuilding of Jerusalem and the Temple (Ezra 3:7; Neh. 2:8). There may have been local difficulties at certain times and certain places but there is no indication that the Jews of *Yehud* had any part in the events of Shushan, or suffered in any way from anti-Jewish sentiment within the central administration. If there was a threat to the Jews in Judaea, it was from internal enemies, such as the Samaritans (Ezra 4:11), and not from the Persian Emperor.

There is also evidence of the friendly attitude of the Persians to the Jews in the papyrus documents from Elephantine at Aswan in Egypt, where there was a Jewish colony and temple. When the Persian Emperor, Cambyses, conquered Egypt in 525 BCE, he destroyed Egyptian temples but not the Jewish one; and when the Jews observed the Passover at their temple in 419 BCE, it was at the express orders of Darius II (Porten 1968,122,130). The situation in Shushan may have been different.

Darius I, father of Xerxes, largely built up the capital by importing craftsmen and materials from all over the empire to work on his great Palace at Susa. According to the Persian records, there was gold, wool and decorators from Egypt and Sudan; cedar and carpenters from Lebanon; stone, wood and stone masons from Asia Minor; mud bricks and bricklayers from Babylon; lapis lazuli from Scythia; gold and decorators from Media; turquoise from Chorasmia; ivory and hardwood from India and Afghanistan; all as recorded in the foundation inscriptions of the royal palace (Roaf 1990, 212; Frye 1976, 108). No doubt these craftsmen included Jews from the west and Babylon, who were known as skilled metal workers. Although the royal officials must have worked with all these foreigners, some perhaps slaves or prisoners of war, it could be there was a xenophobic backlash among the population of Shushan, living with all these "immigrants." Resentment against foreign labor in general may have brought in its wake resentment against other minorities such as the Jews. This in turn may have enabled Haman to exploit public sentiment and to focus his tax reforms on the Jews alone.

▧ SHUSHAN THE CASTLE, SHUSHAN THE CITY

The distinction between the Castle and the City of Shushan is of considerable relevance to the Book of Esther, which speaks of Shushan the Castle (habirah) in 1:2 and of Shushan the City (ha'ir) in 3:15. Mordecai actually lived in the Castle (2:5). The big feast took place in Shushan the Castle, in the garden of the king's palace (ginath bitan hamelekh, 1:5). Queen Vashti's feast was in the royal house (beth ha-malkhut 1:9) and later the virgins were brought into Shushan the Castle for the harem (beth hanashim, 2:3) literally, the house of the women. All of this is much clearer if we have a plan of the palace, the Castle and the City, and indeed one is available, thanks to excavations carried out on the site from 1851 onwards (see figs. 7 & 8).

From the plans we can see that the descriptions are in no way imaginary and we can also identify the gate of the King (sha'ar hamelekh) where Mordecai sat (2:19) and which Haman must have passed many times on his way to the palace. Less clear is the location of the city square (rehov ha'ir, 4:6 and 6:9) but we do know where Esther stood before Ahasuerus in the court (5:2), also called the inner court (hatser hapenimith, 4:11, 5:1) and we can guess where she had her drinking parlor or boudoir (5:5), since it was adjacent to the palace garden (ginath habitan, 7:7); not the king's garden (1:5) this time but the queen's. We can also see that Esther had no access from the royal apartments to the public audience chamber in the outer court, and so had to risk her life by appearing directly in front of Ahasuerus in the throne room, which was "by the entrance of the house" (*pethah habayith*, 5:1), meaning the entrance to the royal quarters.

Some of these details may seem to be added merely for the sake of providing color to the narrative but they reflect an accurate picture of the palace, and the distinction between Shushan the Castle and Shushan the City is essential to the story. This is so at the beginning, where Haman's decree is issued without dissent in the Castle, the king and Haman celebrating its conclusion there, while the City itself is disturbed by these events (3:15). Also at the end of the Book, on the first day of fighting, the battle takes place in the provinces and in Shushan the Castle (9:6, 10), while the fight in Shushan itself, and only there, continues on the next day with the king's special permission (9:15).

Another detail of importance is that Mordecai lived in Shushan the Castle (2:5) and sat in the King's gate (2:19, 21; 6:12), while there is no indication that Haman resided in the Castle. Haman was frequently in and out of the King's gate (3:2, 5:9), which implies that he lived in Shushan the City, beyond the gate and had to pass it to gain entry to the royal quarters within Shushan the Castle. Mordecai, living in the Castle, may well have held higher rank than Haman, have resented Haman's elevation, and so refused to bow to him.

Shushan the Castle was the royal enclosure containing the palace built by Darius on its south side and the great *Apadana* or audience hall to the north. The hall measured 75m. (250ft.) on each side and had a carved cedar roof supported on thirty-six bull-headed pillars (fig. 9). The complex included gardens to the north and east and the gate (King's gate) was to the east, towards the royal city, called here Shushan the City (fig. 8). The plans of the city include an Acropolis, which was the main religious center, not to be confused with Shushan the Castle, and not given a mention in the Book of Esther.

The designation Shushan the Castle (*Shushan habirah*) occurs again in other contexts. Nehemiah meets a deputation of his fellow Jews in Shushan the Castle (Neh.1:1); Daniel receives a vision, in the reign of Belshazzar, while in Shushan the Castle (Dan. 8:2). The word *birah* implies a fortified area of the town and the translation "castle" is appropriate. It occurs in a similar context among the papyrus records from Elephantine, Egypt, where the Jewish colony is located in *Yeb habirta* (the Aramaic for *habirah*) translated as "*Yeb* (Elephantine), the fortress" (Cowley 1923, 112, line 13). The document is from the Persian period and dated to 408 BCE. Clearly the important part of town, which was fortified again within the city walls, is referred to as the *birah*.

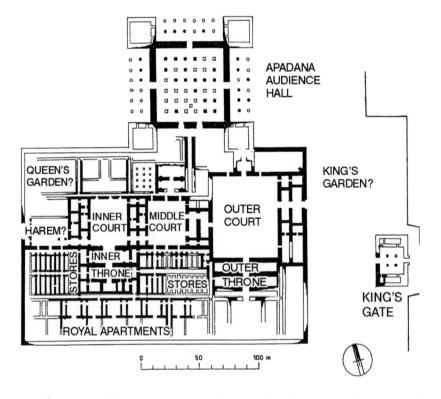

Fig. 7 *Layout of the Palace of Susa, showing the King's gate, the outer and inner Courtyards, the Royal Apartments and the Gardens (from Ferrier 1989, 29).*

Within Shushan the Castle, stood the palace, which was divided into six main sections (fig. 7) as follows:

1. The *Apadana,* or outer Audience Hall, which does not feature in the Book.
2. The Harem (Esther 2:3) with the Queen's Garden (7:7).
3. The Inner Court (4:11; 5:1) leading to the Throne Room to the south; the Royal Entrance (5:1) was between the Middle Court and the Inner Court.
4. The Middle Court (1:9) with the Royal Apartments to the south.
5. The Outer Court (6:4) and the King's Garden (1:5) which may have been to the east or north of it.
6. The King's Gate, entry to the Castle (2:19; 3:2; 5:9; 6:12).

Some of the medieval commentators recognized these features and tried to reconstruct the geography of Shushan in outline. The twelfth-century commentator Abraham Ibn Ezra, of Spain, recognized the distinction between Shushan the Castle and Shushan the City; and Shemariah ben Elijah (1275-1355) of Crete describes the palace as outlined in the feasting scene in Chapter I (Walfish 1993, 97-103). But of course they did not have the benefit of the plans drawn up by the archaeological expeditions of the nineteenth century.

We should also note the location of Shushan itself. The Hebrew name is a direct reflection of the Persian *Shush,* which the Greeks have handed down to us as Susa. The city is not in Persia, but in the adjacent former kingdom of Elam (as Dan. 8:2), that had become the new province of Susiana. Susa may have been the ancestral home of the first Achaemenid ruler Cyrus II (549-530 BCE), but it probably owed more to Darius I (522-486 BCE) who made it the administrative center of his extensive empire and built there the palace that was extended by his son Xerxes I, our Ahasuerus. Darius chose Susa, since it was "midway between the distant eastern and western extremities of the empire" (CAH.1977,IV,192). The royal "Shushan the Castle" (Esther 1:2) was extensive and eminently palatial and, although the Persian palaces at Pasargadae and Persepolis, in Persia itself, may have been more luxurious, the story of Esther rightly takes place in Susa, the administrative capital of the Empire. As Herodotus describes it, Susa was also the terminus of the great royal road that ran from Ionian Sardis in the west to Susa in the east (Herodotus V, 52,53) a distance of some 2,600 km. (1,600 miles).

Susa is located on the east bank of the Shaur River, with another palace and further development on the west bank (fig. 8). It may be

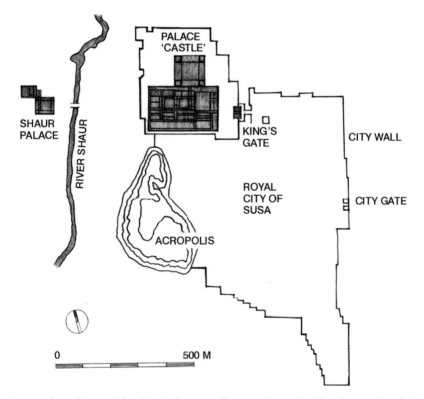

Fig. 8 *Plan of Susa (Shushan) showing the Royal Castle (Shushan Habirah), The Royal City (Ha'ir Shushan) and the Acropolis or Religious Center (plan by M. Piller of the French Expedition, from Roaf 1990, 211).*

that the Jews lived mainly on the west bank and so, when Mordecai goes to instruct them to fast in support of Esther's unsolicited approach to the king, it says "And Mordecai crossed (Heb. *vaya'avor*) and did all that Esther had commanded him" (Esther 4:17). It is not clear what he crossed and it may, in fact, have been that he crossed the river to the Jewish Quarter. In the Talmud the sage Samuel (second century CE) takes the view that the word *vaya'avor* indicates crossing a body of water (B. *Megillah* 15A), and perhaps it was the river Shaur that he crossed on his way to the Jews.

Quite apart from the Book of Esther, the Castle of Shushan played another role in Jewish history. A picture of *Shushan Habirah*, appeared on the eastern gate of the Second Temple, which was used by the High Priest to exit to the Mount of Olives (M. *Middoth* 1:3). It seems that this was a representation carved on the gateway itself or in a room within the gate complex where the standard cubit length was also marked on the wall (M. *Kelim* 17:9). This suggests it was an official symbol placed there by order of the Persian governors to remind the Jews who was in charge; and it was tolerated by the Temple administration, since it was after all the Persian Emperor Cyrus II who had given permission for the Temple to be rebuilt (Ezra 1:2).

ESTHER'S SECOND BANQUET

After Haman's humiliation in having to parade Mordecai around Shushan on the king's horse, we eventually come to the second intimate session between the king, Esther and Haman, when Esther finally reveals her background and her people. It is all done in one curious sentence:

For we are sold, I and my people, to be destroyed, killed and exterminated; and if it was to be sold as slaves, men and women, I would have kept quiet, for the harm would not have been sufficient to trouble the king (Esther 7:4).

Esther does not actually mention the name of her people or how exactly they are going to be destroyed but she puts her finger on it by saying it will not be by slavery. The normal punishment for non-payment of debt or non-payment of taxes would be to be sold into slavery and one's price would go towards canceling the debt (Oppenheim 1977, 75). In the present case, however, it would be different, as Haman had received permission to exercise the death penalty if the tax was not paid. Esther is therefore saying to the king, that the option of slavery, which would be the normal one, 'would not have been enough for me to trouble the king, but as in this case our lives are at stake, I must bring it to Your Majesty's attention.'

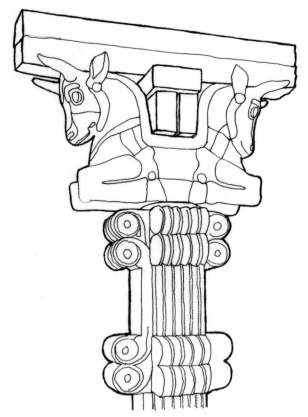

Fig. 9 *Double-headed Bull Capital in the Persian Style from Apadana, the audience hall, in Susa c.500 BCE (from Caubert and Bernus-Taylor 1991, 47).*

By now it will have become clear to Ahasuerus that Haman is collecting the new state tribute exclusively from the Jews. Haman has probably already collected a fair sum from those able to pay, and is preparing to kill off the rest if they do not pay up by 13th Adar. Ahasuerus will realize that this situation is intolerable, especially as the Jews are not just a weak people "scattered and dispersed" through-out the kingdom (3:8) but now actually have a powerful compatriot, Esther, at court! His first thought must have been to find a pretext to remove Haman. And he will have recalled that Haman had revealed his sub-conscious desire for the kingship, when he advised the king how to reward "the man whom the king wants to honor," thinking it to be him-self (6:9). If Ahasuerus could rid himself of Haman he might at one stroke save Esther and her Jews, remove a potential threat to the crown, and lay his hands on the taxes already collected by the chief minister. At Esther's outburst the king, now furious, rushes into the garden to cool off and collect his thoughts (7:7). Coming back and seeing Haman pleading for his life on the queen's couch, gives Ahasuerus the perfect pretext. The king pronounces it to be an attempt on Haman's part to rape the queen. "Does he even assault the queen, while I am in the house?" (7:8), he cries, and Haman's fate is sealed.

THE DENOUEMENT

From here on the rest of the story is downhill. But there are still nine months to go until the fateful day of 13th Adar, when the Jews are due to be killed off, if the tribute is not paid. It has always been difficult to see how Ahasuerus, who now realizes the situation, did not see fit to revoke Haman's decree. The excuse given, "for the decree written in the name of the king and sealed with the ring of the king cannot be reversed" (8:8) is hardly a valid one, but does not seem to have been challenged by the early commentators, not even by Voltaire. We can see how the Persians again and again changed their orders, at least according to Herodotus. For instance the Persian Emperor Cambyses, when in Egypt, ordered the death of Pharoah's son in revenge for the death of the Persian allies at Memphis, but then relented when he saw the father's great self-control in the face of disaster (Herodotus III, 14).

In another case, Xerxes himself spares the lives of two Spartans who came to Susa to offer themselves as atonement for two Persian ambassadors killed earlier at Sparta, whom Darius had vowed to avenge. Xerxes however, is so impressed by their gesture that he lets them live (ibid. VII, 136). An interesting detail in that case is that the two Spartans refuse to bow to the king even when ordered to do so by the royal bodyguard, since "it was not the custom in Sparta to worship a mere man like themselves." So Mordecai may not have been alone in refusing to bow to the mortal Haman, but obviously it was an unusual refusal, even in Jewish eyes.

If, indeed, the king's decree was not irrevocable, why did Ahasuerus not retract it here, as Esther so urgently requested (Esther 8:6)? If Haman's decree really just referred to the slaughtering of the Jews it would have been indefensible for it not to have been revoked. But if it referred to taxation of the Jews, with the death penalty for non-compliance, then it would be understandable that Ahasuerus was reluctant to forego the revenue. It would be in his interest to leave the tax demands in place but to ameliorate the conditions, which is what he did. He may have retained the death penalty as an ultimate sanction, but he gave the Jews the right to self-defense on the fateful day (8:11) and this presumably signaled to his other subjects to rally to the Jews, even in paying a share of the tax. This state of affairs would also explain the difficult verse:

> And many of the people of the land made themselves as Jews (Heb. *mityahadim*) for there fell on them the fear of the Jews (8:17).

The Hebrew word *mityahadim*, which is unique to Esther, is unlikely to mean that the people "became Jews," as some translations render
it. It probably just means that the majority of the population now sided
with the Jews, since the order had been given on 23rd Sivan allowing
the Jews to defend themselves (8:9-12). Siding with the Jews would mean
participating in the tax, and removing the death penalty for those Jews
who did not or could not pay. So much would be made clear when
Mordecai instructs the governors and they in turn help the Jews (9:3).

The majority of the population may have feared the new powers
given to the Jews by Ahasuerus and saw that it would be politic to
participate in the tribute and so they "made themselves as Jews" for
tax purposes. But naturally there was a hard core who did not join
them and who retained the anti-Jewish stance of Haman. They did
not see why they should participate in a tax that was originally restricted to the Jews, even though their governors now sided with the
Jews. These people were "the enemies of the Jews" (9:1) who still expected the Jews to pay all of the new tribute. They included the ten
sons of Haman (9:7-10) which suited Ahasuerus's book. Although he
may have decided to lay his hands on the taxes already collected by
Haman, one presumes the money first reverted to Haman's sons on his
death, and Ahasuerus could not confiscate it, at least not legally, until
the ten sons were out of the way. This may be why the Book makes so
much ado of their death and subsequent hanging, by displaying their
names in the scroll in the unique manner of writing their names in
large script, one name to each line (see fig. 10) as laid down in the
Talmud (B. *Megillah* 16B).

Examples from the time of the earlier Persian emperors suggest
that in the case of convicted criminals their property reverts to the
state. The viceroy of Sardis, Oroetes the Persian – who turned traitor
against Darius – was killed and his "slaves and other possessions were
brought to Susa" (Herodotus III, 128,129). Josephus also relates a case
in the Persian Empire where Cyrus, in a letter to the satraps of Syria

וְאֵת	אִישׁ	וַֽחֲתֹם בְּטַבַּעַת הַמֶּלֶךְ כִּי כְתָב אֲשֶׁר נִכְתָּב בְּשֵׁם
וְאֵת	פַּרְשַׁנְדָּ֫א	
וְאֵת	דַּלְפוֹן	
וְאֵת	אַסְפָּֽתָא	
וְאֵת	פּֽוֹרָתָא	
וְאֵת	אֲדַלְיָ֫א	
וְאֵת	אֲרִידָֽתָא	
וְאֵת	פַּרְמַ֫שְׁתָּא	
וְאֵת	אֲרִיסַי	
וְאֵת	אֲרִידַי	
עֲשֶׂ֫רֶת	וַיְזָֽתָא	

Fig. 10 *The Ten Sons of Haman, as written in oversize letters in a separate column, from a traditional Scroll (Megillah) of Esther, 20th Century.*

regarding the return of the Jews and the rebuilding of the Temple, sets out that all who disobey him shall be put to death and "their posses-sions shall become the property of the king" (Antiquities XI, 17). Nevertheless, if there was still a strong anti-Jewish element in Shushan it is likely that Ahasuerus could more easily lay his hands on Haman's possessions after his sons had been eliminated. What happened to Haman's wife Zeresh, we are not told.

Together with the ten sons, the Jews killed five hundred "enemies" in Shushan the Castle on 13th Adar (9:6) and three hundred in Shushan itself on 14th Adar (9:15). It may be that the anti-Jewish element was concentrated at the headquarters of the Empire, where it had come under the immediate influence of Haman. In the rest of the provinces the "enemies" were killed off in one day, on 13th Adar, and amounted to the alarming total of 75,000 (9:16). How such a number came to be slaughtered so conveniently and so neatly on just one day throughout all the Empire is impossible to comprehend, especially as it took two days to do away with a much smaller number in the reduced area of Shushan the City.

These figures, consisting of large round numbers, can be assumed to be a wild exaggeration. In another context, scholars see the numbers cited by Herodotus, in connection with the count of the troops of Darius and Xerxes, as being greatly overestimated and probably divisible by ten or more (Briant 1996, 543). But even if we take a similar line and divide the numbers of victims by ten, we are still faced with problems.

It is just possible that an attempted pogrom against the Jews in Shushan, Castle and City, lasted for two days and resulted in the death of several hundred people. That there were coordinated attacks in the provinces on just one day, resulting in the death of thousands of non-Jews is implausible and unlikely. One can only suggest that the events of Shushan, which may well have happened, were extrapolated on a wider scale to give literary emphasis to the original historical core. Both in the case of Shushan and the rest of the country, one notes that the Jews did not "put their hands to the spoil" (Esther 9:15, 16) of their enemies. We would surmise that the rabid element of anti-Jewish Persians conducted some kind of pogrom and that the Jews acted out of self-defense and had enough on their hands to protect themselves and counter attack; they were in no position, as their enemies might have been, to lay their hands on any spoil.

The same was not true of the king. From the background of the story, as we have explained it, it is quite clear that Ahasuerus's main concern was not with the Jews, and not even with Esther. He had no complaint against the Jews, he loved Esther and he was happy to promote and reward Mordecai, the Jew. But, besides his own personal welfare and life of luxury, his main concern was to keep the Persian Empire afloat and for that he needed cash, to the tune of ten thousand talents and more. Haman's offer to collect the money, which may indeed have been his responsibility as chief minister for the year, was welcome, and Ahasuerus had not concerned himself too much with Haman's method of obtaining it. Only when Esther alerted him to the consequences did he take action and then he acted very cleverly indeed. He got rid of Haman and later saw to it that the Jews got rid of his sons, so he could lay his hands on the promised ten thousand silver talents plus any surplus that Haman had been able to collect. He then authorized the Jews to defend themselves against that hard core of the population who wanted to see the Jews pay their tribute for them, and who persisted in that attitude. He granted favors to Esther and Mordecai, but he did have a vast empire to maintain and he did need cash.

That is why the Book returns again to the subject of taxes in the last, short, chapter: "And the king Ahasuerus placed a tax on the land and the islands of the sea" (10:1).

The purpose of this line is to show that the king is now imposing the tribute fairly on *all* the provinces and *all* the people, and not just on the Jews. But is this a suitable ending to a fairy tale of oriental intrigue and palace scandal as some see the Book of Esther to be? No, it is the ending to a popular but semi-official record of how the Jews were singled out to pay an extra state tax by a Jew-hating chief minister, who is outflanked by Esther the Queen, and Mordecai the Jew, and finally by King Ahasuerus (Xerxes) of Persia himself.

IN SUMMARY

We conclude that the Book of Esther is an account of a localized incident that happened in Susa, the capital of the Persian Empire.

After his ignominious defeat by the Greeks in 479 BCE, the emperor Xerxes I (486-465 BCE) takes a new queen at his palace in Susa. In 474 BCE, one Haman the Agagite, becomes eponym official, or chief minister, and offers to collect revenue for the king to the tune of ten thousand talents of silver. The offer is attractive to the king who gives Haman the right to extract it from a certain class of foreigners in any way he can. Haman has singled out the Jews to pay the tax and gives them eleven months to pay up, or be killed.

The Jewish courtier, Mordecai, appeals to his ward Esther, the new queen, to intercede with the king. She invites Xerxes and Haman to a drinking feast, but delays her intervention to a second banquet, following the Persian custom. In the meantime the king rewards Mordecai, who had uncovered a court plot against him, and forces Haman to do Mordecai the honors. At the second banquet Esther exposes Haman's anti-Jewish tax plan. Xerxes is furious and manages to get rid of him by claiming that Haman was attempting to rape the queen, when he was actually pleading with her for his life. Haman is executed and his position given to Mordecai, cousin of the queen.

The king cannot afford to revoke the tax order against the Jews, but gives them the right to defend themselves against anyone who tries to impose Haman's original death sentence for non-payment. Things come to a head some months later on the appointed date of 13th Adar, when attacks against the Jews break out in Shushan. The Jews, who are now joined by many Persian sympathizers and officials, turn on their enemies, killing Haman's ten sons and many others involved in the anti-Jewish riots. The Jews rejoice and celebrate victory over their enemies and their release from the victimization of being singled out to pay the state tribute.

The king has now gained all the additional tribute collected by Haman, but still finds it necessary to raise further revenue. This time however, he imposes it on the millions of people of all his vast territories rather than on the Jews alone.

Book of Ruth

1 ¹In the days when the chieftains ruled, there was a famine in the land; and a man of Bethlehem in Judah, with his wife and two sons, went to reside in the country of Moab. ²The man's name was Elimelech, his wife's name was Naomi, and his two sons were named Mahlon and Chilion – Ephrathites of Bethlehem in Judah. They came to the country of Moab and remained there.

³Elimelech, Naomi's husband, died; and she was left with her two sons. ⁴They married Moabite women, one named Orpah and the other Ruth, and they lived there about ten years. ⁵Then those two – Mahlon and Chilion – also died; so the woman was left without her two sons and without her husband.

⁶She started out with her daughters-in-law to return from the country of Moab; for in the country of Moab she had heard that the LORD had taken note of His people and given them food. ⁷Accompanied by her two daughters-in-law, she left the place where she had been living; and they set out on the road back to the land of Judah.

⁸But Naomi said to her two daughters-in-law, "Turn back, each of you to her mother's house. May the LORD deal kindly with you, as you have dealt with the dead and with me! ⁹May the LORD grant that each of you find security in the house of a husband!" And she kissed them farewell. They broke into weeping ¹⁰and said to her, "No, we will return with you to your people."

¹¹But Naomi replied, "Turn back, my daughters! Why should you go with me? Have I any more sons in my body who might be husbands for you? ¹²Turn back, my daughters, for I am too old to be married. Even if I thought there was hope for me, even if I were married tonight and I also bore sons, ¹³should you wait for them to grow up? Should you on their account debar yourselves from marriage? Oh no, my daughters! My lot is far more bitter than yours, for the hand of the LORD has struck out against me."

¹⁴They broke into weeping again, and Orpah kissed her mother-in-law farewell. But Ruth clung to her. ¹⁵So she said, "See, your sister-in-law

מגילת רות

א **וַיְהִי** בִּימֵי שְׁפֹט הַשֹּׁפְטִים וַיְהִי רָעָב בָּאָרֶץ וַיֵּלֶךְ אִישׁ **א**
מִבֵּית לֶחֶם יְהוּדָה לָגוּר בִּשְׂדֵי מוֹאָב הוּא וְאִשְׁתּוֹ וּשְׁנֵי
ב בָנָיו: וְשֵׁם הָאִישׁ אֱלִימֶלֶךְ וְשֵׁם אִשְׁתּוֹ נָעֳמִי וְשֵׁם שְׁנֵי־בָנָיו ׀
מַחְלוֹן וְכִלְיוֹן אֶפְרָתִים מִבֵּית לֶחֶם יְהוּדָה וַיָּבֹאוּ שְׂדֵי־מוֹאָב
ג וַיִּהְיוּ־שָׁם: וַיָּמָת אֱלִימֶלֶךְ אִישׁ נָעֳמִי וַתִּשָּׁאֵר הִיא וּשְׁנֵי
ד בָנֶיהָ: וַיִּשְׂאוּ לָהֶם נָשִׁים מֹאֲבִיּוֹת שֵׁם הָאַחַת עָרְפָּה וְשֵׁם
ה הַשֵּׁנִית רוּת וַיֵּשְׁבוּ שָׁם כְּעֶשֶׂר שָׁנִים: וַיָּמֻתוּ גַם־שְׁנֵיהֶם
ו מַחְלוֹן וְכִלְיוֹן וַתִּשָּׁאֵר הָאִשָּׁה מִשְּׁנֵי יְלָדֶיהָ וּמֵאִישָׁהּ: וַתָּקָם
הִיא וְכַלֹּתֶיהָ וַתָּשָׁב מִשְּׂדֵי מוֹאָב כִּי שָׁמְעָה בִּשְׂדֵה מוֹאָב
ז כִּי־פָקַד יְהוָה אֶת־עַמּוֹ לָתֵת לָהֶם לָחֶם: וַתֵּצֵא מִן־הַמָּקוֹם
אֲשֶׁר הָיְתָה־שָּׁמָּה וּשְׁתֵּי כַלֹּתֶיהָ עִמָּהּ וַתֵּלַכְנָה בַדֶּרֶךְ לָשׁוּב
ח אֶל־אֶרֶץ יְהוּדָה: וַתֹּאמֶר נָעֳמִי לִשְׁתֵּי כַלֹּתֶיהָ לֵכְנָה שֹּׁבְנָה
יָעֳשׂ אִשָּׁה לְבֵית אִמָּהּ יַעֲשֶׂה* יְהוָה עִמָּכֶם חֶסֶד כַּאֲשֶׁר עֲשִׂיתֶם
ט עִם־הַמֵּתִים וְעִמָּדִי: יִתֵּן יְהוָה לָכֶם וּמְצֶאןָ מְנוּחָה אִשָּׁה בֵּית
י אִישָׁהּ וַתִּשַּׁק לָהֶן וַתִּשֶּׂאנָה קוֹלָן וַתִּבְכֶּינָה: וַתֹּאמַרְנָה־לָּהּ
יא כִּי־אִתָּךְ נָשׁוּב לְעַמֵּךְ: וַתֹּאמֶר נָעֳמִי שֹׁבְנָה בְנֹתַי לָמָּה
יב תֵלַכְנָה עִמִּי הַעוֹד־לִי בָנִים בְּמֵעַי וְהָיוּ לָכֶם לַאֲנָשִׁים: שֹׁבְנָה
בְנֹתַי לֵכְןָ כִּי זָקַנְתִּי מִהְיוֹת לְאִישׁ כִּי אָמַרְתִּי יֶשׁ־לִי תִקְוָה
יג גַּם הָיִיתִי הַלַּיְלָה לְאִישׁ וְגַם יָלַדְתִּי בָנִים: הֲלָהֵן ׀ תְּשַׂבֵּרְנָה
עַד אֲשֶׁר יִגְדָּלוּ הֲלָהֵן תֵּעָגֵנָה לְבִלְתִּי הֱיוֹת לְאִישׁ אַל בְּנֹתַי
יד כִּי־מַר־לִי מְאֹד מִכֶּם כִּי־יָצְאָה בִי יַד־יְהוָה: וַתִּשֶּׂנָה קוֹלָן
טו וַתִּבְכֶּינָה עוֹד וַתִּשַּׁק עָרְפָּה לַחֲמוֹתָהּ וְרוּת דָּבְקָה בָּהּ: וַתֹּאמֶר
הִנֵּה שָׁבָה יְבִמְתֵּךְ אֶל־עַמָּהּ וְאֶל־אֱלֹהֶיהָ שׁוּבִי אַחֲרֵי יְבִמְתֵּךְ:
טז וַתֹּאמֶר רוּת אַל־תִּפְגְּעִי־בִי לְעָזְבֵךְ לָשׁוּב מֵאַחֲרָיִךְ כִּי
אֶל־אֲשֶׁר תֵּלְכִי אֵלֵךְ וּבַאֲשֶׁר תָּלִינִי אָלִין עַמֵּךְ עַמִּי וֵאלֹהַיִךְ

has returned to her people and her gods. Go follow your sister-in-law." [16]But Ruth replied, "Do not urge me to leave you, to turn back and not follow you. For wherever you go, I will go; wherever you lodge, I will lodge; your people shall be my people, and your God my God. [17]Where you die, I will die, and there I will be buried. Thus and more may the LORD do to me if anything but death parts me from you." [18]When [Naomi] saw how determined she was to go with her, she ceased to argue with her; [19]and the two went on until they reached Bethlehem.

When they arrived in Bethlehem, the whole city buzzed with excitement over them. The women said, "Can this be Naomi?" [20]"Do not call me Naomi," she replied. "Call me Mara, for Shaddai has made my lot very bitter. [21]I went away full, and the LORD has brought me back empty. How can you call me Naomi, when the LORD has dealt harshly with me, when Shaddai has brought misfortune upon me!"

[22]Thus Naomi returned from the country of Moab; she returned with her daughter-in-law Ruth the Moabite. They arrived in Bethlehem at the beginning of the barley harvest.

2 [1]Now Naomi had a kinsman on her husband's side, a man of substance, of the family of Elimelech, whose name was Boaz.

[2]Ruth the Moabite said to Naomi, "I would like to go to the fields and glean among the ears of grain, behind someone who may show me kindness." "Yes, daughter, go," she replied; [3]and off she went. She came and gleaned in a field, behind the reapers; and, as luck would have it, it was the piece of land belonging to Boaz, who was of Elimelech's family.

[4]Presently Boaz arrived from Bethlehem. He greeted the reapers, "The LORD be with you!" And they responded, "The LORD bless you!" [5]Boaz said to the servant who was in charge of the reapers, "Whose girl is that?" [6]The servant in charge of the reapers replied, "She is a Moabite girl who came back with Naomi from the country of Moab. [7]She said, 'Please let me glean and gather among the sheaves behind the reapers.' She has been on her feet ever since she came this morning. She has rested but little in the hut."

[8]Boaz said to Ruth, "Listen to me, daughter. Don't go to glean in another field. Don't go elsewhere, but stay here close to my girls. [9]Keep your eyes on the field they are reaping, and follow them. I have ordered

יז אֱלֹהָי: בַּאֲשֶׁר תָּמוּתִי אָמוּת וְשָׁם אֶקָּבֵר כֹּה יַעֲשֶׂה יְהוָה לִי

יח וְכֹה יוֹסִיף כִּי הַמָּוֶת יַפְרִיד בֵּינִי וּבֵינֵךְ: וַתֵּרֶא כִּי־מִתְאַמֶּצֶת

יט הִיא לָלֶכֶת אִתָּהּ וַתֶּחְדַּל לְדַבֵּר אֵלֶיהָ: וַתֵּלַכְנָה שְׁתֵּיהֶם

עַד־בּוֹאָנָה בֵּית לָחֶם וַיְהִי כְּבוֹאָנָה בֵּית לֶחֶם וַתֵּהֹם כָּל־הָעִיר

כ עֲלֵיהֶן וַתֹּאמַרְנָה הֲזֹאת נָעֳמִי: וַתֹּאמֶר אֲלֵיהֶן אַל־תִּקְרֶאנָה

כא לִי נָעֳמִי קְרֶאןָ לִי מָרָא כִּי־הֵמַר שַׁדַּי לִי מְאֹד: אֲנִי מְלֵאָה

הָלַכְתִּי וְרֵיקָם הֱשִׁיבַנִי יְהוָה לָמָּה תִקְרֶאנָה לִי נָעֳמִי וַיהוָה

כב עָנָה בִי וְשַׁדַּי הֵרַע־לִי: וַתָּשָׁב נָעֳמִי וְרוּת הַמּוֹאֲבִיָּה כַלָּתָהּ

עִמָּהּ הַשָּׁבָה מִשְּׂדֵי מוֹאָב וְהֵמָּה בָּאוּ בֵּית לֶחֶם בִּתְחִלַּת קְצִיר

א שְׂעֹרִים: ‏ וּלְנָעֳמִי מִידָע* לְאִישָׁהּ אִישׁ גִּבּוֹר חַיִל ב מוֹדָע

ב מִמִּשְׁפַּחַת אֱלִימֶלֶךְ וּשְׁמוֹ בֹּעַז: וַתֹּאמֶר רוּת הַמּוֹאֲבִיָּה

אֶל־נָעֳמִי אֵלְכָה־נָּא הַשָּׂדֶה וַאֲלַקֳטָה בַשִּׁבֳּלִים אַחַר אֲשֶׁר

ג אֶמְצָא־חֵן בְּעֵינָיו וַתֹּאמֶר לָהּ לְכִי בִתִּי: וַתֵּלֶךְ וַתָּבוֹא וַתְּלַקֵּט

בַּשָּׂדֶה אַחֲרֵי הַקֹּצְרִים וַיִּקֶר מִקְרֶהָ חֶלְקַת הַשָּׂדֶה לְבֹעַז

ד אֲשֶׁר מִמִּשְׁפַּחַת אֱלִימֶלֶךְ: וְהִנֵּה־בֹעַז בָּא מִבֵּית לֶחֶם וַיֹּאמֶר

ה לַקּוֹצְרִים יְהוָה עִמָּכֶם וַיֹּאמְרוּ לוֹ יְבָרֶכְךָ יְהוָה: וַיֹּאמֶר בֹּעַז

ו לְנַעֲרוֹ הַנִּצָּב עַל־הַקּוֹצְרִים לְמִי הַנַּעֲרָה הַזֹּאת: וַיַּעַן הַנַּעַר

הַנִּצָּב עַל־הַקּוֹצְרִים וַיֹּאמַר נַעֲרָה מוֹאֲבִיָּה הִיא הַשָּׁבָה

ז עִם־נָעֳמִי מִשְּׂדֵי מוֹאָב: וַתֹּאמֶר אֲלַקֳטָה־נָּא וְאָסַפְתִּי בָעֳמָרִים

אַחֲרֵי הַקּוֹצְרִים וַתָּבוֹא וַתַּעֲמוֹד מֵאָז הַבֹּקֶר וְעַד־עַתָּה זֶה

ח שִׁבְתָּהּ הַבַּיִת מְעָט: וַיֹּאמֶר בֹּעַז אֶל־רוּת הֲלוֹא שָׁמַעַתְּ בִּתִּי

אַל־תֵּלְכִי לִלְקֹט בְּשָׂדֶה אַחֵר וְגַם לֹא תַעֲבוּרִי מִזֶּה וְכֹה

ט תִדְבָּקִין עִם־נַעֲרֹתָי: עֵינַיִךְ בַּשָּׂדֶה אֲשֶׁר־יִקְצֹרוּן וְהָלַכְתְּ

אַחֲרֵיהֶן הֲלוֹא צִוִּיתִי אֶת־הַנְּעָרִים לְבִלְתִּי נָגְעֵךְ וְצָמִת

י וְהָלַכְתְּ אֶל־הַכֵּלִים וְשָׁתִית מֵאֲשֶׁר יִשְׁאֲבוּן הַנְּעָרִים: וַתִּפֹּל

עַל־פָּנֶיהָ וַתִּשְׁתַּחוּ אָרְצָה וַתֹּאמֶר אֵלָיו מַדּוּעַ מָצָאתִי חֵן

יא בְּעֵינֶיךָ לְהַכִּירֵנִי וְאָנֹכִי נָכְרִיָּה: וַיַּעַן בֹּעַז וַיֹּאמֶר לָהּ הֻגֵּד

the men not to molest you. And when you are thirsty, go to the jars and drink some of [the water] that the men have drawn."

[10]She prostrated herself with her face to the ground, and said to him, "Why are you so kind as to single me out, when I am a foreigner?"

[11]Boaz said in reply, "I have been told of all that you did for your mother-in-law after the death of your husband, how you left your father and mother and the land of your birth and came to a people you had not known before. [12]May the LORD reward your deeds. May you have a full recompense from the LORD, the God of Israel, under whose wings you have sought refuge!"

[13]She answered, "You are most kind, my lord, to comfort me and to speak gently to your maidservant – though I am not so much as one of your maidservants."

[14]At mealtime, Boaz said to her, "Come over here and partake of the meal, and dip your morsel in the vinegar." So she sat down beside the reapers. He handed her roasted grain, and she ate her fill and had some left over.

[15]When she got up again to glean, Boaz gave orders to his workers, "You are not only to let her glean among the sheaves, without interference, [16]but you must also pull some [stalks] out of the heaps and leave them for her to glean, and not scold her."

[17]She gleaned in the field until evening. Then she beat out what she had gleaned – it was about an 'ephah of barley – [18]and carried it back with her to the town. When her mother-in-law saw what she had gleaned, and when she also took out and gave her what she had left over after eating her fill, [19]her mother-in-law asked her, "Where did you glean today? Where did you work? Blessed be he who took such generous notice of you!" So she told her mother-in-law whom she had worked with, saying, "The name of the man with whom I worked today is Boaz."

[20]Naomi said to her daughter-in-law, "Blessed be he of the LORD, who has not failed in His kindness to the living or to the dead! For," Naomi explained to her daughter-in-law, "the man is related to us; he is one of our redeeming kinsmen." [21]Ruth the Moabite said, "He even told me, 'Stay close by my workers until all my harvest is finished.'" [22]And Naomi answered her daughter-in-law Ruth, "It is best, daughter, that you go out with his girls, and not be annoyed in some other field." [23]So she stayed

הֻגֵּד לִי כֹּל אֲשֶׁר־עָשִׂית אֶת־חֲמוֹתֵךְ אַחֲרֵי מוֹת אִישֵׁךְ
וַתַּעַזְבִי אָבִיךְ וְאִמֵּךְ וְאֶרֶץ מוֹלַדְתֵּךְ וַתֵּלְכִי אֶל־עַם אֲשֶׁר
יב לֹא־יָדַעַתְּ תְּמוֹל שִׁלְשׁוֹם: יְשַׁלֵּם יְהוָה פָּעֳלֵךְ וּתְהִי מַשְׂכֻּרְתֵּךְ
שְׁלֵמָה מֵעִם יְהוָה אֱלֹהֵי יִשְׂרָאֵל אֲשֶׁר־בָּאת לַחֲסוֹת
יג תַּחַת־כְּנָפָיו: וַתֹּאמֶר אֶמְצָא־חֵן בְּעֵינֶיךָ אֲדֹנִי כִּי נִחַמְתָּנִי
וְכִי דִבַּרְתָּ עַל־לֵב שִׁפְחָתֶךָ וְאָנֹכִי לֹא אֶהְיֶה כְּאַחַת
יד שִׁפְחֹתֶיךָ: וַיֹּאמֶר לָהּ בֹעַז לְעֵת הָאֹכֶל גֹּשִׁי הֲלֹם וְאָכַלְתְּ
מִן־הַלֶּחֶם וְטָבַלְתְּ פִּתֵּךְ בַּחֹמֶץ וַתֵּשֶׁב מִצַּד הַקֹּצְרִים
טו וַיִּצְבָּט־לָהּ קָלִי וַתֹּאכַל וַתִּשְׂבַּע וַתֹּתַר: וַתָּקָם לְלַקֵּט וַיְצַו
בֹּעַז אֶת־נְעָרָיו לֵאמֹר גַּם בֵּין הָעֳמָרִים תְּלַקֵּט וְלֹא תַכְלִימוּהָ:
טז וְגַם שֹׁל־תָּשֹׁלּוּ לָהּ מִן־הַצְּבָתִים וַעֲזַבְתֶּם וְלִקְּטָה וְלֹא
יז תִגְעֲרוּ־בָהּ: וַתְּלַקֵּט בַּשָּׂדֶה עַד־הָעָרֶב וַתַּחְבֹּט אֵת אֲשֶׁר־
יח לִקֵּטָה וַיְהִי כְּאֵיפָה שְׂעֹרִים: וַתִּשָּׂא וַתָּבוֹא הָעִיר וַתֵּרֶא
חֲמוֹתָהּ אֵת אֲשֶׁר־לִקֵּטָה וַתּוֹצֵא וַתִּתֶּן־לָהּ אֵת אֲשֶׁר־הוֹתִרָה
יט מִשָּׂבְעָהּ: וַתֹּאמֶר לָהּ חֲמוֹתָהּ אֵיפֹה לִקַּטְתְּ הַיּוֹם וְאָנָה עָשִׂית
יְהִי מַכִּירֵךְ בָּרוּךְ וַתַּגֵּד לַחֲמוֹתָהּ אֵת אֲשֶׁר־עָשְׂתָה עִמּוֹ
כ וַתֹּאמֶר שֵׁם הָאִישׁ אֲשֶׁר עָשִׂיתִי עִמּוֹ הַיּוֹם בֹּעַז: וַתֹּאמֶר
נָעֳמִי לְכַלָּתָהּ בָּרוּךְ הוּא לַיהוָה אֲשֶׁר לֹא־עָזַב חַסְדּוֹ
אֶת־הַחַיִּים וְאֶת־הַמֵּתִים וַתֹּאמֶר לָהּ נָעֳמִי קָרוֹב לָנוּ הָאִישׁ
כא מִגֹּאֲלֵנוּ הוּא: וַתֹּאמֶר רוּת הַמּוֹאֲבִיָּה גַּם | כִּי־אָמַר אֵלַי
עִם־הַנְּעָרִים אֲשֶׁר־לִי תִּדְבָּקִין עַד אִם־כִּלּוּ אֵת כָּל־הַקָּצִיר
כב אֲשֶׁר־לִי: וַתֹּאמֶר נָעֳמִי אֶל־רוּת כַּלָּתָהּ טוֹב בִּתִּי כִּי תֵצְאִי
כג עִם־נַעֲרוֹתָיו וְלֹא יִפְגְּעוּ־בָךְ בְּשָׂדֶה אַחֵר: וַתִּדְבַּק בְּנַעֲרוֹת
בֹּעַז לְלַקֵּט עַד־כְּלוֹת קְצִיר־הַשְּׂעֹרִים וּקְצִיר הַחִטִּים וַתֵּשֶׁב
ג א אֶת־חֲמוֹתָהּ: וַתֹּאמֶר לָהּ נָעֳמִי חֲמוֹתָהּ בִּתִּי הֲלֹא
ב אֲבַקֶּשׁ־לָךְ מָנוֹחַ אֲשֶׁר יִיטַב־לָךְ: וְעַתָּה הֲלֹא בֹעַז מֹדַעְתָּנוּ
אֲשֶׁר הָיִית אֶת־נַעֲרוֹתָיו הִנֵּה־הוּא זֹרֶה אֶת־גֹּרֶן הַשְּׂעֹרִים

close to the maidservants of Boaz, and gleaned until the barley harvest and the wheat harvest were finished. Then she stayed at home with her mother-in-law.

3 ¹Naomi, her mother-in-law, said to her, "Daughter, I must seek a home for you, where you may be happy. ²Now there is our kinsman Boaz, whose girls you were close to. He will be winnowing barley on the threshing floor tonight. ³So bathe, anoint yourself, dress up, and go down to the threshing floor. But do not disclose yourself to the man until he has finished eating and drinking. ⁴When he lies down, note the place where he lies down, and go over and uncover his feet and lie down. He will tell you what you are to do." ⁵She replied, "I will do everything you tell me."

⁶She went down to the threshing floor and did just as her mother-in-law had instructed her.

⁷Boaz ate and drank, and in a cheerful mood went to lie down beside the grainpile. Then she went over stealthily and uncovered his feet and lay down. ⁸In the middle of the night, the man gave a start and pulled back – there was a woman lying at his feet!

⁹"Who are you?" he asked. And she replied, "I am your handmaid Ruth. Spread your robe over your handmaid, for you are a redeeming kinsman."

¹⁰He exclaimed, "Be blessed of the LORD, daughter! Your latest deed of loyalty is greater than the first, in that you have not turned to younger men, whether poor or rich. ¹¹And now, daughter, have no fear. I will do in your behalf whatever you ask, for all the elders of my town know what a fine woman you are. ¹²But while it is true I am a redeeming kinsman, there is another redeemer closer than I. ¹³Stay for the night. Then in the morning, if he will act as a redeemer, good! let him redeem. But if he does not want to act as redeemer for you, I will do so myself, as the LORD lives! Lie down until morning."

¹⁴So she lay at his feet until dawn. She rose before one person could distinguish another, for he thought, "Let it not be known that the woman came to the threshing floor." ¹⁵And he said, "Hold out the shawl you are wearing." She held it while he measured out six measures of barley, and he put it on her back.

ג הַלָּיְלָה: וְרָחַצְתְּ | וָסַכְתְּ וְשַׂמְתְּ שִׂמְלֹתַךְ* עָלַיִךְ וְיָרַדְתִּי**   *שִׂמְלֹתַיִךְ **וְיָרַדְתְּ

ד הַגֹּרֶן אַל־תִּוָּדְעִי לָאִישׁ עַד כַּלֹּתוֹ לֶאֱכֹל וְלִשְׁתּוֹת: וִיהִי בְשָׁכְבוֹ וְיָדַעַתְּ אֶת־הַמָּקוֹם אֲשֶׁר יִשְׁכַּב־שָׁם וּבָאת וְגִלִּית

ה מַרְגְּלֹתָיו וְשָׁכָבְתִּי* וְהוּא יַגִּיד לָךְ אֵת אֲשֶׁר תַּעֲשִׂין: וַתֹּאמֶר   *וְשָׁכָבְתְּ

ו אֵלֶיהָ כֹּל אֲשֶׁר־תֹּאמְרִי * אֶעֱשֶׂה: וַתֵּרֶד הַגֹּרֶן וַתַּעַשׂ   קְרִי וְלָא כְּתִיב אֵלָי

ז כְּכֹל אֲשֶׁר־צִוַּתָּה חֲמוֹתָהּ: וַיֹּאכַל בֹּעַז וַיֵּשְׁתְּ וַיִּיטַב לִבּוֹ וַיָּבֹא לִשְׁכַּב בִּקְצֵה הָעֲרֵמָה וַתָּבֹא בַלָּט וַתְּגַל מַרְגְּלֹתָיו

ח וַתִּשְׁכָּב: וַיְהִי בַּחֲצִי הַלַּיְלָה וַיֶּחֱרַד הָאִישׁ וַיִּלָּפֵת וְהִנֵּה אִשָּׁה

ט שֹׁכֶבֶת מַרְגְּלֹתָיו: וַיֹּאמֶר מִי־אָתְּ וַתֹּאמֶר אָנֹכִי רוּת אֲמָתֶךָ

י וּפָרַשְׂתָּ כְנָפֶךָ עַל־אֲמָתְךָ כִּי גֹאֵל אָתָּה: וַיֹּאמֶר בְּרוּכָה אַתְּ לַיהוָה בִּתִּי הֵיטַבְתְּ חַסְדֵּךְ הָאַחֲרוֹן מִן־הָרִאשׁוֹן לְבִלְתִּי־לֶכֶת

יא אַחֲרֵי הַבַּחוּרִים אִם־דַּל וְאִם־עָשִׁיר: וְעַתָּה בִּתִּי אַל־תִּירְאִי כֹּל אֲשֶׁר־תֹּאמְרִי אֶעֱשֶׂה־לָּךְ כִּי יוֹדֵעַ כָּל־שַׁעַר עַמִּי כִּי

יב אֵשֶׁת חַיִל אָתְּ: וְעַתָּה כִּי אָמְנָם כִּי אִם* גֹּאֵל אָנֹכִי וְגַם   כְּתִיב וְלָא קְרִי

יג יֵשׁ גֹּאֵל קָרוֹב מִמֶּנִּי: לִינִי | הַלַּיְלָה וְהָיָה בַבֹּקֶר אִם־יִגְאָלֵךְ טוֹב יִגְאָל וְאִם־לֹא יַחְפֹּץ לְגָאֳלֵךְ וּגְאַלְתִּיךְ אָנֹכִי חַי־יְהוָה

יד שִׁכְבִי עַד־הַבֹּקֶר: וַתִּשְׁכַּב מַרְגְּלוֹתָו עַד־הַבֹּקֶר וַתָּקָם בְּטֶרֶום*   *בְּטֶרֶם יַכִּיר אִישׁ אֶת־רֵעֵהוּ וַיֹּאמֶר אַל־יִוָּדַע כִּי־בָאָה הָאִשָּׁה הַגֹּרֶן:

טו וַיֹּאמֶר הָבִי הַמִּטְפַּחַת אֲשֶׁר־עָלַיִךְ וְאֶחֳזִי־בָהּ וַתֹּאחֶז בָּהּ

טז וַיָּמָד שֵׁשׁ־שְׂעֹרִים וַיָּשֶׁת עָלֶיהָ וַיָּבֹא הָעִיר: וַתָּבוֹא אֶל־חֲמוֹתָהּ וַתֹּאמֶר מִי־אַתְּ בִּתִּי וַתַּגֶּד־לָהּ אֵת כָּל־אֲשֶׁר

יז עָשָׂה־לָהּ הָאִישׁ: וַתֹּאמֶר שֵׁשׁ־הַשְּׂעֹרִים הָאֵלֶּה נָתַן לִי כִּי

יח אָמַר * אַל־תָּבוֹאִי רֵיקָם אֶל־חֲמוֹתֵךְ: וַתֹּאמֶר שְׁבִי בִתִּי   קְרִי וְלָא כְּתִיב אֵלָי עַד אֲשֶׁר תֵּדְעִין אֵיךְ יִפֹּל דָּבָר כִּי לֹא יִשְׁקֹט הָאִישׁ כִּי

ד א אִם־כִּלָּה הַדָּבָר הַיּוֹם: וּבֹעַז עָלָה הַשַּׁעַר וַיֵּשֶׁב שָׁם וְהִנֵּה הַגֹּאֵל עֹבֵר אֲשֶׁר דִּבֶּר־בֹּעַז וַיֹּאמֶר סוּרָה שְׁבָה־פֹּה

ב פְּלֹנִי אַלְמֹנִי וַיָּסַר וַיֵּשֵׁב: וַיִּקַּח עֲשָׂרָה אֲנָשִׁים מִזִּקְנֵי הָעִיר

When she got back to the town, [16]she came to her mother-in-law, who asked, "How is it with you, daughter?" She told her all that the man had done for her; [17]and she added, "He gave me these six measures of barley, saying to me, 'Do not go back to your mother-in-law emptyhanded.'"

[18]And Naomi said, "Stay here, daughter, till you learn how the matter turns out. For the man will not rest, but will settle the matter today."

4 [1]Meanwhile, Boaz had gone to the gate and sat down there. And now the redeemer whom Boaz had mentioned passed by. He called, "Come over and sit down here, So-and-so!" And he came over and sat down. [2]Then [Boaz] took ten elders of the town and said, "Be seated here"; and they sat down.

[3]He said to the redeemer, "Naomi, now returned from the country of Moab, must sell the piece of land which belonged to our kinsman Elimelech. [4]I thought I should disclose the matter to you and say: Acquire it in the presence of those seated here and in the presence of the elders of my people. If you are willing to redeem it, redeem! But if you will not redeem, tell me, that I may know. For there is no one to redeem but you, and I come after you."

"I am willing to redeem it," he replied. [5]Boaz continued, "When you acquire the property from Naomi and from Ruth the Moabite, you must also acquire the wife of the deceased, so as to perpetuate the name of the deceased upon his estate." [6]The redeemer replied, "Then I cannot redeem it for myself, lest I impair my own estate. You take over my right of redemption, for I am unable to exercise it."

[7]Now this was formerly done in Israel in cases of redemption or exchange: to validate any transaction, one man would take off his sandal and hand it to the other. Such was the practice in Israel. [8]So when the redeemer said to Boaz, "Acquire for yourself," he drew off his sandal. [9]And Boaz said to the elders and to the rest of the people, "You are witnesses today that I am acquiring from Naomi all that belonged to Elimelech and all that belonged to Chilion and Mahlon. [10]I am also acquiring Ruth the Moabite, the wife of Mahlon, as my wife, so as to perpetuate the name of the deceased upon his estate, that the name of the deceased may not

ג וַיֹּאמֶר שְׁבוּ־פֹה וַיֵּשֵׁבוּ: וַיֹּאמֶר לַגֹּאֵל חֶלְקַת הַשָּׂדֶה אֲשֶׁר
ד לְאָחִינוּ לֶאֱלִימֶלֶךְ מָכְרָה נָעֳמִי הַשָּׁבָה מִשְּׂדֵה מוֹאָב: וַאֲנִי
אָמַרְתִּי אֶגְלֶה אָזְנְךָ לֵאמֹר קְנֵה נֶגֶד הַיֹּשְׁבִים וְנֶגֶד זִקְנֵי
עַמִּי אִם־תִּגְאַל גְּאָל וְאִם־לֹא יִגְאַל הַגִּידָה לִּי וְאֵדַע* כִּי
ה אֵין זוּלָתְךָ לִגְאוֹל וְאָנֹכִי אַחֲרֶיךָ וַיֹּאמֶר אָנֹכִי אֶגְאָל: וַיֹּאמֶר
בֹּעַז בְּיוֹם־קְנוֹתְךָ הַשָּׂדֶה מִיַּד נָעֳמִי וּמֵאֵת רוּת הַמּוֹאֲבִיָּה
ו אֵשֶׁת־הַמֵּת קָנִיתִי* לְהָקִים שֵׁם־הַמֵּת עַל־נַחֲלָתוֹ: וַיֹּאמֶר
הַגֹּאֵל לֹא אוּכַל לִגְאוֹל־לִי פֶּן־אַשְׁחִית אֶת־נַחֲלָתִי גְּאַל־לְךָ
ז אַתָּה אֶת־גְּאֻלָּתִי כִּי לֹא־אוּכַל לִגְאֹל: וְזֹאת לְפָנִים בְּיִשְׂרָאֵל
עַל־הַגְּאֻלָּה וְעַל־הַתְּמוּרָה לְקַיֵּם כָּל־דָּבָר שָׁלַף אִישׁ נַעֲלוֹ
ח וְנָתַן לְרֵעֵהוּ וְזֹאת הַתְּעוּדָה בְּיִשְׂרָאֵל: וַיֹּאמֶר הַגֹּאֵל לְבֹעַז
ט קְנֵה־לָךְ וַיִּשְׁלֹף נַעֲלוֹ: וַיֹּאמֶר בֹּעַז לַזְּקֵנִים וְכָל־הָעָם עֵדִים
אַתֶּם הַיּוֹם כִּי קָנִיתִי אֶת־כָּל־אֲשֶׁר לֶאֱלִימֶלֶךְ וְאֵת כָּל־אֲשֶׁר
י לְכִלְיוֹן וּמַחְלוֹן מִיַּד נָעֳמִי: וְגַם אֶת־רוּת הַמֹּאֲבִיָּה אֵשֶׁת
מַחְלוֹן קָנִיתִי לִי לְאִשָּׁה לְהָקִים שֵׁם־הַמֵּת עַל־נַחֲלָתוֹ
וְלֹא־יִכָּרֵת שֵׁם־הַמֵּת מֵעִם אֶחָיו וּמִשַּׁעַר מְקוֹמוֹ עֵדִים אַתֶּם
יא הַיּוֹם: וַיֹּאמְרוּ כָּל־הָעָם אֲשֶׁר־בַּשַּׁעַר וְהַזְּקֵנִים עֵדִים יִתֵּן יְהוָה
אֶת־הָאִשָּׁה הַבָּאָה אֶל־בֵּיתֶךָ כְּרָחֵל | וּכְלֵאָה אֲשֶׁר בָּנוּ
שְׁתֵּיהֶם אֶת־בֵּית יִשְׂרָאֵל וַעֲשֵׂה־חַיִל בְּאֶפְרָתָה וּקְרָא־שֵׁם
יב בְּבֵית לָחֶם: וִיהִי בֵיתְךָ כְּבֵית פֶּרֶץ אֲשֶׁר־יָלְדָה תָמָר לִיהוּדָה
יג מִן־הַזֶּרַע אֲשֶׁר יִתֵּן יְהוָה לְךָ מִן־הַנַּעֲרָה הַזֹּאת: וַיִּקַּח בֹּעַז
אֶת־רוּת וַתְּהִי־לוֹ לְאִשָּׁה וַיָּבֹא אֵלֶיהָ וַיִּתֵּן יְהוָה לָהּ הֵרָיוֹן
יד וַתֵּלֶד בֵּן: וַתֹּאמַרְנָה הַנָּשִׁים אֶל־נָעֳמִי בָּרוּךְ יְהוָה אֲשֶׁר לֹא
טו הִשְׁבִּית לָךְ גֹּאֵל הַיּוֹם וְיִקָּרֵא שְׁמוֹ בְּיִשְׂרָאֵל: וְהָיָה לָךְ
לְמֵשִׁיב נֶפֶשׁ וּלְכַלְכֵּל אֶת־שֵׂיבָתֵךְ כִּי כַלָּתֵךְ אֲשֶׁר־אֲהֵבָתֶךְ
טז יְלָדַתּוּ אֲשֶׁר־הִיא טוֹבָה לָךְ מִשִּׁבְעָה בָּנִים: וַתִּקַּח נָעֳמִי
יז אֶת־הַיֶּלֶד וַתְּשִׁתֵהוּ בְחֵיקָהּ וַתְּהִי־לוֹ לְאֹמֶנֶת: וַתִּקְרֶאנָה לוֹ

disappear from among his kinsmen and from the gate of his home town. You are witnesses today."

[11]All the people at the gate and the elders answered, "We are. May the LORD make the woman who is coming into your house like Rachel and Leah, both of whom built up the House of Israel!

Prosper in Ephrathah and perpetuate your name in Bethlehem! [12]And may your house be like the house of Perez whom Tamar bore to Judah – through the offspring which the LORD will give you by this young woman."

[13]So Boaz married Ruth; she became his wife, and he cohabited with her. The LORD let her conceive, and she bore a son. [14]And the women said to Naomi, "Blessed be the LORD, who has not withheld a redeemer from you today! May his name be perpetuated in Israel! [15]He will renew your life and sustain your old age; for he is born of your daughter-in-law, who loves you and is better to you than seven sons."

[16]Naomi took the child and held it to her bosom. She became its foster mother, [17]and the women neighbors gave him a name, saying, "A son is born to Naomi!" They named him Obed; he was the father of Jesse, father of David.

[18]This is the line of Perez: Perez begot Hezron, [19]Hezron begot Ram, Ram begot Ammi-nadab, [20]Amminadab begot Nahshon, Nahshon begot Salmon, [21]Salmon begot Boaz, Boaz begot Obed, [22]Obed begot Jesse, and Jesse begot David.

הַשְּׁכֵנוֹת שֵׁם לֵאמֹר יֻלַּד־בֵּן לְנָעֳמִי וַתִּקְרֶאנָה שְׁמוֹ עוֹבֵד

יח   הוּא אֲבִי־יִשַׁי אֲבִי דָוִד: וְאֵלֶּה תּוֹלְדוֹת פָּרֶץ פֶּרֶץ הוֹלִיד

יט   אֶת־חֶצְרוֹן: וְחֶצְרוֹן הוֹלִיד אֶת־רָם וְרָם הוֹלִיד אֶת־עַמִּינָדָב:

כ   וְעַמִּינָדָב הוֹלִיד אֶת־נַחְשׁוֹן וְנַחְשׁוֹן הוֹלִיד אֶת־שַׂלְמָה:

כא כב   וְשַׂלְמוֹן הוֹלִיד אֶת־בֹּעַז וּבֹעַז הוֹלִיד אֶת־עוֹבֵד: וְעֹבֵד הוֹלִיד

אֶת־יִשָׁי וְיִשַׁי הוֹלִיד אֶת־דָּוִד:

ᗡ Ruth ᗡ

Unlike Esther and Jonah, the Book of Ruth contains no overriding mysteries, but like them it is a self-contained narrative that depicts human beings acting out their roles in unusual ways that lead to unusual results. In the case of Ruth, the action is not controlled by God at all, but He is alluded to in the conversations as an element in the players' lives. This is in contrast to Esther, where a supreme power seems to be moving the players around to a divine plan, but is never mentioned as such. While in Jonah, God is much in evidence, directing the prophet, preparing the great fish, accepting Nineveh's repentance and finally rebuking Jonah.

The Book itself is a wonderful record of rural life in Judah at the time of King David. Although it purports to relate events taking place three generations earlier, it would not have been recorded until at least the time of Solomon's reign, because its main significance seems to be the description of his forebears and the events surrounding one particular part of David's family, that came from Moab.

Modern critics see it as a much later composition; while the traditional Jewish view is that the prophet Samuel had written it at an earlier period (B. *Baba Bathra* 14B). One late, but traditional, commentator claims that it must have been written before the Moabite Stone account of Mesha, king of Moab, which dates to the ninth century BCE, and records the victory of Moab over Judah (Melzer 1973, intro. 17). It would then slightly post-date David's reign, but that would still give the Book a very early date. Certainly the events pre-date the history of Mesha, who would have prevented any entry of Israelites into his territory, but the account could well have been written many centuries later. However, the suggestion that the story is a polemic against Ezra and Nehemiah forbidding marriage with foreign wives in the fifth century BCE (as Osterley and Robinson 1934, 84) is unjustified. The Book clearly shows that Mahlon and Chilion, the sons of Naomi who married out, both suffer an early death; hardly a recommendation for taking foreign wives.

The traditional Jewish view considers Ruth to be a simple tale, giving the ancestry of King David that, in itself, just displays the reward for good deeds, such as those of Naomi and Ruth. The Midrash quotes Rabbi Ze'ira (third century CE) as saying: "This scroll [of Ruth] tells us nothing either of ritual purity or impurity, either of prohibition or permission. For what purpose then was it written? To teach how great is the reward of those who do deeds of kindness" (*MR.* Ruth II, 15).

But is the situation really so simple? Are Naomi and Ruth just going through life doing good deeds? Why does Boaz have to be seduced, and who is the mysterious redeemer, *Peloni-Almoni*? Why is it significant that one of David's ancestresses comes from a non-Israelite background? All these essential elements of this "simple" tale require further explanation.

🕮 THE BOOK

Ruth may be the name of the Book and its heroine, but the chief player is her mother-in-law, Naomi. Naomi and her husband, Elimelech, leave Bethlehem in Judah on account of local famine, and cross over to the land of Moab with their two sons. As their stay is extended, the two boys, Mahlon and Chilion, settle down and marry two local girls, Ruth and Orpah, but they have no children. Eventually all three men die (we are not told how and why), and the three women are left without means of support. We presume that as foreigners, Elimelech and his sons did not have the opportunity to acquire land in Moab. On their death, Naomi decides to return to Bethlehem, especially as she has heard that conditions there have now improved. She tries to persuade the girls to remain in their Moabite homeland; both are reluctant, but Orpah finally agrees. Ruth, however, will not leave Naomi and utters the famous words:

> Wherever you go, I will go; where you stay the night, I will stay, your people are my people and your God is my God... (Ruth 1:16).

So Naomi goes back with Ruth to Bethlehem, where they are welcomed, but Naomi is bitter at her fate, having had to return without husband or sons.

It is now the beginning of the barley harvest and Naomi and Ruth manage to survive on the gleanings that Ruth gathers in the fields of Boaz, a rich relative of Elimelech, Naomi's deceased husband. Although Boaz is friendly and kind to Ruth he does not seem to appreciate that, as a close relative of the family, it is his duty to take the girl, the childless widow of his relative Mahlon, under his wing. Naomi goes further and thinks that Boaz has an obligation to marry Ruth and when, after several months of harvest, Boaz shows no sign of approaching Ruth, Naomi decides that direct action is necessary.

She advises Ruth to make the first move and to approach Boaz one night when he is alone in the granary. She tells her to wait until Boaz is asleep and then to go and sleep beside him. Ruth prepares herself and goes to lie with Boaz. When he wakes, she is holding him and asks him to marry her. He now sees the point but says this will have to be part of redeeming Elimelech's property and indicates that there is another closer relative who has the first right of redemption.

Nevertheless, he tells Ruth to stay till daybreak and on parting gives her a handsome present of barley, which she can share with Naomi. Ruth returns and reports to Naomi, who is pleased with events, and persuades Ruth that matters will soon be resolved, since Boaz is anxious not be left in a compromising position. In fact, in the morning, Boaz summons the elders and the other close relative and asks him if he wants to redeem Naomi's land. It is not at first clear whether Boaz is committed to marrying Ruth, and that the land matter is a separate issue, or whether Ruth comes with the acquisition of the land.

After some discussion, the other redeemer declines the offer and the way is clear for Boaz to redeem the land and marry Ruth. The elders witness this happy ending and the people give the couple the blessing that their home should be like that of their ancestor Perez, son of Judah and Tamar. Boaz takes Ruth to his house and they have a son, whom Naomi nurses and whom the people name Obed, who will be the grandfather of David. Finally, David's lineage is traced back through Obed and Boaz to Salmon and to Perez, son of Judah and Tamar (Gen. 38:29).

There are four main strands to this seemingly simple tale, all told in the form of the personal experiences of its three main characters, Naomi, Ruth and Boaz. There is a fourth "hidden" character, the other close relative and redeemer of land, but he is not named, in fact he is deliberately referred to only as *"Peloni-Almoni,"*or Mr. Anonymous, by Boaz (Ruth 4:1), and his identity remains a mystery.

The first of the main strands of the story is the physical relationship between the inhabitants of Judah and Moab. The second is the personal relationship between Naomi and Ruth, the third is that between Ruth and Boaz, and the fourth, the relationship between Boaz and the mystery redeemer. Once these are all resolved, the way is clear for the birth of a child, who will be part of the genealogy of David. The social and religious context includes the agricultural background of life in Bethlehem; the ancient laws of near-levirate marriage, as illustrated by the relationship between Ruth and Boaz and its similarities to that between Judah and Tamar; the methods of courtship; the forms of greeting; the authority of the elders at the gate; the ways of redeeming family property and the symbolic confirmation of a contract. All these subjects are artfully packed into this one short story; to try to understand them we have to consider them one by one.

🕮 NAOMI AND RUTH

In spite of a scene of rural bliss in Bethlehem, the dangers of drought send Naomi's family, her husband and two sons, abroad to Moab. Moab lies not far across the water, the Dead Sea, from Judah and there must have been some kind of ferry system in operation between the Judaean side, near to present-day Masada, and the Lisan, the tongue (Heb. *lashon*) of land that juts out towards Israel from Transjordan (fig. 11). Today, were it not for the security border, it would be possible to walk across from one side to the other. Then, when water levels were higher, it may have been a short boat ride across shallow waters (Aharoni 1979, 290).

The total journey from Bethlehem to the edge of Moab will have been about 55 km. (35 miles) with a few more kilometers to some suitable inland spot, not specified in the text. The journey was certainly not unique, for we are told that David took his parents to safety in Moab, when he was being hunted by Saul (I Sam. 22:4). We can presume that relations with Moab were friendly also at this time, several generations before David. The land of Moab, consisting of hilly slopes facing the prevailing winds from the west, would have had more precipitation than the hills of the Judaean Desert around Bethlehem, and so may not have been suffering the same drought conditions as Bethlehem in Judah.

The relationship between Naomi and Ruth is far from our traditional view of the wife and her mother-in-law. Whereas Orpah eventually goes back to "her people and her gods" (Ruth 1:14), Ruth refuses to leave Naomi, for reasons that are not explained. The chief concern of the widowed woman in Biblical times must have been to find a husband, without whom she was socially and economically helpless, especially if she had no children. Ruth can only expect support from her father or from a levirate (brother-in-law) marriage (on the lines of Deut. 25:5, 6) and there, Naomi cannot help her; she says to her daughter-in-law:

> Even if I were (to spend) this night with a man and (then) give
> birth to sons, would you (be able to) wait until they grew up ?
> (Ruth 1:12, 13).

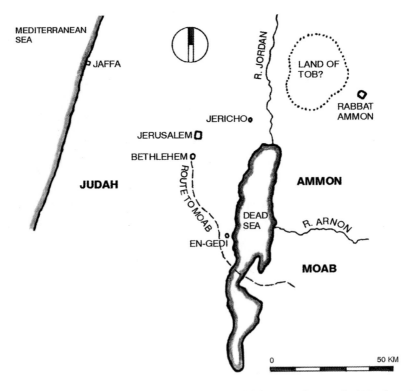

Fig. 11 *Map showing possible Route from Bethlehem to the Land of Moab and probable location of the land of Tob.*

In this, Naomi cannot help Ruth, nor can she support her in other ways, since Naomi left her homeland ten years earlier and it is only later (4:3) that we find out that Elimelech had a field, which may have now passed to Naomi. Ruth, for her part, as a foreigner and a widow, is unlikely to find a husband in Bethlehem. It was different for the two sons, Mahlon and Chilion, coming to Moab. They could choose, were indeed forced to choose, local wives, since no others were available, but it was less possible for a woman to do the same, particularly a widow, on foreign soil. Nevertheless, Ruth is determined to stay with Naomi, for reasons that appear to be quite unselfish. Maybe their common loss of Mahlon, son and husband, had brought the two women close together.

Ruth must have obtained a high opinion of Israelite family life and beliefs from Elimelech, Naomi and her own husband, Mahlon, since she makes that famous declaration to go and do whatever Naomi goes and does, and not to part from her unless it is death itself that separates them (1:17). When indeed they come to Bethlehem, Ruth stays with her mother-in-law, works to feed her by gleaning barley and wheat in the fields for many weeks, and carries out whatever instructions Naomi gives her. It is clear that the two women live in close harmony in the town, although where exactly they are living is not clear. Ruth is still "the Moabitess" (2:2, 6, 21) but to Naomi she is first and foremost her daughter-in-law (2:20) and Naomi's chief concern is to see that Ruth is suitably married in order to secure her future.

Once in Bethlehem, Naomi is keen to make discreet contact with her husband's kinsman, Boaz, who is a man of substance (Heb. *ish gibor ḥayil*, 2:1), presumably to see if he will act as the redeemer (*go'el*) of her husband's land. However, it is only later (4:3) that we are told that Elimelech still has a field in Bethlehem and that Naomi wishes to sell it. Under Israelite tribal law it was the duty of a close relative to "redeem" any land being sold by a member of the tribe, in order to preserve it within the tribal inheritance, and if possible within the family. This law is based on the Biblical passage:

> If your brother becomes poor and sells some of his possession,
> then his close relative shall come and redeem what his brother
> has sold (Lev. 25:25).

The law was extant for many years, as we see from the prophet
Jeremiah when, in spite of being in prison himself, and the kingdom
of Judah being on the verge of defeat by the Babylonians, he "redeems"
a plot of land belonging to his cousin (or uncle) Ḥanamel, in their
home town of Anathoth (Jer. 32:7 - 25).

THE BARLEY HARVEST

At the beginning of Chapter 2, only Boaz is mentioned as a "known"
relative (Heb. *moda*) of Elimelech; we therefore presume that it will be
up to him to buy Elimelech's plot, if Naomi is forced to sell it. As we
are now at the beginning of the barley harvest (1:22), to be followed by
the wheat harvest (2:23), land would not be saleable until the harvests
were in, at mid-summer (when preparations for sowing could begin),
and indeed it is only then, after the end of both harvests (2:23), that the
matter of the purchase of Elimelech's inheritance comes up (4:3). So
Naomi cannot provide for herself and Ruth by selling Elimelech's plot
while the harvests are in full swing, but they must glean in the fields to
provide themselves with food. The Torah (Hebrew Law) puts an obligation on the harvester to leave the corners of the field and the gleanings
for the poor, the widow and the stranger (Lev. 19:9; 23:22 & Deut. 24:19).
Ruth takes the initiative and offers to go out and glean "behind anyone
in whose eyes I will find favor" (Ruth 2:2). Naomi agrees and Ruth luckily happens to start in a field belonging to Boaz, although it seems that
Naomi has not told her of the family connection, and Boaz is unaware
of Ruth's relationship. Only Naomi knows all the details (2:1).

Fig. 12 *The Barley Harvest in Egypt. In the next world, a royal servant, posing as a farmer, cuts the crop while his wife follows behind gleaning; from the tomb of Sennedjem at Deir-el-Medina, nineteenth Dynasty, 1293-1185 BCE (from Giveon 1984, 81).*

When Boaz visits his field, for he is rich enough to have hired reapers and a man in charge of them, he asks him about the girl (2:5). The foreman describes her as the Moabitess who came with Naomi (2:6), but does not actually refer to her as one of the family, so we might think that Boaz is unaware that she is a childless widow and related to him. He obviously likes the look of her as he asks her to continue gleaning in his field (fig. 12) and allows her to take refreshment with his own workers (2:9).

Ruth thanks him for this favor with the rather exaggerated gesture of falling to the ground and with the telling phrase:

Why have I found favor in your eyes, to notice me (*lehakireni*)
and I am a foreign woman (*nokhriyah*)? (2:10).

The two words emphasized have the same Hebrew root (*n-k-r*) but here they have opposite meanings; in one case she is noticed or "recognized," in the other case she is the foreigner, someone who is "unrecognized." The same code or key root of *n-k-r* is present in its different but associated meanings throughout the Joseph story in Genesis (e.g. 37:32, 33) and clearly these key words would have struck a response in native listeners to the story. They certainly evoke one in Boaz, who now reveals that he knows all about Ruth, her relationship to Naomi, Elimelech and Mahlon, and how she elected to stick by Naomi through thick and thin. On parting he wishes her full reward:

> ...from the Lord, the God of Israel, under whose wings you have come for shelter (Ruth 2:12).

But he makes no mention of his own relationship, or his possible responsibility to her as a close relative, although he tells his harvesters to protect Ruth and see that she receives plenty of the gleanings (2:15, 16).

ACKNOWLEDGING THE ONE GOD

It should be noted that Boaz does not hesitate to use the double name of God when wishing Ruth a "full reward from the Lord, the God of Israel" (2:12). He seems to emphasize that the God of Israel will also show kindness to the Moabitess, seeing that she has acknowledged him as her God. "Your God shall be my God," she said to Naomi (1:16). Nor does Boaz hesitate to use the divine name in greeting his workers, as do they in their reply:

> And Boaz... said to the reapers, 'the Lord be with you' and they said to him, 'the Lord bless you!' (2:4).

This could well be to indicate quite clearly that Boaz and his workers, and presumably the whole town of Bethlehem, acknowledged the one and only God. They did not practice the kind of syncretism recorded in some passages in the Book of Judges, where the fertility deity, Ba'al, was still worshipped alongside God, as exemplified in the name of the judge Gideon, who was also called Jerubba'al (Judg. 6:32, 9:1).

The Talmud is not normally happy with the use of the divine name in everyday speech since it looks like using God's name in vain, but in this case it praises Boaz and even recommends his form of greeting for normal use (B. *Berakhoth* 59A). It may be noted that the frequent use of the Tetragrammaton in Ruth points to, but does not prove, an early date for the Book (Bickerman 1967, 266).

On returning from the field, Ruth tells Naomi she has been gleaning in the field of Boaz (2:19), and it is only now that Naomi tells her of their relationship to him. She confirms that Ruth should continue working in Boaz's field and this Ruth does until the completion of the barley harvest, ending in early June, and the subsequent wheat harvest, ending about two months later, in August. We have what looks like a contemporary record of these harvests from the Gezer Calendar (fig. 13), which is a recitation of the agricultural year, dated to the tenth century BCE (Naveh 1987, 63, 65), as follows (the words in parentheses are our additions):

months (two) of gathering fruits	(October and November, approx.)
months (two) of sowing	(December and January, approx.)
months (two) of late sowing	(February and March, approx.)
month (one) of flax	(April, approx.)
month (one) of barley harvest	(May, approx.)
month (one) of harvest (wheat), and survey	(June, approx.)
months (two) of grape harvest	(July & August, approx.)
month (one) of summer fruits	(September, approx.)

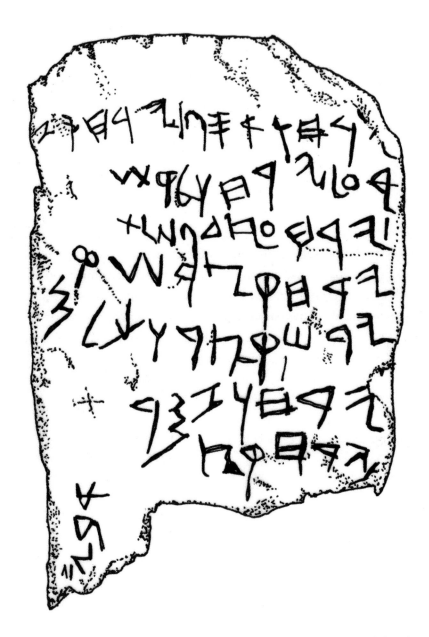

Fig. 13 *The Gezer Calendar, found at Tel Gezer, central Israel, and dated to 10th Century BCE, now in the Istanbul Museum (from Naveh 1987, 63)*

The section we are concerned with is the first harvest, that of barley (*se'orim*), and the second harvest (*qatzir*), which is wheat, although not mentioned as such. June is the month of the wheat harvest and also the month of survey (*ḥil*), showing that this is the month when fields are resurveyed for boundaries (after all the disturbance of harvesting), for replanting and for sale. So the period of gleaning was at least two months (approx. May and June) and perhaps a short period before and after those two months – a total of perhaps ten weeks. Nevertheless, in all this time, Boaz makes no move to approach Ruth or Naomi with a view to discussing marriage with the young widow.

We are not told the status of Boaz except that he was a man of substance (*ish gibor-ḥayil* 2:1). It is unlikely that he was unmarried, but in any case, this would not have prevented him from taking a second wife. The Midrash has it that Boaz's wife died on the day that Naomi and Ruth entered Bethlehem (1:19) and it was because of this that the town was in a state of uproar (*MR. Ruth III, 6*). It also claims that he was quite elderly, being 80 years of age. This may be based on the supposition that Boaz's relationship to Naomi is one of brother-in-law; that Elimelech, Boaz and the other "redeemer," the so-called *Peloni-Almoni* (4:1) were brothers, all sons of Salmon (see 4:21). It would make Boaz uncle to Mahlon and therefore, perhaps, considerably older than Ruth. The same source gives the alternative view that Elimelech was a brother of Salmon (father of Boaz) and of *Peloni-Almoni*, and Boaz would then be a cousin of Mahlon, and therefore, perhaps, not so far removed from Ruth's age (see fig. 14). We shall discuss this further below, in dealing with the mystery character, *Peloni-Almoni*. Suffice is to say that Boaz, elderly or young, makes no move towards Ruth, except to give her preferential treatment amongst the gleaners. Now the harvests are over, what are Ruth and Naomi to do for sustenance?

Naomi sees the problem and decides to take the initiative, since Boaz has not made a move in the right direction. The family relationship between Ruth and Boaz has to be exploited if Ruth is to have a secure future. Naomi will also know that now, after the harvests, would be the time to sell the field. The sale would help to secure some resources for herself, but not enough to guarantee Ruth's future. The field would have been Elimelech's inheritance and on his death would have passed to his sons Mahlon and Chilion, with the firstborn (we presume it is Mahlon) taking a double share.

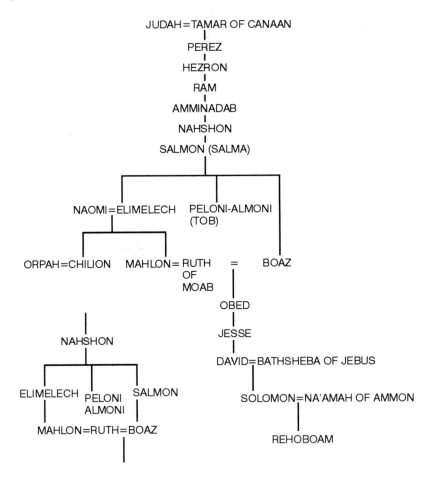

Fig. 14 *Genealogy of the royal line of Judah, showing Elimelech,* Peloni-Almoni, *and Boaz as brothers, all sons of Salmon (as MR. Ruth VI, 3) and alternative with Boaz as nephew of Elimelech and* Peloni-Almoni *(as second opinion of the* Midrash*).*

On the death of the two sons, since there were no children, it looks as if the land would revert to their widows, although this is not the Torah law (see below). Orpah, having remained behind in Moab, is out of the picture, and her childless husband Chilion's portion would revert to Elimelech and then maybe to Naomi, while Mahlon's portion remains with Ruth. Thus, although the sale of the property would benefit Naomi and even more so Ruth, it would only be a one-time gain and unlikely to sustain the women for long. The better option of retaining the land was not a realistic one, because the women could not work it on their own, nor did they have the resources to hire the necessary labor, as Boaz was in a position to do.

A NIGHT IN THE GRANARY

As for the initiative that Naomi now sees to be necessary, she approaches Ruth with her proposal (3:2). That night Ruth is to go to Boaz (again described in that verse as the "known" relative) who will be staying late in the granary (*goren*) to complete the winnowing. She shall make herself beautiful and wait until Boaz has finished sorting the grain, has had his food and drink and lain down to sleep (3:3). She must then go and uncover his feet and lie with him, and he, Boaz, will tell her what to do next (3:4). Ruth agrees to this bold proposal and carries it out to the letter. When Boaz has eaten and drunk, "and his heart was happy" (3:7) and he has gone to sleep, Ruth comes along to lie by him and "uncover his feet". This is a plain euphemism for sexual advance or exposure (as Ezek. 16:25 "you have opened your feet to all that pass by"). A similar expression is used of King Saul, who goes to relieve himself in the cave "to cover his feet" (I Sam. 24:4) and similarly when King David encourages Uriah the Hittite to go home to his wife Bathsheba, he tells him to "wash his feet" (2 Sam. 11:8) that is, to have intercourse with her

(*Metzudat David*, ad loc.). The meaning is underlined in the next
verse:

> And it was midnight, and the man trembled and he was caught
> up (*vayilapheth*) and behold a woman was lying at his feet (3:8).

The key word *vayilapheth* should be translated "he was caught
up" or "he was entwined," from the Hebrew root *l-p-t*, meaning to
bend or incline (Gesenius 1885, 441) and in the passive (as here) it
would mean he was embraced or "entwined" by Ruth. Similarly in the
case of the blind Samson in the temple of the Philistines, "he embraced (*vayilpoth*) the two middle pillars that the temple rested upon"
(Judg. 16:29, trans. JPS. 1985). The Talmud is even more explicit (B.
Sanhedrin 19B) when it derives this rare expression from the word for
turnip, *lepet*, and concludes that Boaz's "skin" became hard like a turnip! The standard translations that use such phrases as "the man was
startled" do so euphemistically and with no other justification.

It is clear that while Boaz was sleeping off his food and drink, Ruth
had worked herself into a compromising position. And when he wakes
and asks who she is, she is so bold as to say immediately:

> I am Ruth. . . and you shall spread your wing (garment) over
> your maidservant, as you are the relative (redeemer) (3:9).

The phrase "spreading your wing" is a symbol of protection and
indeed marriage, as:

> And behold your time was a time of love and I spread my wing
> over you.... and you became Mine (Ezek. 16:8).

Thus, in one phrase Ruth introduces herself, proposes marriage
and reminds Boaz of his obligations. Boaz does not resist and indeed

blesses Ruth in the name of God (3:10) but he does point out one little problem. He is, he says, a near-relative but there is another who is closer (3:12). This is a bolt out of the blue and a blow to Ruth and to Naomi's plan, since it is the first we hear of this closer relative. Presumably this is the first they know of him; so far only Boaz has been described as the "known" relative (2:1 and 3:2). It is inconceivable that Naomi would have gone ahead with her bold plan for Ruth to engage Boaz if there had been another and closer claimant known to her. For it would be up to the closest relative to take Ruth's hand in marriage, if so he desired.

But Boaz reassures Ruth. She is to stay the night and in the morning he will clarify the position with the other relative. Boaz says:

> If he redeems you, good (Heb. *tob*), he will redeem, but if he does not want to redeem you, then I will redeem you, by the life of God (3:13).

This raises a number of basic questions. How can Boaz allow the other relative to "redeem" Ruth, that is, to marry her, when Ruth has already put Boaz and herself in a most compromising position, or are we to understand that Boaz will marry her, and just ask the other relative to redeem the field, hers and Naomi's? This question arises again at the town gate and it is discussed below. The other relative is not named but Boaz uses the term: "if he redeems you, good (*tob*), he will redeem", and as this can also be translated "Good (Tob) will redeem," the Midrash (*MR*. Ruth VI:3) considers his name to have been Tob, which is certainly a possible name, similar to *Tuvya* (as in Zech. 6:10); the idea will be discussed below. For the present, let us call the close relative Tob for the sake of convenience.

Ruth stays the night with Boaz "at his feet," rising before daybreak in order to avoid recognition when returning to the town, but not before Boaz has poured into her mantle a handsome present, "six of barley," and put the mantle back on her (Ruth 3:14,15). The gift may be just to help feed her and Naomi, but it looks mightily like a reward for sexual services, and indeed the Midrash takes it to represent the price of their marriage contract (*MR*. Ruth VII:2). Ruth returns to Naomi, tells her "all that the man had done to her" (Ruth 3:16) and shows her the "six of barley." Naomi seems well pleased with the night's events and tells Ruth not to worry, since Boaz is bound to resolve matters with the other redeemer within the day (3:18).

The account speaks literally of the "six of barley" without mentioning the specific measure. Why it does so is not clear and most translations insert the word "measures." The Midrash (as above) suggests it was either six "*seah*" (about 80 liters), which would be too heavy for a woman to carry, or it was six grains, which seems rather mean, and so the Midrash interprets it as a metaphor to represent the six great men who would result from this marriage, or the six fine qualities of Ruth's heir, David (also enumerated by Rashi, ad loc.). The lack of measure is not just a mistake, because it is deliberately omitted again when Ruth mentions the gift to Naomi (3:17). It therefore makes sense to see it as a bride-price, the exact value of which is not as important as the fact of its transfer from the man to the woman of his choice, and her acceptance of it. There is a suggestion that the Hebrew for barley, which is *se'orim*, be here read as *sha'arim*, which is possible, and which would then mean "gate-measures," as it does in Genesis 26:12, in the story of Isaac at Gerar (Campbell 1975, 128). That solves one problem but creates another, since we would then know the quantity (six measures) but not the product.

Although the night scene in the granary must count as the climax of these events (see fig. 17), and the encounter between Ruth and Boaz seems to have been successfully resolved between them, there remains the question of the mysterious "redeemer," Tob. It seems that Naomi encouraged Ruth to go ahead with the bold proposal to approach Boaz in the safe knowledge that he was the closest relative and the one with an obligation to marry the childless widow and thus "raise up for his brother a name in Israel" (Deut. 25:6). Although in this case Boaz was not the *levir* or brother-in-law, it seems to be assumed by our text that where there is no *levir*, then the duty falls on the nearest male relative. And it is clear that Naomi did not know of this Tob, a relative closer than Boaz.

During the intimate night scene Boaz drops his bombshell. There is he says another relative, even closer than he, Boaz (3:12). He does not name him but just hints that his name may be Tob (3:13, as above). How is it that Naomi knows nothing about this Tob, who must be a very close relative of her late husband, Elimelech? One clue may be in the strange word that is used in connection with Boaz. Both Boaz and Tob are referred to several times as *qarov*, close relative, or *go'el*, redeemer (2:20; 3:12, 13; 4:3, 4) but only Boaz is referred to as *moda*. In fact, the first time we encounter him we read:

> And Naomi had a relative (*moda*) to her husband, a man of substance, of the family of Elimelech, and his name was Boaz (2:1).

Again, Naomi refers to Boaz later as "our relative (*moda'tanu*)" (3:2). This unusual word means, literally, "a known person" (from the Hebrew root *y-d-'*, to know), so we can assume Boaz was a relative "known" to Naomi, while Tob was not. How can this be? To answer that, we have to look further into this man's description.

PELONI-ALMONI

As Naomi has predicted, Boaz wastes no time in confronting the closest redeemer, Tob, and as soon as the man appears by the town gate next morning, he calls him over. "Turn aside, sit here, *Peloni-Almoni*," he says (4:1). This is a most curious appelation; it is the

only time the term is used to describe a person in the Hebrew Bible. It
is used in two other instances, but then in connection with places and
not persons. In one case David, fleeing from Saul, pretends to
Ahimelech the priest, that he has been sent on a secret mission to a
place *"peloni-almoni"* (I Sam. 21:3), and in the other case the king of
Aram (Syria), fighting against Israel, decides to set up camp in a place
"peloni-almoni," (2 Kgs. 6:8). A similar word is used by Daniel to describe his vision of a sacred being speaking to one *"Palmoni"* (Dan.
8:13), which some commentators take to be a combination of the words
peloni and *almoni*.

In all cases the meaning is something like "anonymous" or "so
and so" or "a certain one," but the derivation is far from certain. The
actual words seem to denote something that is distinguished, dis-
tinct or specific (from the root *p-l-'*) and something that is mute or
dumb (as *almon*). The Midrash (*MR*. Ruth VII:7) claims that our
man was ignorant (mute, dumb) of the new law (see below) that it
was permitted to marry a Moabite woman (such as Ruth) even though
a Moabite man was prohibited from "coming into the assembly of
Israel even unto the tenth generation" (Deut 23:4). Further exami-
nation of the term does not really help us to identify this man (whom
we are calling Tob), except perhaps to say that he came from an uncertain place, which seems to be the meaning of *peloni-almoni* in I
Samuel and 2 Kings. The designation *peloni-almoni* came to be pejorative in later Hebrew literature (cf. B. *Yoma* 66b), and even here
its use by Boaz has a definitely dismissive if not pejorative implica-
tion.

If we give some credibility to the man's name being Tob we can
look for further analogies. Again, the direct references are to land rather
than persons. When Jephthah is chased away by his half-brothers, he
goes to live as an outlaw "in the land of *Tob*" (Jud. 11:3, 5) which is
near the territory of Ammon in Transjordan (Aharoni 1979, 109, 443).
This incident occurs in the time of the Judges, as does the story of

Ruth. Some generations later the men of *Tob* (*Ish-Tob*) form an alliance with the people of Ammon against the kingdom of David (2 Sam.
10:6, 8). The term *Tob* can thus be associated with the land of Ammon
(see fig. 11).

If indeed the designation *peloni-almoni* is related to place as much
as to person, and if *Tob* is associated with Ammon, we might suggest
the following. At the time of drought when Elimelech and Naomi go
to Moab (Ruth 1:1), another brother (Tob) also leaves to seek his for-
tune, but this time in neighboring Ammon. The only brother to
remain in Bethlehem is Boaz. The first two brothers do badly.
Elimelech dies abroad but Tob returns, although not in triumph. After
ten years abroad, Naomi is not aware of him; Boaz knows of his existence but is not proud of him. He refers to him, rather dismissively,
as *Peloni-Almoni*. It is inconceivable that Boaz would use such a term
of an uncle, a senior relative, as would be the case according to the
theory that Salmon (father of Boaz), Elimelech and Tob were brothers (see above).

It is much more likely then, on the first opinion of the Midrash,
that Elimelech, Tob and Boaz were brothers (see fig. 14), and so Boaz
felt able to refer to his errant brother Tob as *Peloni-Almoni*. Both
Elimelech and Tob would have been under opprobrium for leaving
Bethlehem in its time of need (as indicated by *MR* Ruth 1:4 in connection with Elimelech) and the irony of the situation may well be that
they are both punished, Elimelech (and his sons) by death, Tob by in-
difference; while Boaz, the youngest who stayed behind, has become
the rich one, the man of substance (2:1). Boaz refers to Tob as being
the closer relative or redeemer, presumably the order of the brothers
in age was Elimelech, Tob and Boaz. The text also suggests that the
three were brothers, since Boaz tells Tob that Naomi is selling the
piece of land "which belongs to Elimelech, our brother" (4:3) although,
as the Midrash (*MR. Ruth VI:3*) and Rashi (ad loc.) point out, this
term could include other close relatives.

🏺 AT THE TOWN GATE

We now have the courtroom drama that takes place at the gate of
the town. Such places are well known from ancient Israelite sites, such
as Tel Dan (fig. 15). The gate was the focal point of entry and exit to
the town and served not only as a point of defense, but also a place of
social contacts. The markets (*hutsot*) were set up just outside the gates
(cf. 2 Kgs. 7:1), King David sat in the gate to receive his people (2 Sam.
19:9), prophets spoke at the gate (Jer. 36:10) and the elders gathered
there (Prov. 31:23). In later times, Mordecai sat in the King's gate of
Shushan (Esther 2:21) and Ezra read the Torah before the Water Gate
in Jerusalem (Neh. 8:3). The fine example at Tel Dan, dating from the
Israelite period of the ninth century BCE, had a paved court between
the middle and the outer gate (Biran 1994, pl. 194), which could have
served well for the kind of case now being heard in Bethlehem.

Boaz and Tob are in place and Boaz assembles ten elders as witnesses and, if necessary, as judges, while the little scene is played out.
He tells Tob that Naomi is selling Elimelech's field and Tob, as the
closest relative, should redeem it, to which Tob immediately agrees
(4:4). Now comes a sentence, which one commentator rightly calls
"the most difficult passage in the book" (Fuerst 1975, 26) and which
has given no end of trouble. Having got Tob's agreement to act as redeemer, Boaz now plays his second card. Literally, the text reads:

> And Boaz said, on the day that you acquire the field from the
> hand of Naomi and from Ruth the Moabitess the wife of the
> dead (man), I have acquired to set up the name of the dead on
> his inheritance (4:5).

As it stands the text is less than clear, and the Masoretic reading
(which standardized the vocalization in the sixth century CE) makes
two small points. The sentence divider (*etnahta*) is placed after

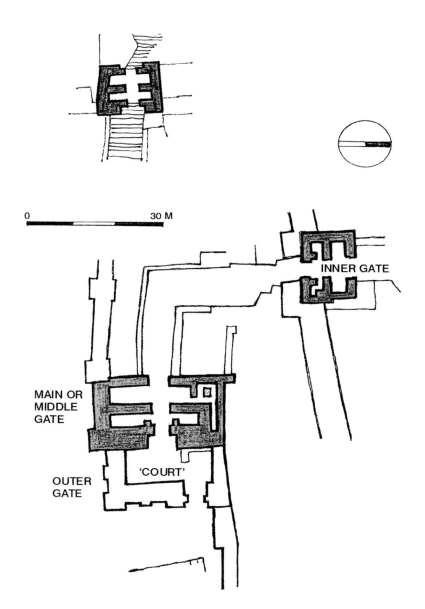

Fig. 15 *The Gates of Dan, northern Israel. The upper plan: the Gate of Laish (early Dan) of the 18th Century BCE. The main plan: the elaborate Gate of Dan of the 9th and 8th Centuries BCE, consisting of outer, main and inner Gates with pathway between them. Judgment may have been conducted in the "Court" between the outer and main Gates, where there was a bench and a canopied seat (from Biran 1994, 78, 236).*

"Naomi" and the word which is written (the *ketiv*) to read "I have acquired *(qaniti)*" is amended (the *qeri*) to read "you have acquired *(qanita)*". The sense is now:

> On the day that you acquire the field from the hand of Naomi, and (then) Ruth the Moabitess, the wife of the dead (man), *you* have acquired to set up the name of the dead on his inheritance.

This makes clear to Tob that *he* will acquire Ruth when *he* acquires the field. It makes sense, and would explain why Tob does not feel it wise to carry on with the purchase, if it means taking Ruth in marriage as part of the deal. He therefore declines the offer, "lest I spoil my inheritance" (4:6) he says, and invites Boaz to go ahead. When the Masoretic authorities gave this reading they relied on the Midrash (*MR*. Ruth VII:10) that explains the "spoiling" of Tob's inheritance. Tob thought that Mahlon and Chilion, the sons of Elimelech, had died because they married Moabite women, prohibited by the Torah law of Deut. 23:4, and he was not willing to meet the same fate by marrying Ruth. The Midrash claims that he had not yet learned the new interpretation (as presumably Boaz had) that it was permitted for a man to marry a Moabite woman but not for a woman to marry a Moabite man, as expounded by the Talmud (B. *Yebamoth* 69A, see below). The Midrash can even take this view of Tob on the basis of the key phrase as spelled or written (the *ketiv*) by making that word *(qaniti)* into a question, thus, "shall I (then) acquire (her) to set up the name of the dead?"

The whole question of whether or not it is permitted to marry a Moabite of either sex is at the heart of this Book. The Torah Law is quite clear:

> The Ammonite and the Moabite shall not come into the congregation of God: even the tenth generation of theirs shall

not come into the congregation of God forever (Deut. 23:4).

The Talmud modifies this by claiming that the law refers to the male Ammonite and the male Moabite but not to the Ammonitess or the Moabitess (B. *Yebamoth* 69A); this distinction is used to justify King David's descent from Ruth the Moabitess (ibid. 76B). At a later period the ancient law is even set aside for a contemporary male Ammonite, who is permitted by Rabbi Joshua (second century CE) to convert to Judaism, as "Sennacherib of Assyria long ago.... mixed up all the nations" he says (B. *Berakhoth* 28A). In our case here, the Rabbis would have agreed to Ruth's entering the community of God as she did, after all, make a sincere conversion in her plea to Naomi:

Let your people be my people and your God, my God (Ruth 1:16).

In fact the Rabbis consider Ruth's words to be the archetypal form of declaration that should be made by the sincere convert (B. *Yebamoth* 47B). As a Moabitess, they say, she was permitted to enter the congregation of God.

However, it is difficult to project these arguments back to Ruth and her times, since it is clear from the Book of Nehemiah that the exiles returning from Babylon in the fifth and sixth centuries BCE read the passage in Deut. 23:4 and put away their foreign consorts (Neh. 13:1) and not only the males, as Ezra refers specifically to the foreign wives, who are to be rejected (Ezra 9:2). Nevertheless, the orthodox rabbinic approach has to reconcile the marriage of Boaz and Ruth with the Torah Law and the Talmud does this by differentiating between the male Moabite and the Moabitess. To take this so far as to claim (as the Midrash does) that Boaz knew of the distinction, and that *Peloni-Almoni* (our Tob) did not, is really unnecessary, as we point out below that the purchase of the field was not, in fact, linked to marrying the girl.

Reverting now to the enigmatic speech that Boaz makes to Tob, the problem with the interpretation, telling Tob that in taking the field he also takes the girl, is that we have been through the elaborate night encounter between Boaz and Ruth and it looks as if they are well and truly betrothed. The deed has been done both by direct sexual contact and by the transfer of the bride price (the "six of barley'"). It can hardly be that Boaz would go back on his words and actions to Ruth. If we look again at the problem verse, in the original, we should read it as follows:

> And Boaz said, on the day that you acquire the field from the hand of Naomi and from Ruth the Moabitess: the wife of the dead (man) I have acquired to set up the name of the dead on his inheritance (4:5).

This is exactly the written text clarified only by putting the sentence divider (*etnaḥta*) after "Moabitess," and it follows the good literary maxim of *difficilior lectio praestat*, "the more difficult reading is to be preferred" (Gordis 1965, 17). The situation is now clear. You (Tob) acquire the field and I (Boaz) acquire the girl. This is perfectly legitimate since in Torah law the redemption of a relative's land (as Lev. 25:25) does not go together with the law of raising the name of the dead brother (Deut. 25:7). However, the question then arises, why does Tob refuse to act as the redeemer of the field, if he is not obliged to acquire the girl?

ELIMELECH'S FIELD

The real question we have to ask is: was there any field to redeem? Certainly Elimelech must have had a parcel of land in Bethlehem, which he left behind. On his death it would have passed to his sons, but as they died childless, who inherited it? Not Naomi and not Ruth or Orpah for, according to Torah law, if there is no son or daughter, it goes to the owner's brother and, if there is none, it goes to his father's (Elimelech's) brother (Numb. 27:10), and that would be Tob! On the other hand, if Ruth were to remarry and have a child, that child is raised in his father's (Mahlon's) name and the land belongs to the child. In fact it would not matter if the child were male or female; where there is no son, the daughter inherits (Numb. 27:8).

So now the difficult verse (see also Sasson 1987, 326) goes as follows: Boaz tells Tob that on the day Tob acquires the field from Naomi and Ruth – it being incumbent on him to give them something for it, even though he is the lawful inheritor – that day I, Boaz, am going to marry Ruth and our child (if any) will be the rightful inheritor of the field. In other words, anything Tob acquires today is likely to be taken from him in nine month's time or so, God willing! No wonder that Tob declines this "inheritance." Now we can make sense of Tob's statement, "I cannot redeem it for me, in case I destroy my inheritance" (4:6). Tob will not enter into an "inheritance" that is most likely to be taken away from him just as soon as he acquires it. Thus he says quite clearly to Boaz, you redeem it "for I am not able to redeem it" (4:6). As he says, quite openly, he *cannot* redeem it. If Ruth is already promised to Boaz, as Boaz says she is, then Tob would have to commit adultery with Ruth to get the field. So it is up to Boaz to redeem it, that is, to pay something for it to Naomi and Ruth; anyway it will become the property of a child of Ruth's, who will be raised in the name of her dead husband, Mahlon.

If we do not accept this explanation, we will have to go along with the idea, as many commentators do, that Elimelech's field has passed to Naomi, his widow, and that Mahlon's portion of it has passed to Ruth, his widow. Although that seems to be the sense of verse 4:3, that Naomi is selling the field of Elimelech, this would be a straight contradiction of the Torah law. Although there are other indications in the Book of variations to the Torah law (the levirate marriage is extended to the previous generation; the action of shoe removal, as below, is extended to all contracts and not just to denial of the levirate contract) this change in land inheritance would be a contradiction of the Torah law and not just a variation of it.

Having proposed this solution to verse 4:5, we can then see that it will also work, though in another way, according to the Masoretic amendment of *qanita* (you have acquired) for *qaniti* (I have acquired). In that case Boaz says to Tob, the day that you acquire the field from Naomi, you must also acquire Ruth, because it is only through her child – "to raise up the name of the dead (man) on his inheritance" – that you can acquire the field legitimately. To this Boaz may have added, "and you should not do that, *Peloni-Almoni*, because I spent last night with her alone in the granary!"

For the sake of the story, it is a pity that Tob backs down so quickly. The sense of tension could have been increased considerably if Tob had stuck to his prior claim and tried to legitimize his redemption by marrying Ruth. His is the better claim, for, unless Ruth has a child in Mahlon's name, the field reverts to Tob. But Naomi has sewn things up nicely against Tob. As a result of her getting Ruth and Boaz to spend the night together, and since Boaz liked what he saw and betrothed Ruth on the spot, Tob has lost out on his previously rightful inheritance, according to Torah law. With Tob out of the way, it is plain sailing to the birth of the all-important baby.

But first the matter has to be formally witnessed by the men at the gate, and Tob and Boaz have to confirm their agreement by a formal act of "redemption and exchange." This is done by one party removing his footwear and giving it to the other "and this was confirmation in Israel" in the old days (4:7). It is not clear who drew off whose shoe and verse 8 makes it no clearer; but the Midrash suggests it was Boaz and thus he was making a symbolic payment to Tob, for the transfer of the redeemer's rights (*MR.* Ruth VII:12). There is just a hint that this matter of removing shoes is related to the "uncovering of the feet" indulged in by Ruth when she approached Boaz in the granary (Ruth 3:4).

But the main interest in this archaic procedure, which the text seems to acknowledge was no longer practiced in Israel, is that it shows similarity to the act of refusal of levirate marriage by the *levir* (brother-in-law), in which case the rejected widow would "withdraw his footgear from his (the *levir's*) foot" in the presence of the elders at the gate (Deut. 25:7-9). The action, the circumstances and even the location are similar but the detail is different. The common elements are the removal of the shoe, which represents an article of value (and perhaps also an element of sexuality) in both cases and the act of confirmation in front of the elders at the gate. As Tob was the closest male relative he should have married Ruth, but Boaz had preempted him. Therefore it would make sense for Boaz to hand to Tob the shoe that Ruth, under a normal levirate refusal, would have taken from him; for why should Tob lose his shoe as well as the girl?

At the same time the action confirmed the transfer of the ownership of the field from Tob's potential child with Ruth, to that of Boaz and Ruth, and so it was also a symbol to confirm the transfer of the field, before the witnesses at the gate. The text tells us that "this was the custom in Israel formerly" to explain that the Deuteronomic law of 25:9 was extended to other forms of contract before witnesses. And Boaz says as much when he makes his final declaration before the elders and calls on them and the people to be witnesses to his acquisition of Elimelech's field and of Ruth the Moabitess (Ruth 4:9,10).

Boaz considers these actions to be total confirmation of his wedding plans and the acquisition of the property of Elimelech, Mahlon and even Chilion. He adds the rider of acquiring the field "from the hand of Naomi" (Ruth 4:9); from which we presume that she did not actually own these properties, she was just the guardian entrusted with the responsibility of seeing that they ended up in the right hands.

By this time it seems that quite a crowd has gathered and the people at the gate, as well as the elders, shout out their approval, "(yes, we are) Witnesses!" (4:11). But they go further and liken Ruth to Leah and Rachel (who incidentally gave birth to Benjamin at Bethlehem, Gen. 35:18,19), and they add the curious blessing that Ruth and Boaz's home shall be like the house of Perez "whom Tamar bore to Judah" (Ruth 4:12). This allusion reveals the significant similarities between the romance of Ruth and Boaz and that of Judah and Tamar; and the importance of both liaisons to the genealogy of David the king.

JUDAH AND TAMAR

The story of Judah and Tamar is given in Gen. 38. Judah marries a Canaanite woman who bears him three sons, Er, Onan and Shelah. Judah arranges for the Canaanitess, Tamar, to be wife to Er, but Er dies early at the hand of God. Onan is called on to perform the duty of the *levir* to Tamar, but refuses to use his seed for his brother's benefit and he also dies. Judah tells Tamar to wait until Shelah grows up but even when he does, Judah does not give Shelah to Tamar. He is afraid that he, the third son, will also die. In the meantime, Judah's wife dies and he goes off to the sheep-shearing festival. Tamar, tired of waiting for a husband, dresses herself as a prostitute on the way to the festival to tempt Judah to come to her. He promises her a sheep in payment, leaving personal pledges as surety for the time being.

The next day, when his servants bring the sheep, the prostitute is nowhere to be found. After three months, Tamar is found to be pregnant and Judah orders her to be burnt for adultery. She produces the pledges saying "please recognize (*haker*)" the owner of these pledges (38:25), for he is the father. "And Judah recognized (*vayaker*) them, saying she is more righteous than I" (38:26). Tamar is saved and delivered of twins, one of whom is Perez, the great-grandfather of the great-grandfather of Boaz (Ruth 4:18). By dint of her disguising herself as a prostitute, Tamar and Judah become ancestors of David, the king.

The similarities are clearly numerous. Two brothers die childless, and Tamar awaits a levirate marriage, as Ruth does in a wider sense.

Tamar has to engineer her union with the father of the *levir*, while
Naomi arranges it for Ruth with a relative who is neither the brother-
in-law nor the nearest relative after him. In both cases the nubile widow
takes the initiative while her intended partner is merry with the harvest (Boaz) or sheep-shearing festival (Judah). Boaz and Judah both
give their ladies a parting gift or pledge and in each case "recognize"
the woman using the key root of *n-k-r* (Ruth 2:10 and Gen. 38:25 &
26). In both cases the women start off as non-Israelites and finish "as
a mother in Israel," as an ancestress of David, the king.

There is a further similarity from a literary point of view. Both
stories are selfcontained, personalized episodes in *"la longue durée"* of
greater events. The story of Judah and Tamar interrupts the much
longer saga of Joseph, from the time of his brother's jealousy until his
appointment as viceroy in Egypt, an account of more than fourteen
chapters in Genesis. As for Ruth, her Book is traditionally placed between those of Judges and Samuel (B. *Baba Bathra* 14B), since it occurs
in the days "when the Judges (leaders) judged" (Ruth 1:1). It is thus a
modest picture of country life that sits between two greater books,
and illuminates a personal tale played out alongside the great events
of war and kingship that the Books of Judges and Samuel record.

DAVID, SOLOMON AND REHOBOAM

When finally the baby is born to Ruth, the local women congratu-
late Naomi, which is natural, seeing that God has now not left her "without
a redeemer" and has given her a surrogate grandchild borne by:

> ...a daughter-in-law who loves you, she has given him birth,
> she who is better to you than seven sons (4:15).

Ruth is greatly praised, as is Boaz, as the redeemer, but we see
Naomi as the real beneficiary, since the line through Elimelech and

Mahlon is continued. That may be why Naomi looks after the child and even nurses it, and the neighbors consider it as her child (4:17). But from the point of view of history, the child, named Obed, is the grandfather-to-be of David and for that Boaz gets the credit (4:21). The name of Mahlon is not mentioned again, even though the purpose of the levirate-type marriage was "to raise up the name of the dead (man) on his inheritance" (4:5). Nevertheless, the field, which was his inheritance, has played a crucial role in the dénouement of the story, and will go to the baby, to Obed.

We finish with the genealogy of David, the king, and we see that the account is careful to count ten generations from Judah to David (4:18 - 22). This puts it on a level of importance with the ten generations from Adam to Noah (Gen. 5:1-32) and the ten from Noah to Abraham (11:10-27). From Abraham to Judah is four generations; we then revert to the ten from Judah to David. This is in line with Biblical and indeed ancient Near Eastern practice, according to which genealogies consist of a general list of prehistoric ancestors of, usually, ten generations, an intermediate list of three or four generations specific to the subject, and then a further list of generations, again usually ten, leading up to the subject in hand (Weinfeld 1973, EJ. XIV, 519). This ancient practice makes it clear that this list of ten ancestors is an integral part of the Book and not tacked on later, as suggested by modern critics (e.g. Campbell 1975, 172).

However, the recitation does have some difficulties, since the generations from Judah to Nahshon are only five. Judah is one of those going down to Egypt (Exod. 1:2) and Nahshon ben Amminadab was leader of the tribe of Judah in the Wilderness (Numb. 7:12); that leaves only a short space of five generations for the Sojourn in Egypt. Also the next five generations leave rather a short time from the Wilderness days to the early Monarchy. But the main point of interest is surely the name of Salmah or Salmon (4:20,21) who is clearly the ancestor who gave his name to David's son, Solomon. He is also mentioned in Chronicles (under the name of Salma) as are Boaz and his son Obed (I Chron. 2:11,12), but here in the Book of Ruth is the first we hear of him in the *Tanakh*.

This makes one realize that the purpose of the book of Ruth, if there is a purpose to it, is to emphasize the genealogical background of Solomon (Heb. *Shlomo*) rather than just David. On this subject the Midrash (*MR*. Ruth 11:2) makes a curious claim. It states that Ruth lived to an advanced age and that she was blessed to see her great-great-grandson, Solomon, on his throne, judging between the two prostitutes fighting over the one live baby. Based on the text, which says "and she sat at his right hand" (1 Kgs. 2:19), the Midrash takes that to be Ruth rather than the more obvious candidate of Bathsheba, the king's mother. The Midrash seems eager to establish a direct link between Ruth and Solomon.

There are further overtones of Solomon in the book. Solomon's mother Bathsheba was probably a Jebusite (Yeivin 1959, 22; Malamat 2001, 221) consistent with being the wife of Uriah the Hittite (2 Sam. 11:3). In her case the sexual initiative came from David, although one could suggest that she was doing something fairly provocative in bathing on the roof within eyeshot of the royal palace (11:2). It may in fact have suited the writer's and Solomon's purpose to show that, although his father had taken the initiative with a foreign lady in a far from proper manner, there was also in Solomon's background a foreign lady, Ruth, who had herself taken the initiative with his ancestor Boaz.

The name Boaz also raises overtones, because it is the name given to one of the two columns set in front of Solomon's Temple (1 Kgs. 7:21), the other being called Jachin (see fig. 16). There is no explanation given for these names, which may just have been the names of donors, rather than the names of deities. But these two pillars, essential elements of the temple doorway, and similar to many other twin-columned portals to a temple (Frankfort 1996, 255,282) must have borne great significance. The name Boaz is not attested elsewhere

in the *Tanakh*; it may conceivably be that Solomon took it in memory
of his ancestor. As for Jachin, that may also have had family connec-
tions, as we find it in the name of one of the last kings of Judah called
Jehojachin (2 Kgs. 24:8, literally "God will establish"). The name also
appears much earlier as plain Jachin, a son of Simeon (Numb. 26:12)
and it has been suggested that David's mother had family connec-
tions with the tribe of Simeon (Yeivin 1959, 22).

Above all, the link with Solomon is most apparent in connection
with his wife Na'amah, the mother of his successor Rehoboam. The

Fig. 16 *Twin Pillars of Solomon's Temple, Jachin and Boaz (based on 1 Kgs.
7:15-22).*

Tanakh says quite simply that Solomon was succeeded by his son, Rehoboam, "and the name of his mother was Na'amah the Ammonitess" (1 Kgs. 14:21,31). It is quite remarkable that Solomon, who boasted of having 700 wives and 300 concubines (11:3), had to choose as his successor the son of a foreign wife, an Ammonitess. His wives included princesses from all the adjoining countries, from Moab, Ammon, Edom, Zidon, and the Hittites (11:1), but surely he must also have had Israelite women in his harem. It is quite extraordinary that the son of an Ammonitess should have been picked as his successor. Some scholars have claimed that the description of Solomon's court and his wealth is considerably exaggerated (Finkelstein & Silberman 2001, 123), but no one has suggested that his successor Rehoboam was not the son of an Ammonitess.

In reality why should the record go out of its way to mention this, if it is giving us an exaggerated picture of the magnificence of Solomon's reign? It is a fact it might have tried to hide but chose not to do so. It is significant that Na'amah the Ammonitess is the only one of Solomon's wives to be named, and it appears that she was married to Solomon before his accession, probably on the orders of his father David (Malamat 2001, 234ff.). Consequently, Rehoboam was the firstborn son with the right to the succession. In this sense, the Book of Ruth is not only a justification for the Moabite ancestry of David but also for the Ammonite origin of his grandson, King Rehoboam.

AN IDYLLIC, BUCOLIC PAST

If it was indeed in the interests of the three first occupants of the Davidic throne, David, Solomon and Rehoboam, to publicize the events surrounding the marriage of Boaz and Ruth, it was also in their interests to hark back to the idyllic country life of a small town, perhaps just a village, like Bethlehem. With the rise of the Davidic dynasty in Jerusalem there must have been the beginnings of the evolution towards a monarchic state structure. Even though that may not have been as great and grandiose as the *Tanakh* suggests, the beginnings were certainly there. There may well have been resentment among the rural population, which was being drawn into larger towns to serve the needs of the monarchy and even being drafted into forced labor gangs, as described in the First Book of Kings (5:28) to build the Temple and the royal apartments. The Book of Ruth would have served to show the humble, pastoral origins of the ancestors of the royal family, the same as that of all the other sectors of the population. It showed their work in the fields, their being subject to the effects of drought, their close family relationships and their resolution of business affairs at the town gate before the elders. Probably by the time the story was publicized, this picture was already a bucolic dream, but one that would resonate well with its audience of city dwellers.

There is indeed one basic element in the story, which does not immediately ring true. Bethlehem is situated in the hill country south of Jerusalem, in a landscape of shallow hills and valleys. With its sparse rainfall and uneven topography it is a land for pasture and grazing of small cattle such as sheep and goats. As a youth, David acted as a shepherd to his father's flock (I Sam. 16:11) and today the Bedouin still roam the area with their flocks of black goats. Was it really a land of barley and wheat harvests as described in our Book (Ruth 1:22; 2:2,23)? At the time in question, specialization in agriculture did not exist. Bethlehem may have been better for herding and for fruit trees and wines (Aharoni 1979, 29) but the days of wider trading were still to come, and each village would have had to grow its own crops, particularly cereals.

It may well be, therefore, that even such hill-country sites as Bethlehem had a limited number of areas where barley and wheat could be grown, albeit in relatively small quantities. The name of the village was, after all, Beth-lehem or "place of bread" (BDB. 111), although its earlier name had been Ephrath (Gen. 35:13). Again, this element of

ancient self-sufficiency within the village would have appealed to listeners to the story of Ruth, who were now probably being forced to
buy their produce in the expensive markets of the town or city.

LESS THAN SIMPLE ?

It appears that the story of Ruth is perhaps not as plain and simple
as the Midrash, quoting Rabbi Ze'ira, had implied. It describes some
quite complex family relationships, laws of inheritance and levirate
marriage not quite in conformity with Torah law, and above all the
interaction between an Israelite village and its foreign neighbors, especially as it concerns intermarriage, and the lineage of the royal house
of David, his son and his grandson. It shows how it is sometimes necessary for the women to take the initiative in the course of history,
and how it happened in this particular case.

Besides the three main characters, Naomi, Ruth and Boaz, it introduces a fourth mystery character referred to only as *Peloni-Almoni*
or Mr. Anonymous. This seemingly unimportant character is now seen
to play a pivotal role in achieving the desired result of Boaz marrying
Ruth and fathering the ancestor of the Davidic dynasty. Moreover,
Peloni-Almoni, if his name was indeed Tob, may himself have had a
connection with the land of Ammon and can therefore be seen as in-
troducing the curious fact that Rehoboam, heir to the throne of
Solomon, was the son of an Ammonite woman.

Unlike the Book of Esther, Ruth makes free use of the name of
God, above all in the greetings between Boaz and his workers (Ruth
2:4) and does not hesitate to describe customs that are not in conformity with Torah laws. Chief among these is the marriage of Boaz with
a Moabitess, Ruth herself, which is in direct contravention of the
Deuteronomic Law. The prohibition against marriage with the Moabite
is linked with that of the Ammonite (Deut. 23:4), and the Book makes
clear that despite this, Boaz, ancestor of David, made a legitimate

marriage to Ruth, the Moabitess. This serves to demonstrate that there was little wrong in the union of Solomon and Na'amah, the Ammonitess (I Kings 14:21) and their son Rehoboam becoming legitimate heir to the kingdom of Judah.

The story is carefully crafted and skilfully arranged, exhibiting a chiastic structure, similar to those of both Esther and Jonah. In this case, the pivotal point is the night scene in the granary, and the events beforehand and afterwards display a pleasing symmetry (see fig. 17, based on Bertram 1965). At the same time, the Book paints a fine picture of village life with a strong and authentic flavor of ancient practices. Its heroine is Ruth, but the prime mover is her mother-in-law Naomi, and the Book describes the happy relationship between the two women. Not for nothing is the name Ruth cognate with the Hebrew word for friendship, re'ut (BDB, 946).

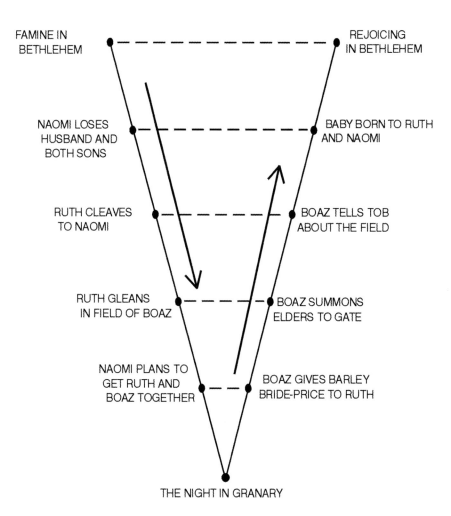

Fig. 17 *Chiastic structure of the Book of Ruth, the events in the second half reflecting those in the first, the turning point being the night that Ruth and Boaz spend together in the Granary.*

Book of Jonah

1 [1]The word of the LORD came to Jonah son of Amittai: [2]Go at once to Nineveh, that great city, and proclaim judgment upon it; for their wickedness has come before Me.

[3]Jonah, however, started out to flee to Tarshish from the LORD's service. He went down to Joppa and found a ship going to Tarshish. He paid the fare and went aboard to sail with the others to Tarshish, away from the service of the LORD.

[4]But the LORD cast a mighty wind upon the sea, and such a great tempest came upon the sea that the ship was in danger of breaking up. [5]In their fright, the sailors cried out, each to his own god; and they flung the ship's cargo overboard to make it lighter for them. Jonah, meanwhile, had gone down into the hold of the vessel where he lay down and fell asleep. [6]The captain went over to him and cried out, "How can you be sleeping so soundly! Up, call upon your god! Perhaps the god will be kind to us and we will not perish."

[7]The men said to one another, "Let us cast lots and find out on whose account this misfortune has come upon us." They cast lots and the lot fell on Jonah. [8]They said to him, "Tell us, you who have brought this misfortune upon us, what is your business? Where have you come from? What is your country, and of what people are you?" [9]"I am a Hebrew," he replied. "I worship the LORD, the God of Heaven, who made both sea and land." [10]The men were greatly terrified, and they asked him, "What have you done?" And when the men learned that he was fleeing from the service of the LORD – for so he told them – [11]they said to him, "What must we do to you to make the sea calm around us?" For the sea was growing more and more stormy. [12]He answered, "Heave me overboard, and the sea will calm down for you; for I know that this terrible storm came upon you on my account." [13]Nevertheless, the men rowed hard to regain the shore, but they could not, for the sea was growing more and more stormy about them. [14]Then they cried out to the LORD:

"Oh, please, LORD, do not let us perish on account of this man's life. Do not hold us guilty of killing an innocent person! For You, O LORD,

ספר יונה

א ב **וַיְהִי** דְּבַר־יְהֹוָה אֶל־יוֹנָה בֶן־אֲמִתַּי לֵאמֹר: קוּם לֵךְ
אֶל־נִינְוֵה הָעִיר הַגְּדוֹלָה וּקְרָא עָלֶיהָ כִּי־עָלְתָה רָעָתָם לְפָנָי:

ג וַיָּקָם יוֹנָה לִבְרֹחַ תַּרְשִׁישָׁה מִלִּפְנֵי יְהֹוָה וַיֵּרֶד יָפוֹ וַיִּמְצָא
אֳנִיָּה | בָּאָה תַרְשִׁישׁ וַיִּתֵּן שְׂכָרָהּ וַיֵּרֶד בָּהּ לָבוֹא עִמָּהֶם

ד תַּרְשִׁישָׁה מִלִּפְנֵי יְהֹוָה: וַיהֹוָה הֵטִיל רוּחַ־גְּדוֹלָה אֶל־הַיָּם וַיְהִי
ה סַעַר־גָּדוֹל בַּיָּם וְהָאֳנִיָּה חִשְּׁבָה לְהִשָּׁבֵר: וַיִּירְאוּ הַמַּלָּחִים
וַיִּזְעֲקוּ אִישׁ אֶל־אֱלֹהָיו וַיָּטִלוּ אֶת־הַכֵּלִים אֲשֶׁר בָּאֳנִיָּה

ו אֶל־הַיָּם לְהָקֵל מֵעֲלֵיהֶם וְיוֹנָה יָרַד אֶל־יַרְכְּתֵי הַסְּפִינָה
וַיִּשְׁכַּב וַיֵּרָדַם: וַיִּקְרַב אֵלָיו רַב הַחֹבֵל וַיֹּאמֶר לוֹ מַה־לְּךָ

ז נִרְדָּם קוּם קְרָא אֶל־אֱלֹהֶיךָ אוּלַי יִתְעַשֵּׁת הָאֱלֹהִים לָנוּ
וְלֹא נֹאבֵד: וַיֹּאמְרוּ אִישׁ אֶל־רֵעֵהוּ לְכוּ וְנַפִּילָה גוֹרָלוֹת

ח וְנֵדְעָה בְּשֶׁלְּמִי הָרָעָה הַזֹּאת לָנוּ וַיַּפִּלוּ גּוֹרָלוֹת וַיִּפֹּל הַגּוֹרָל
עַל־יוֹנָה: וַיֹּאמְרוּ אֵלָיו הַגִּידָה־נָּא לָנוּ בַּאֲשֶׁר לְמִי־הָרָעָה

ט הַזֹּאת לָנוּ מַה־מְּלַאכְתְּךָ וּמֵאַיִן תָּבוֹא מָה אַרְצֶךָ וְאֵי־מִזֶּה
עַם אָתָּה: וַיֹּאמֶר אֲלֵיהֶם עִבְרִי אָנֹכִי וְאֶת־יְהֹוָה אֱלֹהֵי

י הַשָּׁמַיִם אֲנִי יָרֵא אֲשֶׁר־עָשָׂה אֶת־הַיָּם וְאֶת־הַיַּבָּשָׁה: וַיִּירְאוּ
הָאֲנָשִׁים יִרְאָה גְדוֹלָה וַיֹּאמְרוּ אֵלָיו מַה־זֹּאת עָשִׂיתָ כִּי־יָדְעוּ

יא הָאֲנָשִׁים כִּי־מִלִּפְנֵי יְהֹוָה הוּא בֹרֵחַ כִּי הִגִּיד לָהֶם: וַיֹּאמְרוּ
אֵלָיו מַה־נַּעֲשֶׂה לָּךְ וְיִשְׁתֹּק הַיָּם מֵעָלֵינוּ כִּי הַיָּם הוֹלֵךְ וְסֹעֵר:

יב וַיֹּאמֶר אֲלֵיהֶם שָׂאוּנִי וַהֲטִילֻנִי אֶל־הַיָּם וְיִשְׁתֹּק הַיָּם מֵעֲלֵיכֶם
יג כִּי יוֹדֵעַ אָנִי כִּי בְשֶׁלִּי הַסַּעַר הַגָּדוֹל הַזֶּה עֲלֵיכֶם: וַיַּחְתְּרוּ
הָאֲנָשִׁים לְהָשִׁיב אֶל־הַיַּבָּשָׁה וְלֹא יָכֹלוּ כִּי הַיָּם הוֹלֵךְ וְסֹעֵר

יד עֲלֵיהֶם: וַיִּקְרְאוּ אֶל־יְהֹוָה וַיֹּאמְרוּ אָנָּה יְהֹוָה אַל־נָא נֹאבְדָה
בְּנֶפֶשׁ הָאִישׁ הַזֶּה וְאַל־תִּתֵּן עָלֵינוּ דָּם נָקִיא כִּי־אַתָּה יְהֹוָה

טו כַּאֲשֶׁר חָפַצְתָּ עָשִׂיתָ: וַיִּשְׂאוּ אֶת־יוֹנָה וַיְטִלֻהוּ אֶל־הַיָּם וַיַּעֲמֹד

by Your will, have brought this about." ¹⁵And they heaved Jonah overboard, and the sea stopped raging.

¹⁶The men feared the LORD greatly; they offered a sacrifice to the LORD and they made vows.

2 ¹The LORD provided a huge fish to swallow Jonah; and Jonah remained in the fish's belly three days and three nights. ²Jonah prayed to the LORD his God from the belly of the fish. ³He said:

In my trouble I called to the LORD,
And He answered me;
From the belly of Sheol I cried out,
And You heard my voice.
⁴You cast me into the depths,
Into the heart of the sea,
The floods engulfed me;
All Your breakers and billows
Swept over me.
⁵I thought I was driven away
Out of Your sight:
Would I ever gaze again
Upon Your holy Temple?
⁶The waters closed in over me,
The deep engulfed me.
Weeds twined around my head.
⁷I sank to the base of the mountains;
The bars of the earth closed upon me forever.
Yet You brought my life up from the pit,
O LORD my God!
⁸When my life was ebbing away,
I called the LORD to mind;
And my prayer came before You,
Into Your holy Temple.
⁹They who cling to empty folly
Forsake their own welfare,
¹⁰But I, with loud thanksgiving,

הַיָּם מִזַּעְפּֽוֹ׃ וַיִּֽירְא֤וּ הָֽאֲנָשִׁים֙ יִרְאָ֥ה גְדוֹלָ֖ה אֶת־יְהֹוָ֑ה וַיִּזְבְּחוּ־זֶ֙בַח֙ טז

לַֽיהֹוָ֔ה וַיִּדְּר֖וּ נְדָרִֽים׃ וַיְמַ֤ן יְהֹוָה֙ דָּ֣ג גָּד֔וֹל לִבְלֹ֖עַ אֶת־יוֹנָ֑ה **ב** א

וַיְהִ֤י יוֹנָה֙ בִּמְעֵ֣י הַדָּ֔ג שְׁלֹשָׁ֥ה יָמִ֖ים וּשְׁלֹשָׁ֥ה לֵילֽוֹת׃ וַיִּתְפַּלֵּ֣ל יוֹנָ֔ה ב

אֶל־יְהֹוָ֖ה אֱלֹהָ֑יו מִמְּעֵ֖י הַדָּגָֽה׃ וַיֹּ֗אמֶר קָרָ֩אתִי֩ מִצָּ֨רָה לִ֤י ג

אֶל־יְהֹוָה֙ וַֽיַּעֲנֵ֔נִי מִבֶּ֧טֶן שְׁא֛וֹל שִׁוַּ֖עְתִּי שָׁמַ֥עְתָּ קוֹלִֽי׃ וַתַּשְׁלִיכֵ֤נִי ד

מְצוּלָה֙ בִּלְבַ֣ב יַמִּ֔ים וְנָהָ֖ר יְסֹבְבֵ֑נִי כׇּל־מִשְׁבָּרֶ֥יךָ וְגַלֶּ֖יךָ עָלַ֥י

עָבָֽרוּ׃ וַאֲנִ֣י אָמַ֔רְתִּי נִגְרַ֖שְׁתִּי מִנֶּ֣גֶד עֵינֶ֑יךָ אַ֚ךְ אוֹסִ֣יף לְהַבִּ֔יט ה

אֶל־הֵיכַ֥ל קׇדְשֶֽׁךָ׃ אֲפָפ֤וּנִי מַ֙יִם֙ עַד־נֶ֔פֶשׁ תְּה֖וֹם יְסֹבְבֵ֑נִי ס֖וּף ו

חָב֥וּשׁ לְרֹאשִֽׁי׃ לְקִצְבֵ֤י הָרִים֙ יָרַ֔דְתִּי הָאָ֛רֶץ בְּרִחֶ֥יהָ בַעֲדִ֖י ז

לְעוֹלָ֑ם וַתַּ֧עַל מִשַּׁ֛חַת חַיַּ֖י יְהֹוָ֥ה אֱלֹהָֽי׃ בְּהִתְעַטֵּ֤ף עָלַי֙ נַפְשִׁ֔י ח

אֶת־יְהֹוָ֖ה זָכָ֑רְתִּי וַתָּב֤וֹא אֵלֶ֙יךָ֙ תְּפִלָּתִ֔י אֶל־הֵיכַ֖ל קׇדְשֶֽׁךָ׃

מְשַׁמְּרִ֖ים הַבְלֵי־שָׁ֑וְא חַסְדָּ֖ם יַעֲזֹֽבוּ׃ וַאֲנִ֗י בְּק֤וֹל תּוֹדָה֙ ט

אֶזְבְּחָה־לָּ֔ךְ אֲשֶׁ֥ר נָדַ֖רְתִּי אֲשַׁלֵּ֑מָה יְשׁוּעָ֖תָה לַֽיהֹוָֽה׃ וַיֹּ֥אמֶר יא

יְהֹוָ֖ה לַדָּ֑ג וַיָּקֵ֥א אֶת־יוֹנָ֖ה אֶל־הַיַּבָּשָֽׁה׃

Will sacrifice to You;
What I have vowed I will perform.
Deliverance is the LORD's!
¹¹The LORD commanded the fish, and it spewed Jonah out upon dry land.

3 ¹The word of the LORD came to Jonah a second time: ²"Go at once to Nineveh, that great city, and proclaim to it what I tell you." ³Jonah went at once to Nineveh in accordance with the LORD's command.

Nineveh was an enormously large city a three days' walk across. ⁴Jonah started out and made his way into the city the distance of one day's walk, and proclaimed: "Forty days more, and Nineveh shall be overthrown!"

⁵The people of Nineveh believed God. They proclaimed a fast, and great and small alike put on sackcloth. ⁶When the news reached the king of Nineveh, he rose from his throne, took off his robe, put on sackcloth, and sat in ashes. ⁷And he had the word cried through Nineveh: "By decree of the king and his nobles: No man or beast – of flock or herd – shall taste anything! They shall not graze, and they shall not drink water! ⁸They shall be covered with sackcloth – man and beast – and shall cry mightily to God. Let everyone turn back from his evil ways and from the injustice of which he is guilty. ⁹Who knows but that God may turn and relent? He may turn back from His wrath, so that we do not perish."

¹⁰God saw what they did, how they were turning back from their evil ways. And God renounced the punishment He had planned to bring upon them, and did not carry it out.

ג‎ א ב‎ וַיְהִ֧י דְבַר־יְהֹוָ֛ה אֶל־יוֹנָ֖ה שֵׁנִ֥ית לֵאמֹֽר: ק֛וּם לֵ֥ךְ אֶל־נִֽינְוֵ֖ה
הָעִ֣יר הַגְּדוֹלָ֑ה וּקְרָ֤א אֵלֶ֙יהָ֙ אֶת־הַקְּרִיאָ֔ה אֲשֶׁ֥ר אָנֹכִ֖י דֹּבֵ֥ר

ג‎ אֵלֶֽיךָ: וַיָּ֣קָם יוֹנָ֗ה וַיֵּ֛לֶךְ אֶל־נִֽינְוֵ֖ה כִּדְבַ֣ר יְהֹוָ֑ה וְנִֽינְוֵ֗ה הָֽיְתָ֤ה

ד‎ עִיר־גְּדוֹלָה֙ לֵֽאלֹהִ֔ים מַהֲלַ֖ךְ שְׁלֹ֥שֶׁת יָמִֽים: וַיָּ֤חֶל יוֹנָה֙ לָב֣וֹא
בָעִ֔יר מַהֲלַ֖ךְ י֣וֹם אֶחָ֑ד וַיִּקְרָא֙ וַיֹּאמַ֔ר ע֚וֹד אַרְבָּעִ֣ים י֔וֹם וְנִֽינְוֵ֖ה

ה‎ נֶהְפָּֽכֶת: וַיַּֽאֲמִ֛ינוּ אַנְשֵׁ֥י נִֽינְוֵ֖ה בֵּֽאלֹהִ֑ים וַיִּקְרְאוּ־צוֹם֙ וַיִּלְבְּשׁ֣וּ

ו‎ שַׂקִּ֔ים מִגְּדוֹלָ֖ם וְעַד־קְטַנָּֽם: וַיִּגַּ֤ע הַדָּבָר֙ אֶל־מֶ֣לֶךְ נִֽינְוֵ֔ה וַיָּ֙קָם֙

ו‎ מִכִּסְא֔וֹ וַיַּֽעֲבֵ֥ר אַדַּרְתּ֖וֹ מֵֽעָלָ֑יו וַיְכַ֣ס שַׂ֔ק וַיֵּ֖שֶׁב עַל־הָאֵֽפֶר: וַיַּזְעֵ֗ק
וַיֹּ֙אמֶר֙ בְּנִֽינְוֵ֔ה מִטַּ֧עַם הַמֶּ֛לֶךְ וּגְדֹלָ֖יו לֵאמֹ֑ר הָֽאָדָ֣ם וְהַבְּהֵמָ֡ה
הַבָּקָ֣ר וְהַצֹּ֩אן֩ אַֽל־יִטְעֲמוּ֙ מְא֔וּמָה אַ֨ל־יִרְע֔וּ וּמַ֖יִם אַל־יִשְׁתּֽוּ:

ח‎ וְיִתְכַּסּ֣וּ שַׂקִּ֗ים הָֽאָדָם֙ וְהַבְּהֵמָ֔ה וְיִקְרְא֥וּ אֶל־אֱלֹהִ֖ים בְּחׇזְקָ֑ה

ט‎ וְיָשֻׁ֗בוּ אִ֚ישׁ מִדַּרְכּ֣וֹ הָֽרָעָ֔ה וּמִן־הֶֽחָמָ֖ס אֲשֶׁ֥ר בְּכַפֵּיהֶֽם: מִֽי־יוֹדֵ֣עַ

י‎ יָשׁ֔וּב וְנִחַ֖ם הָֽאֱלֹהִ֑ים וְשָׁ֛ב מֵֽחֲר֥וֹן אַפּ֖וֹ וְלֹ֥א נֹאבֵֽד: וַיַּ֤רְא
הָֽאֱלֹהִים֙ אֶֽת־מַ֣עֲשֵׂיהֶ֔ם כִּי־שָׁ֖בוּ מִדַּרְכָּ֣ם הָֽרָעָ֑ה וַיִּנָּ֣חֶם
הָֽאֱלֹהִ֗ים עַל־הָֽרָעָ֛ה אֲשֶׁר־דִּבֶּ֥ר לַֽעֲשׂוֹת־לָהֶ֖ם וְלֹ֥א עָשָֽׂה:

4 ¹This displeased Jonah greatly, and he was grieved. ²He prayed to the LORD, saying, "O LORD! Isn't this just what I said when I was still in my own country? That is why I fled beforehand to Tarshish. For I know that You are a compassionate and gracious God, slow to anger, abounding in kindness, renouncing punishment. ³Please, LORD, take my life, for I would rather die than live." ⁴The LORD replied, "Are you that deeply grieved?"

⁵Now Jonah had left the city and found a place east of the city. He made a booth there and sat under it in the shade, until he should see what happened to the city. ⁶The LORD God provided a ricinus plant, which grew up over Jonah, to provide shade for his head and save him from discomfort. Jonah was very happy about the plant. ⁷But the next day at dawn God provided a worm which attacked the plant so that it withered. ⁸ And when the sun rose, God provided a sultry east wind; the sun beat down on Jonah's head, and he became faint. He begged for death, saying, "I would rather die than live." ⁹ Then God said to Jonah, "Are you so deeply grieved about the plant?" "Yes," he replied, so deeply that I want to die."

¹⁰Then the LORD said: "You cared about the plant, which you did not work for and which you did not grow, which appeared overnight and perished overnight. ¹¹And should not I care about Nineveh, that great city, in which there are more than a hundred and twenty thousand persons who do not yet know their right hand from their left, and many beasts as well!"

ב א וַיֵּרַע אֶל־יוֹנָה רָעָה גְדוֹלָה וַיִּחַר לוֹ: וַיִּתְפַּלֵּל אֶל־יְהֹוָה וַיֹּאמַר
אָנָּה יְהֹוָה הֲלוֹא־זֶה דְבָרִי עַד־הֱיוֹתִי עַל־אַדְמָתִי עַל־כֵּן
קִדַּמְתִּי לִבְרֹחַ תַּרְשִׁישָׁה כִּי יָדַעְתִּי כִּי אַתָּה אֵל־חַנּוּן וְרַחוּם

ג אֶרֶךְ אַפַּיִם וְרַב־חֶסֶד וְנִחָם עַל־הָרָעָה: וְעַתָּה יְהֹוָה קַח־נָא
ד אֶת־נַפְשִׁי מִמֶּנִּי כִּי טוֹב מוֹתִי מֵחַיָּי: וַיֹּאמֶר יְהֹוָה הַהֵיטֵב

ה חָרָה לָךְ: וַיֵּצֵא יוֹנָה מִן־הָעִיר וַיֵּשֶׁב מִקֶּדֶם לָעִיר וַיַּעַשׂ לוֹ
שָׁם סֻכָּה וַיֵּשֶׁב תַּחְתֶּיהָ בַּצֵּל עַד אֲשֶׁר יִרְאֶה מַה־יִּהְיֶה

ו בָּעִיר: וַיְמַן יְהֹוָה־אֱלֹהִים קִיקָיוֹן וַיַּעַל ׀ מֵעַל לְיוֹנָה לִהְיוֹת
צֵל עַל־רֹאשׁוֹ לְהַצִּיל לוֹ מֵרָעָתוֹ וַיִּשְׂמַח יוֹנָה עַל־הַקִּיקָיוֹן

ז שִׂמְחָה גְדוֹלָה: וַיְמַן הָאֱלֹהִים תּוֹלַעַת בַּעֲלוֹת הַשַּׁחַר לַמָּחֳרָת
ז וַתַּךְ אֶת־הַקִּיקָיוֹן וַיִּיבָשׁ: וַיְהִי ׀ כִּזְרֹחַ הַשֶּׁמֶשׁ וַיְמַן אֱלֹהִים
רוּחַ קָדִים חֲרִישִׁית וַתַּךְ הַשֶּׁמֶשׁ עַל־רֹאשׁ יוֹנָה וַיִּתְעַלָּף

ט וַיִּשְׁאַל אֶת־נַפְשׁוֹ לָמוּת וַיֹּאמֶר טוֹב מוֹתִי מֵחַיָּי: וַיֹּאמֶר
אֱלֹהִים אֶל־יוֹנָה הַהֵיטֵב חָרָה־לְךָ עַל־הַקִּיקָיוֹן וַיֹּאמֶר הֵיטֵב

י חָרָה־לִי עַד־מָוֶת: וַיֹּאמֶר יְהֹוָה אַתָּה חַסְתָּ עַל־הַקִּיקָיוֹן אֲשֶׁר
לֹא־עָמַלְתָּ בּוֹ וְלֹא גִדַּלְתּוֹ שֶׁבִּן־לַיְלָה הָיָה וּבִן־לַיְלָה אָבָד:

יא וַאֲנִי לֹא אָחוּס עַל־נִינְוֵה הָעִיר הַגְּדוֹלָה אֲשֶׁר יֶשׁ־בָּהּ הַרְבֵּה
מִשְׁתֵּים־עֶשְׂרֵה רִבּוֹ אָדָם אֲשֶׁר לֹא־יָדַע בֵּין־יְמִינוֹ לִשְׂמֹאלוֹ
וּבְהֵמָה רַבָּה:

🕮 Jonah 🕮

Like the Books of Esther and Ruth, the Book of Jonah is a self-contained tale of adventure and travel but, in contrast to the former books, God is given a major role in the story. God is part of the action, rather than just instructing Jonah to be His messenger.

The Book of Jonah tells one of the best-known stories of the Hebrew Bible, but much of it remains an enigma. That fabulous creature, the "whale," fires our imagination. We marvel to see how it rescues and swallows Jonah and later disgorges him as a better man and a more obedient prophet (fig. 18). When Jonah suffers outside Nineveh and the gourd springs up and gives him shade, we feel mightily relieved but then we are suddenly plunged into despair, with Jonah, when a worm attacks the plant, and it withers and dies. For some reason, we eagerly follow the fortunes and misfortunes of poor Jonah; we respond sympathetically to these vicissitudes and that makes his Book so attractive to us all, and to our children. It is as if we were reading a fascinating fairy-tale, like Snow White and the wicked Witch, or Little Red-riding Hood and the Wolf. There is the little person beset by huge problems, one of them God Himself, although in the end, it is Nineveh that is left happy while Jonah does not live happily ever after. So is it just a fairy tale or is there more to it than that? As we shall see, the fantastic elements in the Book produce a political allegory related to the trials and tribulations of the northern kingdom of Israel.

In a larger sense, Jonah shows us a certain moral that we should allow to seep into our hearts. The moral would be one of repentance: that even the wicked people of a wicked city such as Nineveh can be made to repent and receive God's forgiveness. This is a nice idea and many commentators accept it (Driver 1891, 302; Oesterley and Robinson 1934, 375), suggesting it was a message written in the time of the scribe, Ezra, to show that God's acceptance will apply to all people and is not exclusive to the Jews, as Ezra was implying when he asked all Jews to put away their foreign partners (Ezra 9:2). That would be a fine universalistic idea, but what interest does it have for a Jewish prophet? We shall see there is no other Hebrew prophet who is interested in saving only a gentile people or city.

If the tale is not told for moral reasons, then why is it told at all? If it relates to actual circumstances in the history of Israel, as in the relationship between the kingdom of Northern Israel and the Assyrian Empire, how can we reconcile that with the introduction of fabulous creatures and plants?

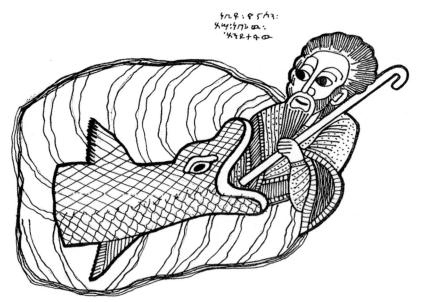

Fig. 18 *Jonah rescued by the Great Fish (from an Ethiopian orginal).*

It is our purpose to show that Jonah is not a fairy tale and not even a moral tale, but a political one, dressed up in the distinctive guise of allusion and allegory. One way to understand this approach is to recognize that it may be a very rare piece of Biblical Hebrew literature, the writing of a prophet from the camp of Northern Israel.

THE STORY

The story is short and the language simple. Jonah ben Amittai is commanded by God to go to Nineveh to warn its people to repent, because God has seen their evil doings. Jonah, however, gets on a boat to Tarshish, which is in the opposite direction, pays his fare and goes to sleep in the hold. A fearful storm arises, the ship is in danger and all the sailors pray to their god but without success. They wake Jonah who admits the storm is his fault and the sailors, albeit most reluctantly, throw Jonah overboard. The storm subsides and God instructs a great fish to swallow Jonah. Once inside the belly of the fish Jonah prays to God and vows to pay his respects to God's sanctuary. After three days the fish spews Jonah onto dry land and this time our hero makes the journey to Nineveh (see fig. 19).

Once there, he proclaims that the city will be destroyed within forty days unless the population repents from their evil ways. The people do repent, they and the king and even the animals fast and wear sackcloth. Their change of heart is so sincere that God alters his intentions and the city is saved. This displeases Jonah, who tells God he wishes to die.

Now Jonah goes and sits in a hut outside the city to see what will happen. A curious *qiqayon* plant grows overnight to protect him from his troubles, but by the next day it is gone, destroyed by a worm, and Jonah is left to suffer the scorching wind and sun, without shade or shelter. He again tells God he is ready to die, but God only replies that Jonah should stop mourning the loss of the *qiqayon*, think less of his own condition and realize that God is more concerned to save Nineveh, the great city, with "one hundred and twenty thousand people...and many cattle" (Jon. 4:11).

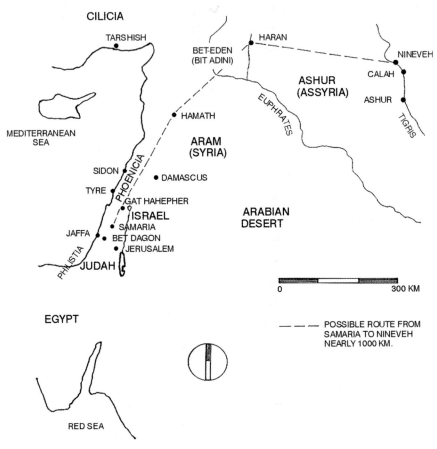

Fig. 19 *Map of Locations associated with Jonah, showing birthplace of Jonah ben Amittai (Gat Haḥepher) and possible route to Nineveh.*

JONAH AMONG THE PROPHETS

This account of Jonah's adventures is totally unlike the books of any other of the Hebrew prophets, whether the three major prophets Isaiah, Jeremiah and Ezekiel or the eleven other minor prophets. In fact, it is quite a surprise that Jonah is included among the Twelve (minor) Prophets and it is not clear why he has been placed between Obadiah and Micah. As mentioned, the Book of Jonah is a kind of novella, giving God a prominent place in instructing Jonah, and conducting a dialogue with him, but also in producing the great fish and a fabulous plant, and even personally accepting the repentance of Nineveh. The element of prophecy is restricted to just five Hebrew words: "another forty days and Nineveh will be overthrown" (Jon. 3:4) which are indeed given on God's instructions (3:2) but, outside of that short diatribe, God acts on Jonah alone, directing him hither and thither. It is not at all like the other prophets mentioned above, known as the "writing" prophets, but more like the early ones, Elijah and Elisha, whom God directs on their business, and who have not left us long speeches or visions of the future.

As Jonah appears in Nineveh, so Elijah appears to king Ahab, out of the blue, without warning but with an unsettling message (I Kgs. 17:1). He moves around the country and then appears again to Ahab and arranges the great cultic challenge to Ba'al on Mt. Carmel (18:20). When he flees to Horeb (Mt. Sinai) God meets him and charges him to carry out three duties (19:15,16). Like Jonah, it is a matter of jobs to do, rather than words to preach, and all the time Elijah has a direct link with God.

With his pupil, Elisha, it is similar. Elisha carries out a series of miracles rather than making pronouncements. He sweetens the waters at Jericho (2 Kgs. 2:22), he fills the widow's pots with oil (4:7), he promises the Shunammite a child and cures him of a fatal disease (4:16,35), he cures Na'aman of leprosy (5:14) and he saves the city of Samaria from siege (7:1). Elisha is a man of action, even political action, as when he instructs Hazael how to become king of Aram (Syria) by murdering his master, Ben-Hadad, the reigning monarch (8:10,15). His activities are all carried out in the name of God (13:17) rather than by making pronouncements in God's name. One action in particular has to be mentioned. On God's instructions, one of the three originally given to Elijah, Elisha sends "one of the sons of the prophets" to anoint the army commander, Jehu, to take on the role of regicide and seize the kingship from Joram, son of Ahab (9:1). This was the action, in the name of the Lord (9:6), of one of Elisha's trainees, "one of the sons of the prophets" whom the Midrash actually designates as Jonah (Rashi on 9:1 and cf. *MR.* Bereshith 21:5). Be that as it may, it was an action that changed the course of Israelite history. For Jehu was to kill off all the house of Ahab and their Ba'al worshippers, and in return, he would be allowed to set up his own dynasty of kings of Israel for four generations, as promised by God (2 Kgs.10:30).

Another unusual feature in Jonah is that he composes a prayer to God, while in the belly of the big fish. This prayer, comprising nearly the whole of Chapter 2, is in the form of a psalm, with many features and sentiments similar to several chapters of the Book of Psalms (particularly Psalm 116). This is not quite without parallel among the prophets, seeing that the last chapter of Habakkuk is also in the form of a psalm (3:1-19) but, with that one exception, Jonah's prayer-psalm is unique.

God not only plays a major role in Jonah, but he also has the last word. Several prophets commence their work at the personal invitation of God, a tradition going back to Moses (Ex. 3:4) whom God meets at the "burning bush." Isaiah has a vision and speaks to God and his angels (Isa. 6:8-11), Jeremiah is personally appointed by God and converses with Him (Jer. 1:4-19), while Ezekiel is instructed by God (Ezek. 2:1) but cannot respond in dialogue. In fact, once initiated, the prophets (except Moses and Elijah) only receive their words from God and cannot reply direct to Him. Jonah, however, is different. He is able to hear God and respond instantly and, at the end, even to converse with Him (Jon. 4:2-4, 8-11). Most unusually, the Book finishes with this second dialogue between Jonah and God. This is another unique feature.

However, not only does God play a large role in the Book, so also does evil (Heb. *ra'ah*). The books of the prophets are full of evil-doers and evil-doings but in Jonah there is a curious accent on evil itself, and especially the evil in Nineveh. The *evil* of Nineveh has come before God (Jon. 1:2); *evil* has come from somewhere to affect the sailors and their ship (1:8); the men of Nineveh turn away from their way of *evil* (3:8); God sees they have turned away from their ways of *evil* and He changes from His intention to do them *evil* (3:10). Jonah becomes *evil* with anger, and complains that God has turned away from doing His *evil* to Nineveh (4:1 & 2) and, finally, the fast-growing plant shades Jonah to save him from (literally, in Hebrew) his *evil* (4:6). There appear to be several forms of this *evil*, although all are called (in Hebrew) *ra'ah*, as we shall explain.

Unlike many of the other prophets, Jonah's language is simple and straightforward; it can hardly be called "poetic", except perhaps in the psalm sequence in Chapter 2. The language is plain early Hebrew, except for a few Aramaic terms, which could be taken as a reason to give it a late date when Aramaic became more common. These "late" terms include *sephinah* (ship) in 1:5; *shathaq* (to be still) in 1:12; and *amal* (to labour) in 4:10. If they really are Aramaicisms, they might suggest a post-Exilic date for Jonah in the 5th century BCE (see Allen 1976, 187, 188) but it may well be that the Book originates, as we have said, from a northern (Israel) prophet, who would be using Aramaic terms, owing to his proximity to Syria (Aram), well before his southern colleagues were adopting them.

PROBLEMATIC IMAGES AND EVENTS

As has been noted, the Book throws up a considerable number of problematic terms and situations, of which the most obvious is the role of the "big-fish," usually referred to as the "whale." But first there is a bigger problem, which we have already mentioned. Of what interest was the repentance of Nineveh to an Israelite prophet or to an Israelite audience? There is no parallel situation in the *Tanakh*, except perhaps Abraham's concern for the evil cities of Sodom and Gomorrah.

The dialogue of God and Abraham before the destruction of the two sinful cities (Gen. 18:23-32) is indeed remarkable for its length and detail. Abraham tries to persuade God to cancel the destruction of Sodom and Gomorrah for the sake of the number of good people (*tzadiqim*) in the cities, even if it were only ten, to which God agrees (18:32). As the destruction goes ahead we conclude there were not even ten good men and true in the twin cities. Abraham's concern was for the *tzadiqim,* not for the cities, and he accepts their destruction. In the case of Jonah it is not a question of numbers of people; he in fact is happy to see the city *and its people* destroyed and is only upset to see them escape punishment. He did not want the people to repent and then to see his prophecy proved wrong (Jon. 4:2).

And why choose Nineveh? It can hardly be an historical fact that it was saved by repentance and even if it was, how long did it last? If it is just a moral tale, would it not have been more telling to choose somewhere closer to home like Samaria or Dan or Beersheba, all cities which practiced idolatry?

As for other prophets concerning themselves with the fate of foreign states, we have the case of Amos, who inveighs against Damascus, Gaza, Tyre, Edom, Ammon and Moab (Amos 1:3- 2:3), but these are all kingships bordering on Israel and Judah; therefore, of immediate concern to Amos. And Amos does go on to criticize Judah and Israel as well at some length (2:4-16). So his case is quite different from Jonah and Nineveh. Nearer home is the case of Jeremiah, who gives a general description similar to that of Nineveh. He says:

At one moment I will say that a nation or kingdom be plucked up, pulled apart and destroyed; but if that nation turns from

the evil that I spoke about it, I will repent on the evil which I
calculated to do to it (Jer. 18:7,8).

The Midrash Rabbah (Exodus 45:1), recognizing the similarity of
wording, goes so far as to refer this general statement to Jonah's
Nineveh. But there is a fundamental difference, because Jeremiah
immediately gives the converse: that God will also destroy a good nation if it turns to evil, and he applies this to Judah and Jerusalem (Jer.
18:9-11). In the case of Jonah however no such connection is made
and why God chooses Nineveh as an example for repentance remains
a mystery.

Our explanation lies in the "evil" that God sees in Nineveh, "for
their *evil* has come up before Me" (Jon. 1:2). This means the evil of
Nineveh in relation to Israel and can represent either the evil of Assyria
in attacking Israel or the evil of Assyria in not coming to Israel's help.
Why Assyria? Because Nineveh became the military capital of Assyria
in the time of Sennacherib (705-681 BCE) and before that it was the
headquarters of the army of Shalmaneser III (858-824 BCE) and before him of Ashurnasirpal II (Saggs 1984, 98, 73). Nineveh was already
the site of an early temple of Ishtar that needed restoration in the time
of Shalmaneser I (c. 1260 BCE, Luckenbill 1989, I, 47). Consequently,
Nineveh is an ancient city and intimately linked to the Assyrian army
from at least 870 BCE.

Jonah always refers to it as "Nineveh, that great city," (Jon. 1:2;
3:2,3; 4:11) which harks back to its original mention in the Biblical
worldview:

From that land went out Ashur and built Nineveh .....the same
is the great city (Gen. 10:11,12).

"Nineveh, that great city" therefore represents in our view the great
army of the Assyrian Empire.

The Assyrian army was a trained force of well over 100,000 men. Shalmaneser III, who had made Nineveh its headquarters, mentions "crossing the Euphrates westwards (that is to the Levant) with an army of 120,000 men in 845" (Saggs 1984, 253: as Luckenbill 1989, I, 240). This is one of the few occasions on which Shalmaneser mentions the size of his own army, although he constantly boasts of the numbers he has defeated and captured.

If Nineveh is the Assyrian army and its evil is in relation to Israel, let us assume for the moment that the Assyrians were *evil* in not coming to the help of Israel. Jonah, however, does not go to Nineveh for help but first tries to go to Tarshish instead (Jon. 1:3). Tarshish is connected with the name of a city in Spain, Tartessus, thanks to Herodotus (I:163), who says the Phoenicians sailed there. But there is no need to go so far afield, since the famous port of Tarsus in southern Anatolia (fig. 19) is much closer and its local name is exactly equivalent to the Hebrew *Tarshish*. Although Tarshish (Tarsus) is a renowned ancient port, it is also the name given to a kind of boat well known in Biblical times (see fig. 20). Solomon had a combined "Tarshish navy" with Hiram, the Phoenician king of Tyre, going east for luxury goods (I Kgs.10:22); Jehoshaphat, some hundred years later, tried the same thing, but his "ships of Tarshish" were broken and foundered at Ezion-geber (22:49). The east wind has the power of "breaking the boats of Tarshish" (Psalms 48:8), while the prophet Ezekiel describes the boats of Tarshish and their rich merchandise:

> Tarshish was your merchant because of all its riches, in silver, iron, tin, and lead, they gave (you) their goods (Ezek. 27:12); and
> The ships of Tarshish were your masters for your exchange (27:25).

Ezekiel tells us the ships of Tarshish brought their rich goods to

Tyre, Sidon, Gebal and Arvad (27:3-11) and also further afield, but the specified towns are all on the Lebanese coast in ancient Phoenicia. These Phoenicians were the great merchant sailors of the Levant; it would seem that Jonah, in trying to proceed to Tarshish, was going to elicit help from the Phoenicians, who were settled on the coast just north of Israel. If Jonah was looking for help for Israel (as we will suggest) it would be much easier and quicker to seek it in nearby Phoenicia than to travel one thousand kilometers (six hundred miles or so) to Nineveh.

Fig. 20 *"Ships of Tarshish", a Phoenician two-level Galley equipped for War. Note the two levels of oars and a third upper level protected by shields. This ship was built and manned by Phoenicians but employed by the Assyrian Emperor Sennacherib (704-681 BCE). From the Palace of Nineveh, now in the Assyrian Salon in the British Museum (from Casson 1994, 56).*

But Jonah did not succeed in reaching the Phoenician coast. "God thrust a great wind at the sea," which threatened to break the boat (Jon. 1:4). This wind was, in fact, a storm (Heb. *sa'ar*), a wind of gigantic proportions commanded by God, as in, "fire and hail. . . stormy wind (*ruah se'arah*) do His bidding" (Psalms 148:8). To the local peoples of the Levant and Mesopotamia the god of storm is Adad or Hadad (see fig. 21). In the Epic of Gilgamesh "a black cloud rose up. . . inside it Adad thunders"; the code of Hammurabi talks of a field that "Adad has inundated," and Shalmaneser III offered "sacrifices before the Adad of Aleppo" (Pritchard 1958, 68, 144, 190). It seems, therefore, that the god of storm, Hadad, is preventing Jonah from reaching the Phoenician coast. This Hadad can really only be Ben-Hadad, king of Aram (Syria).

There were probably three Ben-Hadads ruling Syria throughout the years of the ninth century BCE. Ben Hadad I (ben Tabrimmon) in the time of Baasha (908-885), Ben-Hadad II, ruling in the time of Ahab (873-852) and Ben-Hadad III in the time of Jehoahaz (819-803). The *Tanakh* mentions them in constant conflict with their neighbor, the northern kingdom of Israel (I Kgs. 15:18-20; 20:1,26; 2 Kgs. 6:24) but also once in friendly relationship with them, as when Ahab makes a covenant with Ben-Hadad (probably Ben-Hadad II) in Samaria (I Kgs. 20:34). For this, however, he is heavily criticized by an anonymous prophet (20:42), which indicates that the Ben-Hadads were always seen as potential enemies of Israel, the northern kingdom. Some historians doubt the existence of Ben-Hadad II and give that title to the one contemporary with Jehoahaz (Miller and Hayes 1986, 263, 264). Others agree that there was a Ben-Hadad III (Galil 1996, 54,55).

The storm (Ben-Hadad) prevents Jonah from reaching Tarshish (the Phoenicians) and forces the sailors to throw him overboard (Jon. 1:15) into the sea, from which he is rescued by the great fish (2:1). This fish is not a whale, although that is the popular notion, based on the Greek translation of "great fish" which is *kitos*, meaning both large fish and whale. But the Hebrew is clear: it is *dag gadol* or great fish. An equivalent Hebrew term would be *dag-on*, also translated as "great fish" (Gesenius 1885, 189) or "mighty fish," spelled with or without the Hebrew letter *aleph*. Such a creature represents *Dagon*, chief god of the Philistines, as described in the Books of Judges and Samuel. For example, Samson was finally captured and brought in chains before the Philistines, who were gathered together to offer "great sacrifice to *Dagon* their god" (Judg. 16:23).

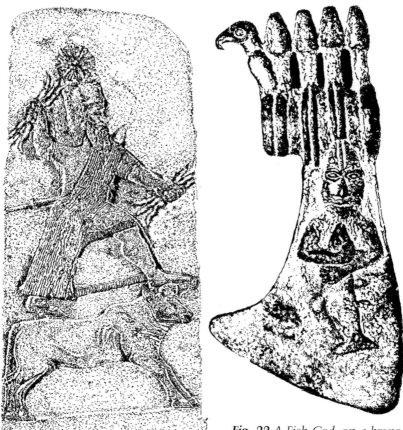

Fig. 21 *Adad, the Storm God riding on a Bull and grasping Thunderbolts in his hands. 8th Century BCE from Arslan Tash, Syria, now in the Louvre (from Pritchard 1958, ill. 40).*

Fig. 22 *A Fish God, on a bronze Axe from a tomb in Luristan (Iran), the blade decorated by a fabulous figure holding a fish, "symbol of the Mesopotamian god EA and the Canaanite god Dagon" (Godard 1965, 48 and fig. 13).*

Modern authorities claim that the name of the god *Dagon* is equivalent to *Dagan* (lit. corn) and that he is a corn or harvest god. But in
Biblical terms he is a fish-form god (cf. fig. 22), as is made clear when
the Philistines capture the Ark of the Covenant and place it in the
House of *Dagon*. There, the Ark causes the idol of *Dagon* to break into
two parts, with the head and arms fallen to the ground and "only his
fish-part *(dagon)* left standing" (I Sam. 5:4). Not far inland from the
coast of Jaffa (Joppa) is the village of *Bet-Dagon*, the House of *Dagon*,
which Sennacherib conquered in his advance on Jerusalem (Luckenbill
1989, II, 119) and which presumably housed a temple to *Dagon*. The
"dag-gadol" is thus *Dag-on*, and represents the Philistines.

As an aside, we note that Robert Graves considered that "the whale
in the Book of Jonah is clearly a metaphor of the sea-power of Tyre and
Sidon, Phoenician maritime cities lying to the north-west of Israel"
(Graves 1972, 32). To our mind this was an inspired comment even if
slightly off the mark.

Although Jonah has not been able to reach the Phoenicians to gain
their help, it seems that he succeeds in reaching *Dagon*, or the Philistines, to receive their protection for a short period, represented by the
three days that he is reported to be in the belly of the great fish (Jon.
2:1). This, however, is only a temporary reprieve, after which Jonah is
spewed out and finally realizes that only from Nineveh can he get the
help he so desperately needs, as God tells him for the second time
(3:2). Now he finally goes to Nineveh and, on arrival, threatens it with
destruction within forty days (3:4). The men of Nineveh take this very
seriously and start to fast and to put on sackcloth (3:5). The king hears
of the threat and also puts on sackcloth; and the royal decree commands the men, the cattle and the flocks all to fast and don sackcloth,
and to cry to God (3:6-8). They all turn from their ways of *evil*, and
when God sees this, He also turns away from the *evil* He had intended
to do to Nineveh (3:9,10).

When the men and cattle of Nineveh turn away from their *evil*, this means they realize their fault in not coming to the aid of Israel and they get ready to do so. How is that achieved? By fasting and donning sackcloth (3:5). Fasting was recommended before the start of battle. Saul called a fast of all his men before engaging battle with the Philistines (I Sam. 14:24) and nearly killed his own son Jonathan for unwittingly breaking that command (14:44,45). But even clearer than that, was the act of donning sackcloth. Although it is often taken as a sign of mourning or abasement (for example Gen. 37:34) here it has military overtones. Sackcloth was regularly worn under suits of armor, which were liable to cut the flesh. We know that the Assyrian army had sophisticated coats of chain mail that could be molded to the contours of the human body (Mitchell 1988, 57) but which required an undergarment of hair or sack to protect the skin. The Philistines also wore armor that was similar to the scales of a fish; Goliath was protected by body-armor of scales (*qasqasim*, I Sam. 17:5), which must have also required a protective undergarment. The Hebrew word used for sackcloth is *saq*, which equates to the Greek *sakkos*. The related Greek word *sagos* means a soldier's cloak, being made of sack-like material; and in Latin, *saga sumere*, "to put on the saga" meant to go to war, to take up arms (Lewis and Short 1879, 1617).

It should be noted that the cattle and sheep also put on sackcloth (Jon. 3:8). Is that believable? This seems to make it clear that we are not talking literally of mourning or repentance, for why should the animals get involved in that? But as we are talking of the Assyrian army preparing to take up arms, it is possible that the cattle and sheep refer to the auxiliary units of the army, the non-fighting units such as the supply and transport units. Alternatively, it can be taken more literally, as the large herds of animals that accompanied the ancient armies to draw wagons and to act as a food supply to the troops, the whole army marching, as one says "on the hoof." For instance, after one battle, the Assyrian Emperor Sargon II destroys the enemy's settlement, saying, "like swarming locusts I turned the beasts of my camps into its meadows" (Luckenbill 1989, II, 85). These auxiliary units had to prepare themselves in the same way as the fighting men, and so they too "put on sackcloth," on the orders of the king (Jon. 3:8).

At this stage, the great Assyrian army has been mustered and is ready for battle (see fig. 23). And then, nothing. Chapter 3 stops abruptly. We hear nothing further concerning the army's destination or its activities. At this point, we need to go back and explain the reason for Jonah having run (finally) to Nineveh to summon the Assyrian army.

Fig. 23 *The Assyrian Army on the march; pairs of sling-shooters c. 700 BCE, note the scale armor protecting the body. From Lachish Relief in the Palace of Sennacherib at Nineveh, now in British Museum (see Mitchell 1988, 60).*

▧ *THE SIEGE OF SAMARIA*

Here we have come to the crux of our explanation. What was the event that prompted God to see the *evil* of Nineveh, which in our terms made it necessary for Jonah to seek the help of Assyria and press them to take up arms on behalf of Israel? It must have been at a time when Israel was in great peril from an enemy, who could only be defeated or at least drawn off by that great super-power, Assyria.

Assyria dominated the Near East for some three hundred years from about 900 to 612 BCE (Roaf 1990, 164,179) and during that time its power over the Levant waxed and waned with the power and energy of its own emperors. From about 740 BCE, the Assyrian Emperor Tiglath-Pileser III started to invade Israel; by 722 BCE the whole of the northern kingdom of Israel had been wiped out by Sargon II and his predecessor Shalmaneser V. But before Tiglath-Pileser, Assyria's power was less direct and it managed to protect Israel from its closer enemies, such as Aram (Syria), by exerting a restraining influence on local conflicts. So much is clear from the famous Black Obelisk of Shalmaneser III, which shows Jehu, king of Israel (842-815 BCE), among others, paying tribute to the Assyrian Emperor, who had come to the West (the Levant) to check on his client kingdoms (fig. 24). That was in the year 841 or 842 BCE, when he defeated Damascus of Syria but not Israel, since Jehu, who had recently ascended the throne, had paid him sufficient tribute (Miller and Hayes 1986, 260).

However, after the death of the energetic Shalamaneser III in 824 BCE, the power of Assyria declined for a period and it did not again exercise an active role in the West, that is in Syria, Lebanon and Israel, until the rise of Tiglath-Pileser III in 744 BCE (ibid. 296, 318). In those 80 years from 824 to 744, Israel (and Judah) was relatively free of Assyrian domination but, on the other hand, they did not enjoy Assyria's protection from their local enemies, the chief of whom was Aram (Syria) on the northern border of Israel.

As mentioned above, the Ben-Hadads of Aram were active in attacking Israel from the time of Israel's King Baasha onwards. In the Books of Kings, which record this period, the worst crisis in the northern kingdom of Israel was the siege of Samaria, conducted by Ben-Hadad (2 Kgs. 6:24), most probably our Ben-Hadad III, who came to the throne in about 810 BCE (Miller & Hayes 1986, 301). The name of the king of Israel however is not given in the account. He is just referred to as "the king" (6:28, 30). The siege was so terrible that:

> The head of an ass sold for eighty pieces of silver and a quarter-kab of bird-dung for five (6:26).

In desperation women were forced to eat their own children and the king was powerless to help them (6:28-30).

The king blames the prophet Elisha for this tragedy, and tries to have him killed, but Elisha, calling the king "this son of a murderer" (6:32) predicts that the siege will be lifted the next day (7:1). Elisha's description of the king gives us a small clue. The "murderer" seems to be king Ahab,

Fig. 24 *King Jehu of Israel paying homage to Shalmaneser III of Assyria (858-824 BCE). Detail from the Black Obelisk showing the "tribute of YAUA ben Humri" (Jehu son of Omri) in 841/2 BCE from Nimrud, now in the British Museum (EA 28).*

who murdered Naboth by a false judicial process (1 Kgs. 21:13) and his son would be Jehoram, who reigned from 851-842 BCE. But the death of Naboth was more the concern of Elijah (21:20) than that of his successor, Elisha; moreover, Ahab had made a treaty with Ben-Hadad (20:33,34) which makes it unlikely that that Ben-Hadad, that is Ben Hadad II, would have come back to besiege Ahab's son in Samaria.

It is much more likely that it was Hazael's son, Ben-Hadad III, who besieged Samaria in the reign of Israel's king Jehoahaz (819-803) son of Jehu (as Rofé 1988, 73; *contra* Hallo 1998, 124). Jehu was also a famous murderer. Originally, at the behest of Elisha, he was told that the house of Ahab was to be destroyed (2 Kgs. 9:8). However, Jehu went far beyond his instructions and murdered not only Jezebel, wife of Ahab, and Jehoram, his son, but also his brother-in-law, Ahaziah, king of Judah (9:27); in cold blood he ordered the slaughter of Ahab's other seventy sons (10:7), forty-two of Ahaziah's close relatives (10:14) and finally all the priests of Ba'al, whom he put to the sword (10:25). Jehu was a murderer indeed, perhaps even in the eyes of Elisha, who had given instructions for him to be anointed king (9:2,3). Furthermore, this murderer's son, Jehoahaz, was well and truly harassed by Aram (Syria) throughout his reign:

> And the anger of God burned against Israel, and He gave them into the hand of Hazael, king of Aram, and that of Ben-Hadad son of Hazael all their days. And Jehoahaz sought the face of God, and God heard him, for He saw the oppression of Israel, that the king of Aram oppressed them. And God gave Israel a savior and they came out from under the hand of Aram and the children of Israel lived in their tents (homes) as yesteryear and before (13:3-5).

This passage describes the oppression of Jehoahaz by Ben Hadad III and how Israel was finally delivered by a mystery "savior," and not by God alone. Many commentators consider that savior to have been Assyria, in the person of Adadnirari III and his army, who came to the West on several campaigns in the years between 805 and 796 BCE (Miller and Hayes 1986, 292; Hallo 1998, 126). Could one of these campaigns have drawn off Ben-Hadad and the Syrians (Aram) from the siege of Samaria to go and protect their northern border and Damascus from the Assyrian army? It is more than likely that this was so.

The Book of Kings, in a passage just after the one quoted above, tells us that:

> There was not left to Jehoahaz (any) people except fifty horsemen and ten chariots and ten companies (*aluphim*) of foot soldiers, for the king of Aram destroyed them and made them like dust (2 Kgs. 13:7).

This sounds uncommonly like the few troops left to the king at the siege of Samaria:

> Let them take five of the remaining horses...for they are all that are left of the multitudes of Israel....and they took two chariots....to go and see (if the enemy had withdrawn), (7:13,14).

As we have said, in the time of Jehu, the Assyrian Emperor Shalmaneser III had come to the West, conquered Damascus and kept Aram from attacking Israel. Jehu had paid tribute to Shalmaneser to keep the Assyrians on his side. But when Shalmaneser withdrew and later died, Aram was able to regroup and resume its attacks on Israel, under Hazael and his son Ben-Hadad III. Samaria was then at the mercy of Aram, with no one to save them. Where was Assyria, who had helped them some forty years previously? Why was Assyria so *evil* as to leave its army in Nineveh and not come to the help of Jehoahaz, king of

Israel? It appears that eventually Adadnirari III did march onto the borders of Aram and act as the "savior" of Israel (Galil 1996, 56; Hallo 1998, 126). This is the salvation described in the Second Book of Kings (13:5) and engineered by our hero Jonah.

🕮 THE HISTORY OF JONAH

We can now reconstruct the events alluded to in the Book of Jonah. The siege of Samaria is under way and famine is biting hard. The king Jehoahaz is helpless and his army seriously depleted. The prophet Elisha, though at loggerheads with the king, is personally involved and realizes that the only help in the long term would be the Assyrian army, which has been absent from the area for forty years. He (playing God) therefore decides to dispatch his pupil, Jonah, to contact the Assyrians, to Nineveh. Jonah thinks Nineveh, some thousand kilometers away, is too far to be of help and opts instead for Phoenicia (*Tarshish*). However, Phoenicia cannot help, as Jonah is prevented by the long arm of Ben-Hadad (the *storm*) from reaching them, and he is saved by getting aid from the Philistines (*Dag-on*, the great fish); but it is only temporary relief and Jonah is forced to return to Elisha, who tells him again it must be *Nineveh* – that is, the Assyrian army, which has to come to the rescue.

At this period it could well be that the Assyrian army, at least in part, was stationed at *Bit Adini*, or Beth Eden (see fig. 19) to the north of Syria, where the local Assyrian ruler was Shamshi-ilu, the *turtanu* or general of the Emperor Adadnirari III (Hallo 1998, 128; CAH.1982, III Pt.1,405). If indeed the army was there, then Jonah had a journey of only 560 kilometres (350 miles) from Samaria. With the benefit of relays of horses over good routes, he might just have achieved the journey in three days:

And Nineveh was a great city to God, a journey of three days (Jon. 3:3).

Presumably Jonah was able to bring pressure of some sort to bear on the Assyrians to induce them to advance towards Syria (Aram). It is equally, if not more, likely that it suited the Assyrians to come West again anyway, and the help to Israel was a by-product of their actions rather than the prime motive. The Assyrian Emperor Adadnirari III reigned from 810 to 783 BCE and conducted at least three campaigns to the West, in 805, 803/2 and 796 BCE (Miller and Hayes 1986, 292). The last one, recorded by Adadnirari on his stela at Rimah (Northern Iraq) is dated to 796 (see fig. 25) and records tribute received from Jehoash (Joash) of Samaria, the son of Jehoahaz (Miller and Hayes 1986, 299), so presumably it was one of his earlier campaigns that helped to lift the siege of Samaria for Jehoahaz (819 to 803 BCE). We can there-fore date the end of the siege to about 804 or 803 BCE. Confirmation of these events seems to be contained in the set of cryptic verses of 2 Kgs. 13:3-5 quoted previously.

The account of the siege and its aftermath also gives us clues. It seems Elisha was able to predict the siege would be over on a certain day (2 Kgs.7:1); perhaps he was briefed by his faithful acolyte Jonah. But more than that, the description of the raising of the siege describes the following curious scene:

> God had made the camp of Aram hear the voice of chariot and horse, the voice of a great army, and the men (had) said to each other, 'Behold, the king of Israel has hired against us the kings of the *Hittim* (Hittites) and the kings of *Mitzrayim* (Egypt) to come at us'; and they rose and fled (7:6,7).

Furthermore, they fled towards the east, to the Jordan, for when the Israelite soldiers came to check the retreat of the Aramean army, they followed them all the way "to the Jordan" (7:15). Taken together, these accounts allow us to reconstruct the lifting of the siege. The soldiers *did* hear the sounds of the Hittites and the Egyptians. The

Fig. 25 *Adadnirari III (810-783 BCE) on the Rimah (Iraq) stele reporting his expeditions to Hatti land (the West, Syria) when he received tribute from King IA'ASU (Joash son of Jehoahaz) of Samaria, Israel. The stele is 1.3m. high and stands in the British School of Archaeology in Iraq (from Miller and Hayes 1986, 288, 299).*

"Hittites," being in the north, could really have been the northern Phoenicians of *Tarshish* whom Jonah had tried to contact, and the "Egyptians" in the south, would have been the Philistines of *Dagon* coming to his aid from the south. The Arameans fleeing to the Jordan, would have been rushing to the north, via the Jordan valley, to protect their border from the Assyrians of Adadnirari III, or more probably his general, Shamshi-ilu. This cryptic verse then makes sense in the context of Jonah's attempts to lift the siege.

This concludes Chapter 3 of Jonah: Samaria is saved and Israel is saved. However, in Chapter 4, Jonah is suddenly very displeased again (Jon. 4:1) and we have to look at the subsequent events in the history of Israel, the northern kingdom, to understand why this is so.

THE DYNASTY OF JEHU AND ITS AFTERMATH

The dynasty of Jehu started in blood and ended, four generations later, in blood. Jehu came to the throne of Israel by murdering Joram (Jehoram) son of Ahab in 842 BCE. He not only killed the reigning king but he wiped out the whole house of Ahab, the priests of Ba'al and even Ahaziah, king of Judah, who happened to be related to the house of Ahab (2 Kgs. 9 and 10). Elijah had been told in prophecy that he should anoint Jehu as king (I Kgs.19:16), but in the circumstances it was his successor Elisha, who took the necessary steps (2 Kgs 9:1-3). Furthermore, God spoke directly to Jehu to promise him that his dynasty would rule for four generations (10:30) and so it was (see fig. 26).

Jehu reigned for 28 years (10:36) from 842 to 815 BCE and was succeeded by his son Jehoahaz, who suffered greatly from marauding attacks by the Arameans (Syrians) under Hazael, who had already cut Transjordan off from Israel at the time of Jehu (10:33). After Hazael, Ben-Hadad his son, who was Ben-Hadad III, continued to harass Israel (13:3) and it was under him that Samaria suffered the terrible siege that is described in 2 Kgs. 6 and 7 (see above). That siege was lifted with the help of an outside power, as enigmatically described in Second Kings:

> And the Lord gave to Israel a savior, and they went out from under the hand of Aram, and the children of Israel dwelt in their tents as yesteryear and before (13:5).

This seems indeed to describe the Assyrians coming to the aid of Israel, who were reduced to a very sorry state, to a tiny army (13:7), whose description is parallel to the deficiencies of the Israelite army during the siege. There the king is persuaded to send out scouts with only five of the remaining horses and just two chariots, most of what was left of his army (7:13).

Jehoahaz's successor Jehoash or Joash (805-790 BCE) had an easier time. The prophet Elisha, by then an old man, foretold that he would "smite Aram three times" and in the course of three battles he regained "out of the hand of Ben-Hadad" the cities that his father had lost to Aram (13:25). The power of Aram had been broken and Joash's son Jeroboam II (790-750 BCE) was able to expand Israel's northern border to Lebo-Hamath (modern Hama, on the Orontes, in Syria) in his long and successful reign of 41 years (14:23). But his success was not to last. Although the power of Aram had been broken, Assyria was now in the ascendant. This giant had been slumbering since the time of Adadnirari III (810 - 783 BCE) but was now reawakening under the vigorous Tiglath-Pileser III (744-727 BCE) who resumed forays to the West, taking territory and tribute as he came. Whereas Adadnirari III had saved Israel by threatening Aram on its northern border in about 803 BCE, the collapse of Aram left a territorial vacuum that Israel, under Jeroboam II, was to fill from the south and that later Assyria was to fill from the north. Assyria was by far the stronger party and, after Jeroboam II, Israel was forced to give way to its former "savior."

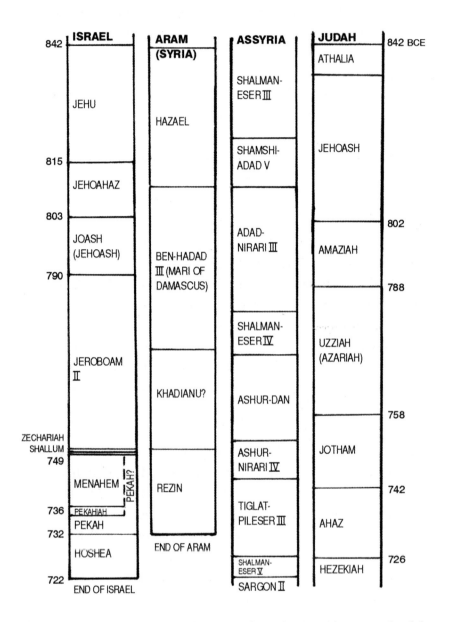

Fig. 26 *Comparative Chart of the Kings of Israel, Aram, Assyria and Judah, 840-720 BCE. For the sake of clarity, co-regencies have been omitted (Israel and Judah based on Galil 1996; Aram and Assyria on Miller and Hayes 1986 and CAH. III, Pt. 1, 1982).*

Jeroboam's son, Zechariah, was the last of the dynasty of four promised by God to Jehu, and he reigned for only six months (2 Kgs.15:8).
It can be assumed that his father had reigned in relative harmony with
his powerful neighbor, Assyria, which at the time was not asserting
itself in the "West," on the Levantine coast, that included the kingdom of Israel. His weak son Zechariah will have followed in his father's
footsteps, in this pro-Assyrian policy.

That, however, will not have been to the people's liking, since they
could see the awesome might of Assyria looming on the horizon. They
will have wanted to see an alliance with Egypt, the only other super-
power in the area, and the only one capable of facing up to Assyria. So
the reign of Zechariah was not to last and came to a quick end after
six months, when he was murdered and the throne usurped by one
Shallum ben Jabesh (15:10) in the year 749 BCE. Like so many other
usurpers in the kingdom of Israel, including Jehu himself (9:5), this
Shallum was predictably a tough military man who, in contrast to
Zechariah and his father, favored the Egyptian connection as a bul-
wark against Assyria. But his moment of power was brief indeed; after
only one month he was murdered by Menahem ben Gadi (15:14) who
reigned in his stead for ten years (749-738 BCE). This Menahem bore
the full brunt of the Assyrian ascendancy under Tiglath-Pileser, "king
of Ashur who came up against the land (of Israel)." So he bought him
off with a bribe of :

...a thousand talents of silver, for his hands to be with him to
strengthen the kingdom in his hands (15:19).

In other words, Menahem paid Tiglath-Pileser to strengthen his
(Menahem's) grip over the kingdom of Israel and also to buy him off
from attacking the land. He did this in a rather shrewd way, by ex-
tracting the necessary silver from the population itself (15:20). It was
a deeply unpopular move. He also perpetrated the most monstrously

cruel act of punishing the city of Tiphsah, which had refused to cede to him:

...so he smote it... and cut open all its pregnant women (15:16).

Menahem terrorized the people and taxed the landed gentry, forcing all into a mold acceptable to the Assyrians. His son Pekahiah reigned after him for only two years, until he was killed by another ambitious army commander, Pekah ben Remaliah (15:25). We can assume that Pekahiah had followed his father's pro-Assyrian policy, for which he was murdered by his general, Pekah, responding to the people's demand for an end to Assyrian accommodation, and a rapprochement with Egypt.

So much is also clear from the account in Isaiah, which describes the alliance of Pekah ben Remaliah with Rezin, king of Aram. They try to force Jerusalem and Judah to join them in a confederation against Assyria, which Isaiah wisely advises against (Isa.7:1-6). In fact, the king of Judah, Ahaz, saves himself from their attack by appealing directly to Assyria for help (2 Kgs.16:7) and later going to Damascus to meet Tiglath-Pileser, who had by that time conquered it from Aram and killed Rezin its king (16:9-10). As for Pekah ben Ramaliah, most of his territory of Israel was captured by Tiglath-Pileser and the people taken into captivity (15:29). Pekah, though pro-Egypt, survived, but only to be murdered by Hoshea ben Elah, who took over the throne of Israel in 732 BCE. Hoshea served as a client king of Assyria, sending annual tribute to the Emperor Shalmaneser V (17:3) but, after some years of apparent Assyrian disregard, he was tempted to throw off the Assyrian yoke and made overtures to the Egyptian king So, perhaps Pharaoh Osorkon IV (Miller and Hayes 1986, 336). The Assyrians uncovered this act of treason and put Hoshea in prison and besieged his capital, Samaria. After three years of siege, the city fell (2 Kgs.17:4,5). Thus came to an end the kingdom of Israel in the year 722 BCE, when Shalmaneser's successor, Sargon II captured the city and exiled its inhabitants (17:6; Miller and Hayes 1986, 338; Pritchard 1958; 195). From the accession of Jehu to the fall of the kingdom of Israel, had been a tumultuous period of one hundred and twenty years (see fig. 26).

📜 *JONAH AFTER NINEVEH*

In our brief history of the last one hundred and twenty years of Israel, we have seen only one outstanding reign, that of Jeroboam ben Joash or Jeroboam II. He reigned for forty-one years and:

> He restored the border of Israel from Lebo-Hamath to the sea
> of the Arabah, as the word of the Lord, God of Israel as He
> (had) instructed by the hand of His servant, Jonah ben Amittai
> the prophet, who was from Gath Hahepher (2 Kgs.14:25).

Before proceeding further with Chapter 4 of Jonah, we shall examine this Jonah ben Amittai to see what correlation there is, if any, with the Jonah ben Amittai claimed to be the author of the Book of Jonah.

So far we have tried to demonstrate that the events of Chapters 1 to 3 are related to the siege of Samaria during the reign of Jehoahaz, and to salvation by Assyria taking place in about the year 803 BCE. If Jonah was involved in contacting the Assyrians, he must have been at least twenty years old at the time, placing his birth at the latest in, say, 823 BCE. Jeroboam II, the grandson of Jehoahaz, reigned from 790 to 750 BCE; so Jonah would have been about 33 years of age at the beginning of his reign and 73 if he survived it. Although that is a good age for the period, it is not an impossible one. Curiously enough, Jewish tradition has it that Jonah lived to a very good old age, and his merit was to enter paradise alive (Ginzberg 1968, IV,253). Be that as it may, he could well have been court prophet to Jeroboam II, as the Book of Kings states, being between 33 and 73 years old at the time.

He will have experienced the great saving of Samaria by Assyria in 803 BCE and, towards the end of Jeroboam's reign, he will have seen the potential danger of an Assyrian empire growing steadily stronger and more assertive.

Second Kings 14:25 says Jonah ben Amittai came from a place called Gath-Hahepher. The site is mentioned as Gath-hepher in the inheritance of the tribe Zebulun (Josh. 19:13), which supports its generally accepted identification with the village of Mash-ḥad, located 4 miles (6 km.) north-east of Nazareth, in the Lower Galilee (Aharoni 1979, 257, 434). There is a small *tel* (ancient mound), called Tel Gath-ḥepher (Arabic - *Khirbet ez-Zurra'a*) just above the village, overlooking the entire central Lower Galilee from the Carmel in the west to Qarnei-Ḥittim in the east. According to recent surveys, the *tel* was occupied almost continuously from the Early Bronze Age to the Byzantine Period, a time line of some two thousand years.

During the Iron Age, the period we are interested in, it was a fortified town of four-roomed houses, destroyed in the later eighth century BCE by one of the Assyrian campaigns of Tiglath-Pileser III, when he devastated the Galilee. Thereafter, the site was abandoned for about three hundred years until the Persian period (Alexandre et al. 2003). Today the village retains several Jonah relics. An ancient large oak on the outskirts is named *Batmet Nebi Yunas* (oak of the prophet Jonah) and there is a heavily restored tomb in Jonah's name beside the local mosque (fig. 27).

The site identification shows that Jonah ben Amittai came from a town well into the territory of the northern kingdom of Israel, as ruled from the capital in Samaria. If he was born, as we have said, around 823 BCE, it is most unlikely that he lived to see the terrible destruction meted out to his home town and to the Galilee in general by Tiglath-Pileser in his campaign of 733 BCE (Gal 1992, 108, 9; Hallo 1998, 132), but he may well have lived beyond the reign of Jeroboam II and seen the rapid decline of Israel that followed. Jeroboam's son, Zedekiah, reigned for only six months, his murderer and usurper

Shallum ben Yabesh for only one month, and he was murdered in turn by the cruel Menahem, as mentioned above. In other words one year saw the reign of four monarchs (Jeroboam II, Zedekiah, Shallum, Menahem), a real sign of turmoil and weakness, and Jonah would have recognized the warning signs.

If Jonah ben Amittai, court prophet to Jeroboam II, was indeed the Jonah of the Book, he would have been that rare bird, a writing prophet of the northern kingdom. Although the origin of many of the Twelve (minor) Prophets is obscure, they really all came from the south, from Judah. The later ones lived after the destruction of the northern kingdom and, of the earlier ones whose origins are not given, only Hosea is likely to have come from the north. His preoccupation with the Valley of Jezre'el (Hos.1:5) points to a northern origin, but on the other hand his superscription (1:1), saying he was active in the time of four kings of Judah (as well as one king of Israel) suggests he was allied more with the south than the north.

Fig. 27 *The so-called Tomb of Jonah at the mosque of Mash-ḥad, ancient Gath Hepher, near Nazareth in northern Israel (photograph 1996).*

There were, of course, other true prophets in the north, such as Ahijah of Shiloh, at the time of Jeroboam I (1 Kgs.11:29), Micaiah ben Imlah, who so vexed Ahab (22:8), and indeed Elisha ben Shaphat from Abel-Meholah, in the north near Bet-Shean (19:16). However, they were not writing prophets, those whose words were recorded in their own separate books. We do not have any indication of their literary style and output. Therefore, it could well be that the Book of Jonah represents a unique example of the words and work of a northern prophet, as recorded in a separate book. As such, it is quite possible that its literary style and genre would be different from that of the other prophetic works. We suggest that the events of the turmoil and weakness of the kingdom of Israel, following the reign of Jeroboam II, were not only witnessed by Jonah ben Amittai, but were recorded metaphorically in Chapter 4 of the Book in his name.

ᗰᗩ JONAH, CHAPTER 4

The beginning of Chapter 4 is a short interchange between Jonah and God. Jonah is feeling the effects of "evil," in fact a great evil (Heb. *ra'ah gedolah*) and prays to God saying, 'all this explains why I fled to Tarshish, for I knew You would forgive them, and You would regret the "evil" you planned to do to them; so please, God, take my life.' To which God simply answers, "Are you so well and truly angry?" (Jon. 4:1-4). After this little dialogue, Jonah goes out and sits to the east of the city in a little booth "until he would see what was to be in the city" (4:5). The implications are clear. Jonah is upset that Nineveh has repented – that God has refused to destroy it and that his prophecy has proved false. He wishes to die but waits outside the city to see what will happen.

The curious thing is that we never hear any more about what happens to the city, except in the last verse, which confirms that God wanted all along to save "Nineveh, that great city" (4:11). In between, Jonah suffers a series of trials, which can be summarized in five stages as follows:

1. Jonah sits to the east of the city, in a temporary shelter (*sukkah*),
2. God prepares a special plant (*qiqayon*) to give Jonah shade (presumably the *sukkah* shelter has disappeared),
3. God prepares a crimson worm (*tola'ath*), which destroys the plant the next day,
4. God prepares a cutting east wind (*ruaḥ qadim*) and hot sun (Jonah blacks out and asks to die),
5. God criticizes Jonah for regretting the death of the *qiqayon* plant.

To enable us to relate these trials to Israelite history, we first have to clarify the meaning of "the city" in 4:5. It is not Nineveh at all; which has been described throughout as "Nineveh, that great city" (1:2; 3:2; 4:11), and never as "the city." It is that other city which concerns Jonah: Samaria, capital of Israel. When Jonah sits to the east of it, it implies that he is looking east, towards Assyria, to see what will happen to Samaria from that quarter.

So much is also implied from that little interlude of four verses where Jonah and God discuss Jonah's feelings of anger at "the great evil" (4:1-4). Here we are back to the "evil" of Assyria, but now it is "great evil" (4:1). The *evil* of Assyria had been its unwillingness to come to the aid of Israel in its time of need, at the siege of Samaria by Aram in about 804 BCE. That *evil* was assuaged when the Assyrian army marched to the West in 803 BCE. But now there is a greater *evil*, as Assyria itself seems to be preparing to march on Israel, perhaps even on Samaria, the capital. That is the "great evil" that Jonah now fears.

ᗧ JONAH, THE HISTORICAL CONTEXT

Looking at the five trials suffered by Jonah we can see that from the time of Jeroboam II onwards, the events of Israelite history and the trials of Jonah correspond convincingly well:

1. Jonah sits in his shelter: this is the end of Jeroboam's reign, the shelter (*sukkah*) being Jehu's dynasty, just as the revival of the dynasty of David is referred to as the restoration of "the tabernacle (*sukkah*) of David that has fallen" (Amos 9:11). The last king of the line of Jehu is Zechariah, who continued his father's pro-Assyrian stance, but who lasted only six months on the throne. The end of the dynasty is the end of the *sukkah*.

2. The special plant (*qiqayon*) that shelters Jonah represents Shallum ben Jabesh (2 Kgs.15:10), the regicide and usurper who has popular support as he looks to Egypt to throw off the Assyrian yoke. The purpose of the plant was to save Jonah "from his evil," (4:6) quite clearly from the great *evil* of Assyria. The plant's name, usually translated as gourd, is unknown from elsewhere in Jewish literature. The Talmud, describing oils unsuitable for Sabbath use, talks of *shemen qiq* or oil of *qiq* and one Rabbi, Resh Lakish of the third century CE, says this is the oil of Jonah's *qiqayon* plant; while another, Rabbah bar Bar Huna, a great traveller, claims he has seen it, and it is an oily tree that grows in ditches and its branches give shade to the sick (B. *Shabbath* 21A). However, the best description comes from Herodotus, who talks of the *kiki* plant, growing in the Egyptian marshes, from which oil can be extracted (Herodotus II, 94). It seems that the plant produces a form of castor oil for which the Egyptian term is *keke* (the vowels in hieroglyphics are uncertain) which is equivalent, it appears, to our *qiqayon*

and to the Greek term *kiki* used by Herodotus (Porten 1968, 92). The point of all this is that the *qiqayon* is clearly an Egyptian plant. Thus it can be taken to represent Egypt and the "shade" or cover that Egypt can provide against Assyria. Jonah's *qiqayon* plant lasts for only one day before it is destroyed by the crimson worm (4:7). Similarly, Shallum ben Jabesh reigned for only one month before being murdered in his turn by Menahem ben Gadi (2 Kgs. 15:13,14). Shallum's was the shortest reign in the history of Israel and Judah except for that of Zimri who lasted on the throne of Israel for only seven days (I Kgs.16:15). The short reign of Shallum and his pro-Egyptian leanings makes him eminently suitable to be represented by that Egyptian reed, the *qiqayon* plant, "which came up one night and disappeared the next" (4:10).

3. The *qiqayon* is destroyed by the *tola'ath*, the crimson worm. The *tola'ath* is a worm which produces a deep red dye, used to color the curtains of the Tabernacle and the clothes of the priests that served in it, there called *tola'ath shani* (Exod. 25:4; 26:1; 28:5). It is equivalent to the cochineal insect that produces a scarlet dye. Here it destroys the *qiqayon* and represents Menahem ben Gadi, who killed Shallum and took the throne from him (2 Kgs.15:14). Menahem was a strong monarch and a cruel one. In consolidating his grip on the kingdom, he besieged and took the town of Tiphsah because it continued to support Shallum; he destroyed it and "all its pregnant women he split open" (15:16). This unnecessary detail is only recorded once as actual fact in the *Tanakh*. Elsewhere it is given only as a threat and not an action. Elisha predicted that Hazael of Aram was capable of such an act (2 Kgs.8:12). Amos accused the people of Ammon of it (Amos 1:13) and Hosea prophesied such a fate for Samaria at the hands of its besiegers (Hosea 14:1),

but of no other Israelite or Judaean king is such an atrocity recorded. Menahem's bloody cruelty is well exemplified by the crimson worm. He obviously sympathized with Assyria or at least was forced to accommodate them. Moreover, he used Assyria to strengthen his own position:

Menahem gave Pul (Tiglath-Pileser III) a thousand talents of silver, that his hands would be with him, to strengthen the kingdom in his (Menahem's) hand (2 Kgs.15:19).

Menahem was astute. This tribute came not from the state coffers but was a tax on the people, and particularly the wealthy, each of whom was forced to contribute fifty shekels of silver (15:20). With this bribe in his pocket Tiglath-Pileser stayed out of the country, but at a very heavy price to the people of Israel.

4. After the *qiqayon* had gone, no wonder Jonah suffered from the cutting east wind (*ruah qadim*, Jon. 4:8). This is not just an east wind, but a cutting one (*harishith*). This form of the word occurs in the Bible only here, but its root *h-r-sh* can mean to engrave, fabricate, plough, be deaf or silent (Gesenius 1885, 309). All imply some form of cutting, or cutting off, and so we translate it as "cutting." Whatever its exact meaning, it is clearly a very severe and painful wind. And what in political terms is the east wind? Hosea tells us:

Ephraim...follows after the east wind (*qadim*)...and makes a covenant with Ashur" (Hos. 12:2); and,
An east wind (*qadim ruah*) shall come... and spoil the treasure of all fine vessels (13:15).

Both references imply the Assyrian (*Ashur*) invasion that will eventually hit Israel. Similarly Isaiah (27:8) refers to the saving of Israel and Jacob from the Assyrian enemy when he says that God has moved her (Israel) away "on the day of the east wind (*qadim*)." The east wind is a destructive wind:

With the east win*d (ruaḥ qadim*) you break up the ships of Tarshish (Psalms 48:8).

In addition, Jeremiah (18:17) claims that God will scatter "the virgin of Israel" with "the east wind (*ruaḥ qadim*)." In our case the "cutting east wind" can only mean Assyria, now breathing heavily on Israel in the reign of Menahem (749-738 BCE) and his son Pekahiah (738-736 BCE) but so far not overrunning the country. Nevertheless the pressure for tribute is so great that no doubt many of the people pined after the short reign of Shallum when an alliance with Egypt may have been in the offing.

5. When God criticizes Jonah for hankering after the *qiqayon* plant, this mirrors exactly the situation, where Israel hankers after an Egyptian alliance to counter Assyria. And it could well be for this reason that his general Pekah ben Ramaliah murders the young Pekahiah after only two years on the throne (2 Kgs.15:25). Pekahiah, following his father Menahem, would have supported Assyria, and we know that his successor Pekah ben Ramaliah sided with Egypt, for he joined his former arch-enemy Aram (Syria), then ruled by Rezin, to march on Jerusalem to force Judah to join their alliance against Assyria (15:37). Judah's Ahaz was saved by the advice of Isaiah (Isa. 7:4) and an appeal for help to the Assyrians, who came up, captured Damascus and killed Rezin (2 Kgs. 16:9). Here Assyria is helping Judah and, by defeating Aram, it is threatening Israel, Aram's ally for the time being.

🐚 LIGHT ON A CONFUSED PERIOD

In Israel, it was indeed a confused period, when there must have been factions inside Israel itself siding with Assyria on the one hand and with Egypt on the other. The confusion is compounded by the fact that Pekah is given a reign of twenty years in the Bible (2 Kgs.15:27) and yet the Assyrian annals show that Menahem (his predecessor) paid tribute to Tiglath-Pileser III in 738 and Hoshea (his successor) paid it in 731, so that at most, he could have only ruled for five years, since Menahem's son Pekahiah ruled for two years before Pekah (see fig. 26). It is suggested that Pekah may have acted as the Israelite king's governor in Gilead (Transjordan) from the end of Jeroboam's reign and then counted this period into his own later reign, which would have been the five years 736-732 BCE (Galil 1996, 65,66). If so, there may well have been a pro-Egypt faction following Pekah in one part of the kingdom while the official line under Menahem (749-738 BCE) and his son Pekahiah remained a pro-Assyrian one. It certainly seems that the population as a whole favored an Egyptian connection for which they were roundly criticised by Isaiah (8:6-16), who also threatens them with retribution from Assyria (8:4).

We would suggest that it was in this period that the work of Jonah, even if not the Book itself, was recorded. Jonah, as the little Israelite man, hankers after the freedoms hoped for from Egypt, but he realizes that power remains in the hands of Assyria; and God makes it clear to him that when it comes to *qiqayon* (Egypt) versus Nineveh (Assyria), then Nineveh must take precedence (Jon. 4:11).

In summary, we see Jonah's Chapter 4 as his view of events at the end of Jeroboam II's reign and afterwards, in the ten years from say 750 to 740 BCE, by which time Jonah may have been about 83 years old. This train of events starts some fifty years after Assyria's saving of Samaria in about 803 BCE and now the original form of "evil" changes to a "greater evil." Jonah sees the danger coming from Assyria and hankers for a bit of Egyptian shade, he regrets the loss of the *qiqayon* and longs for its return. But it is not to be, as God makes abundantly clear. The Assyrian army can muster 120,000 troops and this time God is on the side of the big battalions. You grieved (*ḥasta*) for the *qiqayon*, God says:

..and I, shall I not grieve (*aḥus*) for Nineveh, the great city, in which there are more than 120,000 men, who do not know their right from their left, and much cattle ? (Jon. 4:11).

Jonah's message, following God, is clear. Israel may want to run away to Egypt out of the clutches of Assyria, but it is a policy of disaster. This became clear a few years later, surely after Jonah's death, when Israel's last king, Hoshea, rebelled against his Assyrian masters and conspired with Egypt against them (2 Kgs.17:4). When Assyria becomes aware of this, it leads to the final siege of Samaria by the Assyrian Shalmaneser V, and to its total defeat, three years later, by his successor Sargon II, who took Israel into exile (17:6) in the year 722 BCE.

We have said that Jonah must have been an old man when he witnessed the conflicting Assyrian and Egyptian factions within Israel. His younger colleague, the prophet Hosea, saw the same dilemma:

They make a covenant with Ashur (Assyria) and oil is diverted to Egypt (Hos. 12:2).

That kind of double game will be disastrous, Hosea says, Israel should rather forgo alliances and trust in God (12:7). Jonah is different. He sees Assyria as the dominant world power, and Israel will have to submit to its superior might if it is to survive.

Jonah differs from the other prophets and indeed his book is very different from theirs. It is a racy account of events, not a collection of speeches and diatribes. It tells a story, which we have tried to show corresponds to events in Israelite history in the period from about 800 to 730 BCE. That the Book of Jonah is a book apart is already noted in the Midrash, which singles it out as a special case on account of its entire preoccupation with a foreign people (as *MR. Bamidbar* 18:21). This may perhaps be explained by its authorship in the northern kingdom, by the only northern prophet from whom we have a book (as above). If that is correct, then we have no other work of that genre with which to compare it, and thus its singularity stands strikingly alone.

ᗡ JONAH BEN AMITTAI, A NORTHERN PROPHET

The traditional view is that the Book of Jonah (ben Amittai) is indeed the work of the prophet Jonah ben Amittai, described as serving at the court of Jeroboam II of Israel (2 Kgs.14:25). The Talmud takes the view that they are one and the same person, comparing God's direction to Jonah at Nineveh to those He gave him to transmit to Jeroboam (B. *Yebamoth* 98A). So how is it possible that the Israelite prophet should take an interest in the repentance of a gentile city such as Nineveh? The Midrash solves this problem by claiming that Jonah was first sent to Jerusalem to announce its destruction and when that city repented, its downfall did not happen. He was therefore reluctant to see the same thing happen in Nineveh, and so tried to flee to Tarshish away from God (Midrash *Jonah*, 218). Such an interpretation would explain the relevance of Jonah's Book to an Israelite or Judaean audience, but it is only an interpretation and not the reality of the Book itself.

As it stands, the repentance of Nineveh from its evils is of no interest to our audience unless we can conclude that this "evil," as we have said, is *evil* in relation to Israel. To this there are certain parallels. Isaiah speaks of the evil of Aram (Syria):

Because Aram has advised evil (*ra'ah*) against you (Judah), with Ephraim and Ben-Ramaliah (Isa. 7:5),

and that of Babylon, in a chapter on Babylon:

And I will appoint on the world (their) evil (*ra'ah*, 13:11).

And Jeremiah speaks also of the evil of Babylon:

From the north the evil (*hara'ah*) will break out on all the inhabitants of the land (Jer. 1:14).

These are all statements of other nation's evil in relation to Israel or Judah. Elsewhere it has been suggested that "the great evil" committed by Edom (inscribed on an ostracon from Arad) is their treachery in abandoning Judah for Assyria (Aharoni 1979, 419 n.5). This would be dated to Sennacherib's entry to Judah in about 700 BCE.

Once the significance of the *evil* of Nineveh (the Assyrian army) is established, then the story of Jonah takes on a covert historiographic meaning. We have tried to show how the events of the story, both plain and fabulous, are related to the siege of Samaria in about 803 BCE and to subsequent events. Jonah's participation in all this means that he may have been born, as we have said, in about the year 823 BCE, and helped as a young man to get Assyria to save Samaria; he lived through the reign of Jeroboam II, and then carried on until he was over 80, to see the decline of the northern kingdom and the growing threat of the Assyrian Empire. In this case the named author of the Book of Jonah could well be the Jonah ben Amittai of Chapter 14 of the Second Book of Kings.

This does not mean that he necessarily wrote the Book as we have it. We are talking of the period from 800 to 730 BCE and it would be surprising to find literature such as this at this early stage. We know that Jonah is mentioned as one of the "twelve" (minor prophets) in

Ben Sirach (Ecclesiasticus 49:10) and possibly also in The Book of Tobit (14:4), so the Book's composition must have taken place before the end of third century BCE. When exactly it was written down and by whom we cannot say, but we would claim that it records, in an accurate but covert and allegorical way, events of Israelite history of the first half of the eighth century BCE.

The question then remains concerning the form or style of the Book, and particularly its fabulous elements. It could be that this was a standard literary form in the northern kingdom, of which this is our sole example. That it is a contemporary record would imply an incredibly early date, before the fall of Samaria in 722 BCE. We would not make such a bold claim, but we suggest that the elements of the Book derive from this early period, the time of the Jonah ben Amittai of the Second Book of Kings; and that they were recorded by scribes of the northern kingdom at a later period, after 722 BCE, when Samaria was attached to the kingdom of Judah (2 Chron. 30:10).

A further question remains; why was the Book written in this covert form, if it is indeed a record of the last years of Samaria and Israel, the northern kingdom? The answer must be that the elderly Jonah was living out his last years in the reign of Pekah (736-732 BCE), who was pursuing an aggressive anti-Assyrian stance. Jonah saw this as fatally flawed and a policy that would bring the full might of the Assyrian army back onto the head of Israel. But he may not have dared to say this publicly, it would have been lèse-majesté to defy the royal party, and might have led to his early death for treason. So he chose to cloak his predictions in allegory and to describe the ultimate inevitable victory of Assyria in cryptic terms.

🗢 A SUMMARY

The literature on the Book of Jonah is extensive (see Wolff 1986, 88-93). Besides the classical Jewish and Christian works, medieval commentaries and archaeological parallels of the ninetcenth century, new articles and books on the subject continue to appear. The June 2000 Edition of Old Testament Abstracts, which covers a period of only four months, records ten articles in learned journals and one book-length commentary, all on Jonah. These scholarly works concentrate on minutiae of the text and often offer excellent parallels and insights. As far as we are aware, however, not one of them has linked the Book to the known events of any period of Israelite history, nor have they been able to explain what interest the repentance of Nineveh can have for an Israelite or Judaean audience.

It has been our thesis that the whole story of Jonah can only be understood in relation to the events of Israelite history from about 800 to 730 BCE. The story starts with the terrible siege of Samaria by the Arameans, when Jonah tries to get help from Phoenicia (ship to *Tarshish*) but is frustrated by the great storm god *Adad*, or Ben-Hadad of Aram, and is rescued temporarily by the Philistines, worshippers of *Dagon*, the mighty fish. The *evil* of Nineveh is the *evil* of the Assyrian army in not coming to the help of Israel, but eventually they put on sackcloth (don the sack) to go to war and Adadnirari III saves Samaria in 803 BCE. Later, Jonah regrets this obligation, since he now sees Assyria as a potential threat. He seeks the shade of the *qiqayon* plant, representing help from Egypt. But the plant (Shallum ben Jabesh) dies and the crimson *worm* (Menahem ben Gadi) leads Israel back to Assyrian domination. Jonah hankers for the *qiqayon*, the Egyptian connection, but God has other ideas. Nineveh must take precedence, and its standing army of 120,000 will sweep all before them. To flirt with Egypt is attractive but fatally dangerous; there is no point in opposing Assyria, for now God is on the side of the big battalions.

Jonah delivers this message in the period of turmoil after the death of Jeroboam II when Israel is split into pro-Assyrian and pro-Egyptian factions. By then Jonah is an old man, but the hero of his Book may well be the same prophet as Jonah ben Amittai, the court prophet of

Jeroboam II. That he himself wrote the book is doubtful, but it records, in a covert way, the highly unstable period of Israelite history that precedes, by only a generation, the final destruction of the northern kingdom of Israel in 722 BCE.

The Book of Jonah is constructed in symmetrical fashion and exhibits a chiastic structure (see fig. 28) similar to that of Esther and Ruth, though not as pronounced as in their case. The turning point is Jonah's time in the belly of the great fish, when his psalm to God brings the action back to Nineveh (the Assyrian army). Before that Jonah had fled to Tarshish (Phoenicia); now he goes to Nineveh, but after Nineveh he again suffers torments. Before it was the storm (Ben-Hadad), now it is the cutting east wind (Assyria); before he was temporarily protected by the big fish (Philistia), now by the short-lived *qiqayon* plant (Egypt). Just as God commands Jonah at the beginning, so now He rebukes him at the end. At first it was to warn Nineveh of its destruction, now finally it is to see Nineveh preserved.

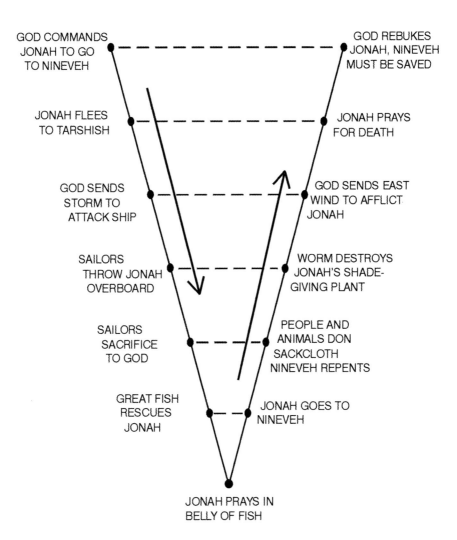

GOD COMMANDS
JONAH TO GO
TO NINEVEH

GOD REBUKES
JONAH, NINEVEH
MUST BE SAVED

JONAH FLEES
TO TARSHISH

JONAH PRAYS
FOR DEATH

GOD SENDS
STORM TO
ATTACK SHIP

GOD SENDS EAST
WIND TO AFFLICT
JONAH

SAILORS
THROW JONAH
OVERBOARD

WORM DESTROYS
JONAH'S SHADE-
GIVING PLANT

SAILORS
SACRIFICE
TO GOD

PEOPLE AND
ANIMALS DON
SACKCLOTH
NINEVEH REPENTS

GREAT FISH
RESCUES
JONAH

JONAH GOES TO
NINEVEH

JONAH PRAYS IN
BELLY OF FISH

Fig. 28 *Chiastic structure of the Book of Jonah, showing symmetrical arrangement of the main events, with the turning point being the three days that Jonah spends in the belly of the great fish.*

☞ ABBREVIATIONS

ad loc.	at that place
approx.	approximate, approximately
ASOR.	American Society for Oriental Research
B.	Babylonian Talmud (Babli, see References)
BCE.	Before Common Era
BDB.	Brown, Driver and Briggs (see References)
c.	circa (about)
CAH.	Cambridge Ancient History (see References)
CE.	Common Era
cf.	compare
chap.	chapter
Dan.	Daniel (Bible)
Deut.	Deuteronomy (Bible)
ed.	editor, edited, edition
EJ.	*Encyclopaedia Judaica,* Jerusalem: Keter, 1971
Esth.	Esther (Bible)
et al.	and others
Ezek.	Ezekiel (Bible)
ff.	following
fig.	figure
Gen.	Genesis (Bible)
Heb.	Hebrew
Hos.	Hosea (Bible)

ibid.	same (source)
ill.	illustration
introd.	introduction
Isa.	Isaiah (Bible)
Jon.	Jonah (Bible)
Josh.	Joshua (Bible)
Jr.	Junior
Judg.	Judges (Bible)
JPS.	Jewish Publication Society (trans. *Tanakh*, 1985)
Kgs.	Kings (Bible)
km.	kilometers
Lev.	Leviticus (Bible)
lit.	literally
M.	Mishnah (trans. H. Danby, *The Mishnah*, 1933)
mm.	millimeters
MR.	*Midrash Rabbah* (see References)
Neh.	Nehemiah (Bible)
op.cit.	work quoted
p., pp.	page, pages
Prov.	Proverbs (Bible)
R.	Rabbi
Sam.	Samuel (Bible)
trans.	translated
v., vv.	verse, verses
vol.	volume
Zech.	Zecheriah (Bible)

SHORT BIBLIOGRAPHY & REFERENCES

Aharoni, Y. 1979,	*The Land of the Bible*, trans. & ed. A.F. Rainey, Burns and Oates, London.
Alexandre, Y., Covello-Paran, K., and Gal, Z. 2003,	Excavations at Tel Gat Hefer in the Lower Galilee, Areas A and B, In *Atiqot* 44: 143-170.
Allen, L.C. 1976,	*The Books of Joel, Obadiah, Jonah and Micah*, The New International Commentary on the Old Testament. Eerdmans, Grand Rapids, Michigan.
Bardtke, H. 1973,	Zusätze zu Esther, in *Historische und Legendarische Erzählungen*, ed. W.G. Kümmel et al. 15-62. Gütersloh.
Bartlett, J.R. 1973,	*The First and Second Books of Maccabees*, Cambridge Bible Commentary, Cambridge University, London.
Bertram, S. 1965,	Symmetrical Design in the Book of Ruth, in *Journal of Biblical Literature*, No. 84: 165-168.
Bickerman, E. 1967,	*Four Strange Books of the Bible, Jonah, Daniel, Koheleth, Esther.* Schocken, New York.
Biran, A. 1994,	*Biblical Dan.* Israel Exploration Society, Jerusalem.

Bolin, T.M. 1997,

Freedom, beyond Forgiveness, the Book of Jonah Re-examined.
Copenhagen International Seminar 3, Sheffield Academic, Sheffield.

Briant, P. 1996,

Histoire de l'Empire Perse de Cyrus à Alexandre. Fayard, Paris.

Brown, F., Driver, S.R. and Briggs, C.A. 1966,

A Hebrew and English Lexicon of the Old Testament. Clarendon, Oxford.

Cambridge Ancient History, 1977,

Vol.IV (first ed.) The Persian Empire and the West, ed. J.B.Bury et al. Chap. 7, The Reign of Darius: 173-228. Cambridge University, Cambridge.

Cambridge Ancient History 1982,

Vol. III, Pt.1 (second ed.) The Prehistory of the Balkans; and the Middle East and the Aegean World, Tenth to Eighth Centuries B.C., ed. J. Boardman et al.
Chap.9, The Neo-Hittite States in Syria and Anatolia, J.D.Hawkins: 372-441.
Chap.10, Israel and Judah from Jehu until the Period of Assyrian Domination (841-750 B.C.), T.C.Mitchell: 488-510, Cambridge University, London.

Campbell Jr., E.F. 1975,

Ruth, The Anchor Bible.
Doubleday, New York.

Casson, L. 1994,

Ships and Seafaring in Ancient Times.
University of Texas, Texas.

Caubert, A., and Bernus-Taylor, M. 1991,

The Louvre, Near Eastern Antiquities.
Scale, Paris.

Collins, R. 1974,

The Medes and Persians.
Cassell, London.

Cook, J.M. 1983,   *The Persian Empire*. Dent, London.

Cowley, A. 1923,   *Aramaic Papyri of the Fifth Century BC*. Oxford University, Oxford.

Daube, D. 1995,   *Esther*. Yarnton Trust, Oxford Centre for PostgraduateStudies, Oxford.

Driver, S.R. 1891,   *Introduction to the Literature of the Old Testament*. Clark, Edinburgh.

Esther, Apocrypha   The Rest of the Chapters of the Book of Esther, in *New English Bible, the Apocrypha*, 1970: 116-133. Oxford and Cambridge University.

Ferrier, R.W. (ed.) l989,   *The Arts of Persia*. Yale University, New Haven.

Finkelstein, I. and Silberman, N.A. 2001,   *The Bible Unearthed, Archaeology's New Vision of Ancient Israel*. Free Press, New York.

Frankfort, H. 1996,   *The Art and Architecture of the Ancient Orient*, Fifth ed. rev. M. Roaf and D.Matthews. Yale University, New Haven.

Frye, R.N. 1976,   *The Heritage of Persia*. Cardinal, London.

Fuerst, W.J. 1975,   *The Books of Ruth, Esther, Ecclesiastes, Song of Songs, Lamentations*, Cambridge Bible Commentary. Cambridge University, London.

Gal, Z. 1992,   Lower Galilee in the Iron Age, ASOR Dissertation Series 8. Winona Lake, Minnesota.

Galil, G. 1996,   *The Chronology of the Kings of Israel and Judah*. Brill, Leiden.

Gesenius, W. 1885, *Hebrew and Chaldee Lexicon to the Old Testament Scriptures*, trans. S.P.Tregelles. Samuel Bagster, London.

Ghrishman, R. 1964, *Persians, from the Origins to Alexander the Great*, trans. S.Gilbert and J.Emmons. Thames and Hudson, London.

Ginzberg, L. 1968, *Legends of the Jews*, 7 vols. JPS. Philadelphia.

Giveon, R. 1984, *The Footsteps of Pharaoh in Canaan, Essays on the Relations between Israel and Ancient Egypt.* Sifriat Poalim, Tel Aviv (Heb.).

Godard, A. 1965, *The Art of Iran*, trans. M. Heron. George Allen and Unwin, London.

Gordis, R. 1965. *The Book of God and Man, a Study of Job.* University of Chicago, Chicago.

Graves, R. 1972. *Difficult Questions, Easy Answers.* Cassell, London.

Grayzel, S. 1949. The Origins of Purim, in *The Purim Anthology*, ed. P. Goodman: 3-13. JPS, Philadelphia.

Ḥakham, A. 1973. Esther, in *Five Megilloth, Da'at Mikra*, ed. A. Mirsky et al. Mossad Rav Kook, Jerusalem (Heb.).

Hallo, W.W. 1983, The First Purim, in *Biblical Archaeologist*, Vol. 46, No. 1: 19-29.

Hallo, W.W. and Simpson, W.K. 1998, *The Ancient Near East, a History,* Second Ed. Harcourt Brace, Fort Worth.

Herodotus, *The Histories*, Books I to IX. trans. A. Godfrey. 4 vols. Revised 1960. Loeb Classical Library, London.

Herodotus 1972,   *The Histories*, trans. A. de Selincourt,
                                       rev. A.B. Burns. Penguin,
                                       Harmondsworth. [The quoted
                                       passages are from this translation.]

Huart, C. 1927,   *Ancient Persian and Iranian Civilization*,
                                       trans. M.R. Dobie. Routledge and
                                       Kegan Paul, London.

Ibn Ezra, A. (born 1092),   Commentary on Bible, in *Mikraoth
                                       Gedoloth* (Heb.).

Josephus, F. (34-c.100 CE),   *Antiquities of the Jews*, trans. R.
                                       Marcus, 6 vols. Reprinted 1961.
                                       Loeb Classical Library, London.

Kuhrt, A. 1995,   *The Ancient Near East, c. 3000-330
                                       BC*, 2 vols. Routledge, London.

Levenson, J.D. 1997,   *Esther, a Commentary*, Old Testament
                                       Library. SCM, London.

Lewis, C.T. and Short, C. 1879,   *A Latin Dictionary*. Clarendon Press,
                                       Oxford.

Luckenbill, D.D. 1989,   *Ancient Records of Assyria and
                                       Babylonia*, reprint of 1926 ed.
                                       Histories and Mysteries of Man,
                                       London.

Malamat, A. 2001,   *History of Biblical Israel, Major Problems
                                       and Minor Issues.*
                                       Brill, Leiden.

Melzer, F. 1973,   Ruth, in *Five Megillot, Da'at Mikra*,
                                       ed. A.Mirsky et al. Mossad Rav Kook,
                                       Jerusalem (Heb.).

Metsudat David,   Commentary on Book of Samuel,
(D. Altschuler, 18th Century),   in *Mikraoth Gedoloth* (Heb.).

Midrash Jonah,   in *Ozar Midrashim*, ed. J.D.Eisenstein,
                                       1915: 218. Eisenstein, New York
                                       (Heb.).

Midrash Rabbah (MR),   *Bereshith*, trans. H.Freedman.
                            Exodus, trans. S.M.Lehrman.
                            Numbers, trans. J.J.Slotki.
                            Ruth, trans. L.Rabinowitz.
                            Esther, trans. M.Simon.
                            all 3rd. ed. 1983, Soncino, London.

Miller, J.M. and Hayes,   *A History of Ancient Israel and Judah.*
J.H. 1986,   SCM, London.

Mitchell, T.C. 1988,   *The Bible in the British Museum.*
                            British Museum, London.

Modrzejewski, J.M. 1995,   *The Jews of Egypt from Rameses II to
                            Emperor Hadrian*, trans. R. Cornman.
                            Clark, Edinburgh.

Moore, C.A. 1971,   *Esther, the Anchor Bible.*
                            Doubleday, New York.

Moore, C.A. 1992,   Esther in *Anchor Bible Dictionary*,
                            ed. D.N.Freedman, vol. 2: 633-643.
                            Doubleday, New York.

Naveh, J. 1987,   *Early History of the Alphabet, an
                            Introduction to West Semitic Epigraphy
                            and Palaeography.* Magnes Press,
                            Jerusalem.

Oates, J. 1986,   *Babylon.* Thames and Hudson,
                            London.

Osterley, W.O.E. and   *An Introduction to the Books of the Old
Robinson, T.H. 1934,   Testament.* SPCK, London.

Oppenheim, A.L. 1977,   *Ancient Mesopotamia*, rev. E.Reiner.
                            Chicago University, Chicago.

Porten, B. 1968,   *Archives from Elephantine, the Life of
                            an Ancient Jewish Military Colony.*
                            University of California, Berkeley.

Pritchard, J.B. 1955,   *Ancient Near Eastern Texts.*
                            2nd ed. Princeton, New Jersey.

Pritchard, J.B. 1958,   *The Ancient Near East, an Anthology of Texts and Pictures.* Princeton University, Princeton.

Rashi (Reb Shlomo ben Yitzhak, 1040-1105)   Commentary on the Bible, in *Mikraoth Gedoloth* (Heb.).

Roaf, M. 1990,   *Cultural Atlas of Mesopotamia.* Equinox, London.

Rofé, A. 1988,   *The Prophetical Stories, the Narratives of the Prophets in the Hebrew Bible, their Literary Types and History.* Magnes Press, Jerusalem.

Saggs, H.W.F. 1984,   *The Might that was Assyria.* Sidgwick and Jackson, London.

Sasson, J.M. 1989,   *Ruth, a new Translation & Philological Commentary and Formalist-Folklorist Interpretation.* 2nd ed. Sheffield Academic Press, Sheffield.

Talmud Babli (B.),   *The Babylonian Talmud, Baba Bathra,* trans. M.Simon and I.W.Slotki, 1976. *Berakhoth,* trans. M.Simon, 1972. *Megillah,* trans. M.Simon, 1984. *Shabbath,* trans. H.Freedman, 1971. *Yebamoth,* trans. I.W.Slotki, 1984. *Yoma,* trans. L.Jung, 1974. all ed. I.Epstein, Soncino, London.

Trible, P. 1992,   Ruth, in *Anchor Bible Dictionary,* ed. D.N. Freedman, Vol. 5: 842-847. Doubleday, New York.

Voltaire. 1878,   *Oeuvres Complètes de Voltaire,* Siècle de Louis XIV, Pt.1.Garnier Frères, Paris.

Walfisch, B.D. 1993,   *Esther in Medieval Garb.* State University of New York, New York.

Walker, C.B.F. 1987,   *Reading the Past, Cuneiform.* British Museum, London.

Weinfeld, M. 1971,   Ruth, in *E J.* ed. G. Wigoder. Vol XIV:
                         518-522. Keter, Jerusalem.

Wolff, H.W. 1986,   *Obadiah and Jonah, a Commentary,*
                         trans. M. Kohl.
                         Augsburg, Minneapolis.

Yamauchi, E.M. 1990,   *Persia and the Bible.* Baker Book
                         House, Grand Rapids, Michigan.

Yeivin, S. 1959,   Jachin and Boaz, in *Palestine
                         Exploration Quarterly,* No. 91: 20-22.